T0339836

Self and Other

PSYCHOANALYTIC CROSSCURRENTS
General Editor: Leo Goldberger

THE DEATH OF DESIRE: A STUDY IN PSYCHOPATHOLOGY
by M. Guy Thompson

THE TALKING CURE: LITERARY REPRESENTATIONS OF
PSYCHOANALYSIS
by Jeffrey Berman

NARCISSISM AND THE TEXT: STUDIES IN LITERATURE AND
THE PSYCHOLOGY OF SELF
by Lynne Layton and Barbara Ann Schapiro, Editors

THE LANGUAGE OF PSYCHOSIS
by Bent Rosenbaum and Harly Sonne

SEXUALITY AND MIND: THE ROLE OF THE FATHER AND THE
MOTHER IN THE PSYCHE
by Janine Chasseguet-Smirgel

ART AND LIFE: ASPECTS OF MICHELANGELO
by Nathan Leites

PATHOLOGIES OF THE MODERN SELF: POSTMODERN
STUDIES ON NARCISSISM, SCHIZOPHRENIA, AND
DEPRESSION
by David Michael Levin, Editor

FREUD'S THEORY OF PSYCHOANALYSIS
by Ole Andkjær Olsen and Simo Koppe

THE UNCONSCIOUS AND THE THEORY OF
PSYCHONEUROSES
by Zvi Giora

CHANGING MIND-SETS: THE POTENTIAL UNCONSCIOUS
by Maria Carmen Gear, Ernesto César Liendo, and Lila Lee Scott

LANGUAGE AND THE DISTORTION OF MEANING
by Patrick de Gramont

THE NEUROTIC FOUNDATIONS OF SOCIAL ORDER
by J. C. Smith

SELF AND OTHER: OBJECT RELATIONS IN PSYCHOANALYSIS
AND LITERATURE
by Robert Rogers

SELF AND OTHER
Object Relations in Psychoanalysis and Literature

Robert Rogers

NEW YORK UNIVERSITY PRESS
New York and London

Library of Congress Cataloging-in-Publication Data

Rogers, Robert, 1928–
Self and other : object relations in psychoanalysis and literature
/ Robert Rogers.
p.   cm.—(Psychoanalytic crosscurrents)
Includes bibliographical references and index.
ISBN 0-8147-7418-0
1. Object relations (Psychoanalysis)   2. Object relations
(Psychoanalysis) in literature.   I. Title.   II. Series.
BF175.5.O24R64   1991
155.9′2—dc20   91-25953
CIP

New York University Press books are printed on acid-free paper,
and their binding materials are chosen for strength and durability.

For my mother and father: in memoriam

This is most strange,
That she whom even but now was your best object,
The argument of your praise, balm of your age,
The best, the dearest, should in this trice of time
Commit a thing so monstrous to dismantle
So many folds of favor.
                    — France to Lear, in *King Lear*

Being a self with others entails a constant dialectic
between attachment and self-definition, between
connection and differentiation, a continual negotiation
between one's wishes and will and the wishes and will
of others, between one's own subjective reality and
a consensual reality of others with whom one lives.
                    — Stephen Mitchell, *Relational*
                        Concepts in Psychoanalysis

CONTENTS

FOREWORD

The *Psychoanalytic Crosscurrents* series presents selected books and mono-graphs that reveal the growing intellectual ferment within and across the boundaries of psychoanalysis.

Freud's theories and grand-scale speculative leaps have been found warning, if not disturbing, from the very beginning and have led to a succession of derisive attacks, shifts in emphasis, revisions, modifications, and extensions. Despite the chronic and, at times, fierce debate that has characterized psychoanalysis, not only as a movement but also as a sci-ence, Freud's genius and transformational impact on the twentieth cen-tury have never been seriously questioned. Recent psychoanalytic thought has been subjected to dramatic reassessments under the sway of contem-porary currents in the history of ideas, philosophy of science, epistemol-ogy, structuralism, critical theory, semantics, and semiology as well as in sociobiology, ethology, and neurocognitive science. Not only is Freud's place in intellectual history being meticulously scrutinized, but his texts, too, are being carefully read, explicated, and debated within a variety of conceptual frameworks and sociopolitical contexts.

The legacy of Freud is perhaps most notably evident within the narrow confines of psychoanalysis itself, the "impossible profession" that has served as the central platform for the promulgation of official orthodoxy. But Freud's contributions—his original radical thrust—reach far beyond the parochial concerns of the clinician psychoanalyst as clinician. His writings touch on a wealth of issues, crossing traditional boundaries—be they situated in the biological, social, or humanistic spheres—that have profoundly altered our conception of the individual and society.

A rich and flowering literature, falling under the rubric of "applied psychoanalysis," came into being, reached its zenith many decades ago, and then almost vanished. Early contributors to this literature, in addition to Freud himself, came from a wide range of backgrounds both within and outside the medical/psychiatric field, and many later became psychoanalysts themselves. These early efforts were characteristically reductionist in their attempt to extrapolate from psychoanalytic theory (often the purely clinical theory) to explanation of phenomena lying at some distance from the clinical. Over the years, academic psychologists, educators, anthropologists, sociologists, political scientists, philosophers, jurists, literary critics, art historians, artists, and writers, among others (with or without formal psychoanalytic training), have joined in the proliferation of this literature.

The intent of the *Psychoanalytic Crosscurrents* series is to apply psychoanalytic ideas to topics that may lie beyond the narrowly clinical, but its essential conception and scope are quite different. The present series eschews the reductionist tendency to be found in much traditional "applied psychoanalysis." It acknowledges not only the complexity of psychological phenomena but also the way in which they are embedded in social and scientific contexts that are constantly changing. It calls for a dialectical relationship to earlier theoretical views and conceptions rather than a mechanical repetition of Freud's dated thoughts. The series affirms the fact that contributions to and about psychoanalysis have come from many directions. It is designed as a forum for the multidisciplinary studies that intersect with psychoanalytic thought but without the requirement that psychoanalysis necessarily be the starting point or, indeed, the center focus. The criteria for inclusion in the series are that the work be significantly informed by psychoanalytic thought or that it be aimed at furthering our understanding of psychoanalysis in its broadest meaning as theory, practice, and sociocultural phenomenon; that it be of current topical interest and that it provide the critical reader with contemporary insights; and, above all, that it be high-quality scholarship, free of absolute dogma, banalization, and empty jargon. The author's professional identity and particular theoretical orientation matter only to the extent that such facts may serve to frame the work for the reader, alerting him or her to inevitable biases of the author.

The *Psychoanalytic Crosscurrents* series presents an array of works from the multidisciplinary domain in an attempt to capture the ferment of scholarly activities at the core as well as at the boundaries of psychoanalysis. The books and monographs are from a variety of sources: authors will be psychoanalysts—traditional, neo- and post-Freudian, existential, object relational, Kohutian, Lacanian, etc.—social scientists with quantitative or qualitative orientations to psychoanalytic data, and scholars from the vast diversity of approaches and interests that make up the humanities. The series entertains works on critical comparisons of psychoanalytic theories and concepts as well as philosophical examinations of fundamental assumptions and epistemic claims that furnish the base for psychoanalytic hypotheses. It includes studies of psychoanalysis as literature (discourse and narrative theory) as well as the application of psychoanalytic concepts to literary criticism. It will serve as an outlet for psychoanalytic studies of creativity and the arts. Works in the cognitive and the neurosciences will be included to the extent that they address some fundamental psychoanalytic tenet, such as the role of dreaming and other forms of unconscious mental processes.

It should be obvious that an exhaustive enumeration of the types of works that might fit into the *Psychoanalytic Crosscurrents* series is pointless. The studies comprise a lively and growing literature as a unique domain; books of this sort are frequently difficult to classify or catalog. Suffice it to say that the overriding aim of the editor of this series is to serve as a conduit for the identification of the outstanding yield of that emergent literature and to foster its further unhampered growth.

Leo Goldberger
Professor of Psychology
New York University

PREFACE

A memorable comic moment in the psychological high jinks of *High Anxiety* occurs when the psychiatrist protagonist, played by Mel Brooks, becomes able to recall the childhood origin of his uncontrollable fear of heights. He visualizes a dreamlike scene of angry conflict between his parents. He remembers sitting in his high chair, fearful of it being tipped over, as his father speaks harshly to his mother, complaining that the baby keeps them prisoners in their own household. She responds with defensive fury: "Whaddya want me to do? Get rid of him?" Then the high chair begins to topple over. On the basis of this memory Dr. Thorndike has a sudden insight into the real meaning of his acrophobia: "It's not heights I'm afraid of; it's parents!"

The shifts of theoretical perspective I have experienced over the past two decades that moved me to write this book have not taken the form of any sudden illuminations such as the one dramatized by Mel Brooks, but in at least one respect the alteration of my viewpoint parallels that of Dr. Thorndike: instead of seeing behavioral problems in terms of impersonal forces (in the movie, the force of gravity, shall we say), I now look at them in terms of the effect of interpersonal relationships.

I cannot take much credit for this improvement for the simple reason that my altered perspectives surely correspond to changes that have been taking place on a far broader scale in the field of psychoanalysis. When I was working on *The Double in Literature* (1970) it seemed perfectly acceptable to base my discussion of splitting and dissociation largely on the foundation of Freud's structural theory. I did not realize at the time that my working knowledge of object relations theory was almost entirely confined to oedipal configurations and was almost exclusively drive-oriented. As I wrote *Metaphor: A Psychoanalytic View* (1978), I was only beginning to have doubts about Freud's doctrine that individual motivation is largely fueled by libidinal drives, so it still seemed meaningful to try to account for the powerful effects of the language of poetry in terms of certain assumptions about the operations of what Freud calls the primary and secondary processes. At that time my methodology remained locked into the dynamic, economic, and structural metapsychological points of view. Then, as I wrote a series of papers about the interpretive process during the years that followed, I eventually began to repudiate psychoanalytic drive theory—under the guidance of others, of course— even though I was not altogether clear about what there was to replace it. By the mid-1980s the principal new resource available to me, I thought, was Bowlby's attachment theory. But there were certain problems. Relatively few people in psychoanalytic circles appeared to be paying much attention to Bowlby at that time, and my attempts to interest colleagues in his work fell flat. I also began to realize at this time that in some ways Bowlby's theory did not match well with my convictions about internalized object relations, especially as they are represented in literature. Worse yet, I no longer felt very secure about where I stood regarding the etiology of neurosis. Worst of all, I became increasingly aware of the lack of consensus concerning object relations theory in the psychoanalytic community.

The more I thought about these problems, the more it made sense to me to try to explore the possibility of making some sort of contribution, however limited, toward the integration of a science-oriented, person-oriented theory of object relations—one purged of drive theory but merged with the best features of attachment theory and with what I refer to as *self theory* so as to distinguish it from Kohutian self psychology.

The limits of this undertaking will be more or less apparent from the following prospectus. Chapter 1 begins with an account of the mixed legacy we inherit from Freud, offers a brief overview of the principal contributions to object relations theory from Klein to Kohut, summarizes some of the major arguments against drive theory, and concludes by taking a firm stand in favor of a person-oriented theory of object relations. Chapter 2 attempts to integrate the most meaningful features of traditional object relations theory with attachment theory, with recent findings deriving from the observation of early mother-infant interaction, and with self theory. Chapter 3 provides a critical rereading of all of Freud's major cases in a way that deemphasizes sexual factors while stressing interpersonal conflict and attachment deficits. Chapter 4 continues the same strategy using published case histories of Winnicott, Lichtenstein, Sechehaye, and Bettelheim. Chapters 5 through 8 deal with object relations represented in literary fantasy. Chapter 5 emphasizes the permutations of attachment behavior depicted in the text of *Moby Dick*. Chapter 6 focuses on the special, essentially unsuccessful adaption to aberrant infant-parent relations exhibited by Meursault in *The Stranger*. Chapter 7 treats creative uses of the self as a facilitating environment in the poetry of Emily Dickinson. And chapter 8 traces patterns of attachment, separation, anxiety, and loss in four Shakespearean tragedies.

I am grateful to those who in various ways have assisted me in this endeavor. I especially want to thank the friends and colleagues who have read and commented on one or more chapters of this work: Peter Heller, Joseph Masling (whose high standards concerning what constitutes empirical evidence have remained beyond my reach, I fear), Charles Proudfit, David Richards (whose response has been so constructive and sustaining), and David Willbern. Their efforts helped me to avoid innumerable blunders, yet it goes without saying that they can in no way be held in the least degree responsible for any of the faults that doubtless remain. I am also grateful to Arthur Efron for his willingness to share discoveries with me, to Bruce Jackson for his sound advice, and to Claire Kahane and Ronald Ruskin for their friendly collegiality. I want to thank all of my students, graduate and undergraduate, for their patience in hearing me out and for the stimulation our interactions afforded me. I thank Jonathan Havey especially for the benefits of the many hours we spent discussing object relations theory. My sense of indebtedness to the late Emanuel Peterfreund runs deep. He was a source of strength for many years. I thank Joan Cipperman as much for allowing me to bask in the warmth of her presence as for her labor in typing the manuscript. To Leo Goldberger I am greatly obliged for his willingness to include this book in the *Psychoanalytic Crosscurrents* series. And I want to thank Jason Renker and Despina Gimbel, at New York University Press, for all their help. Finally, and most important of all, I want to thank my wife for her untiring support.

I

MODELING INTERPERSONAL RELATIONS

1.

DRIVE VERSUS PERSON: TWO ORIENTATIONS

One's choice of terms always has consequences. So does one's selection of explanatory frameworks. An instance from one of Winnicott's case histories illustrates the distance between an orthodox, drive-oriented perspective on object relations and one that assumes that interpersonal relationships may reflect forms of attraction not necessarily fueled by sexual urges. A little girl called Gabrielle, only two years and ten months old, goes immediately to the toy box at the beginning of her sixth therapeutic consultation with Winnicott: "She put the two big soft animals together and said: 'They are together and are fond of each other' "(1977, 77). Winnicott responds in this instance with a sexual interpretation, one highly characteristic of his former mentor and supervisor, Melanie Klein: "And they are making babies." Gabrielle, who has already glossed her own play in a very different way ("They are ... fond of each other"), remarks, "No, they are making friends." Would Winnicott's customary, person-oriented mode of interpretation have been more accurate, and functional, at this point than the sexually oriented one? Many contemporary analysts might think so.

When it comes to selecting explanatory frameworks in the field of object relations theory, there is God's plenty to choose from. To whose work do we turn for guidance? Even if we go first to the theory of object relations explicit and implicit in Freud, we cannot fail to be aware that the ensuing history of the development of object relations theory constitutes a complex and often conflicting response to his work in this area. Can we rely on the innovations of Melanie Klein, who still has many

3

followers? Or can we perhaps find better guidance in the work of Fairbairn, or Winnicott, or Guntrip, or Sullivan, or Bowlby, or Kohut? Practitioners of various kinds frequently associate themselves with the object relations theory of a particular individual, Winnicott and Kohut being popular choices these days. Alternatively, many choose to be eclectic, often without thinking about it, by adopting a casual mixture of views: some Freud, for instance, with a helping of Klein, a dollop of Winnicott, and a lacing of Kohut. More commendable than passive eclecticism, surely, are deliberate attempts on the part of theoreticians to effect syntheses of earlier views, such as Kernberg's attempted integration of "object-relations theory with psychoanalytic instinct theory and a contemporary ego psychological approach" (1976, 131). The problem in this case is that the proposed synthesis may prove to be unworkable because of incompatibilities inherent in the explanatory frameworks.

Virtually all current psychoanalytic schools of thought agree substantially on the fundamental importance of object relations, yet no consensus about these matters exists at present according to Greenberg and Mitchell (1983). To be more precise, they say that "underlying the apparent diversity of contemporary psychoanalytic theory there is a convergence of basic concerns" (2). It would be still more exact to speak not of "a convergence" but, in the plural, of convergences, or groups, of basic concern. Thus, for convenience, one may designate two major groups of object relations theory as drive oriented and person oriented. It may then be asked, should we select a person-oriented theory like those of Sullivan and Fairbairn, or a drive-oriented one like those of Freud and Melanie Klein? Or can we live with *both,* in a state of enlightened complementarity analogous to living with both wave and corpuscle theories of the behavior of light, as Greenberg and Mitchell imply is possible—and perhaps even desirable insofar as it may give rise to a "creative dialogue" between the two (408; cf. Mitchell, 1988)? Collateral questions then unfold. Is it possible to invest heavily in a person-oriented theory while retaining some interest in drive theory, as Winnicott appears to do? And if we totally reject drive theory, as Bowlby does, how satisfactory is attachment theory, which he considers to be a theory of object relations (1969, 17)? Does the strength of its empirical basis compensate for an orientation to outer reality that slights the inferable existence, volatility, and complexity of intrapsychic constellations of internalized objects, and that in rejecting libido theory neglects to account in any detail for sexual behavior?

The essential problem for the psychoanalyst, as Schafer sees it, is the problem of "finding the right balance" (1983, 293). He refers specifically to how much emphasis should be placed on the "inner world" and the "outer world." "How much do you talk about real interactions and how much do you talk about the analysand's fantasizing, particularly the un-conscious infantile aspects of what is fantasized?" (292). One can think of other "balancing acts" that need to be considered as well, such as the possible "correct balance" between a self-oriented theory of object rela-tions, such as Stern's (1985), which not only regards an emergent self-hood as being present in neonates from virtually the beginning of life outside the womb but also privileges self over other in modeling object-relational interactions, and, in contrast, an other-oriented theory such as that of Lacan, for whom autonomy is unthinkable because "man's desire is the desire of the Other" (1977, 158). Another balancing act would have to deal with the possible equilibrium between models of object relations relying on the concept of a coherent, specialized, centered ego, as in ego psychology, as distinguished from models depending on a decentered conception of self, or "subject," one dispersed in language and culture, like Lacan's—or, to take a less extreme and very different in-stance, the comparatively decentered, systemic conceptualization of be-havioral control envisioned by Peterfreund (1971), who rejects the con-cept of ego in its structural sense.

All terms remain suspect. This chapter, which does not aspire to be a "balanced," neutral account, or a systematic survey, endeavors to compare the two broad orientations in object relations theory already referred to as drive oriented and person oriented. Other writers employ different sets of terms to make a comparable distinction. Greenberg and Mitchell use "drive/structure model" and "relational/structure model" (20), phrasings that seem to me not only awkward but seriously problematic because of the way they imply a commitment to Freud's structural theory, a difficulty Mitchell finesses later (1988, viii) by treating object relations as part of a "relational theory" that excludes drive theory and ego psychology. Eagle provides another instance of inconsistent terminology when he writes dichotomously of "Freudian instinct theory" as against "a psychology of object relations" (1984, 19)—as though there were no overlap. In one sense, of course, there is no middle ground here. Yet we need to make room, as Eagle does in his discussions, for elements of object-relational theory in Freud, a situation I try to account for by speaking of the "drive-oriented" object relations theory of Freud and some of his followers without excluding the possibility of the presence of traces of drive theory in the positions of figures who are fundamentally person-oriented, like Winnicott. A clearer, more precise sense of what the terms "drive-oriented" and "person-oriented" are meant to convey will unfold as discussion proceeds. Meanwhile these two categories are intended to provide a set of coordinates in terms of which to argue the claim that contemporary psychoanalysis needs to adopt a person-oriented theory of object relations, more unreservedly than it already has, in order to be free of the defects of Freud's drive-oriented emphasis and to be responsive to empirical findings and clinical evidence concerning the formative role of interpersonal relationships in human development.

FREUD'S MIXED LEGACY

The origins of many of the intractable difficulties of Freud's early theorizing can be located in the formulations of *Three Essays on the Theory of Sexuality* (1905b). One of the most momentous of these derives from Freud's insistence on isolating "the sexual aim" from "the sexual object" (1905b, 135–36). He argues that abnormal sexuality shows that "the sexual instinct and the sexual object are merely soldered together" (148). He urges us to "loosen the bond" in our minds because "it seems probable that the sexual instinct is in the first instance independent of its object," and shortly thereafter he stresses that under a great many circumstances "the nature and importance of the sexual object recedes into the background" (149). This emphasis allows Freud to valorize sexuality at the expense of object relations, such as when he remarks that children behave "as though their dependence on the people looking after them were in the nature of sexual love," adding, "Anxiety in children is originally nothing other than an expression of the fact that they are feeling the loss of the person they love" (224). Freud's language also performs the maneuver of constituting *all* objects as *sexual* objects, by definition, with the paradoxical result that while sexuality can be discussed more or less independently from objects, objects themselves can never be divorced from sexuality, a position that soon hardens into doctrine. Further instances of Freud's perspective can be found in the following statements, some of them from late in his career. After claiming that "sexual life does not begin only at puberty, but starts . . . soon after birth" (1940, 152), Freud goes on to characterize the child's tie to his mother as an *erotic* one: "A child's first erotic object is the mother's breast that nourishes it; love has its origin in attachment to the satisfied need for nourishment" (1940, 188). He adds, in the language of seduction theory, "By her care of the child's body she becomes its first seducer" (188). Thus it is that Freud comes to regard all initial object relations as incestuous in their essential character, all subsequent relations as tainted by the lingering psychological influence of the earliest ones (1905b, 225–28), and he even goes so far as to think of "an excess of parental affection" (223) as potentially harmful.

Freud's conceptualization of sexual behavior as instinctive does not, in itself, constitute a problem within the scope of the issues being considered here, though it should be noted that in place of speaking of "the sexual instinct," as Freud does, I shall try to speak instead of "sexual behavior" in order to remain closer to the actualities of human experience and to avoid the common tendency in psychoanalysis to reify abstractions (as in the case of such nominative phrases as "the unconscious," "the ego," "the libido," and so on). Neither does Freud's construction of a general theory of the development of human sexuality from particular bodily zones and events and experiences and stages into the more complex design of adult sexuality constitute a stumbling block, though judgment may be reserved with regard to specific features of this developmental theory. Nature does not make jumps, as an ancient proverb reminds us, so adult sexuality cannot be supposed to blossom overnight out of nowhere. What do constitute major problems with Freud's early theories are, first, his assumption that sexual experience, including fantasy, serves as a privileged arena of psychological conflict; and, second, his metapsychological suppositions known collectively as libido theory. I address the latter problem first.

An endless source of confusion in psychoanalysis results from the common practice of casually using "libidinal" as a synonym for "sexual." Doing so effectively blurs two levels of discourse, the high level of abstraction belonging to libido theory and the clinical, everyday level of immediate observation and experience. Freud himself obscures the difference at the outset of *Three Essays* by equating the term *libido*, Latin for "pleasure," with "sexual instinct" (1905b, 135). Later he calls it "the energy of the sexual instinct" (163). He thinks of this sexual energy as a psychic, or "mental" energy, a "force" (177). Freud's inclination to describe the action of the libido in the naively concrete language of hydraulic flow has been a target of widespread criticism. Freud depicts "the libido" as flowing through "channels" that are like "inter-communicating pipes" (151n); these "mental forces" can be dammed up, and "diverted" (178), and of course "repressed"; in some cases "the libido behaves like a stream whose main bed has become blocked. It proceeds to fill up collateral channels which may hitherto have been empty" (170). Elsewhere Freud describes libido in highly abstract ways: "We have defined the concept of libido as a quantitatively variable force which could serve as a measure of processes and transformations occurring in the field of sexual excitation" (217) and as "a measure of the demand made upon the mind for work" (168). Freud explicitly distinguishes "libidinal and other forms of psychical energy" from the energy made available by metabolic processes (217), lest there be any question on that score. But the more one reads, the more difficult it becomes to decide just exactly what Freud did have in mind by the concept of libido—quite apart from the problem of whether or not this concept can be found to correspond to anything in the real world, a problem to be addressed late in this chapter in the context of considering various published critiques of libido theory. In any case, it becomes understandable that even those discriminating and indefatigable lexicographers, Laplanche and Pontalis, lamely concede that "the concept of libido itself has never been clearly defined" (1973, 239).

Although related ideas of Freud involving such distinctions as those between the sexual instincts and the ego instincts, and the distinction between ego-libido and object-libido, will be passed over for the time being, it will be useful to dwell for a moment on the comparison Freud makes between the sexual instinct and what he refers to as "the herd instinct" (1923, 257). Freud doubts the innateness of any social instinct, but he believes that even if it were innate it could probably "be traced back to what were originally libidinal object-cathexes" (258). He claims that the social instincts belong to a class of aim-inhibited sexual impulses. "To this class belong in particular the affectionate relations between parents and children, which were originally fully sexual, feelings of friendship, and the emotional ties in marriage which had their origin in sexual attraction" (258). These assumptions on his part stand in stark contrast to those of person-oriented object relations theory in general and to attachment theory in particular, as later discussion will emphasize.

The underlying purpose of Freud's theory of sexuality is to account for neuroses, "which can be derived only from disturbances of sexual life" (1905b, 216). In "My Views on the Part Played by Sexuality in the Aetiology of the Neuroses" (1906) Freud summarizes his position. Although he says he had earlier attributed to sexual factors "no more significance than any other emotional source of feeling" (1906, 272), he eventually arrives at a different decision: "The *unique* significance of sexual experiences in the aetiology of the psychoneuroses seemed to be established beyond a doubt; and this fact [in midsentence an opinion becomes a "fact"] remains to this day one of the cornerstones of my theory [of neurosis]" (1906, 273; italics added). These experiences lie in "the remote past" of the developmental continuum (274). Freud mentions one further constraint: for childhood sexual experiences to be pathogenic, they must have been conflictful (have been repressed), the reason being that some individuals who experience sexual irregularities in childhood do not become neurotic (276–77). This qualification can be regarded as a pivotal one. If the essential etiological factor is the presence of *conflict*, as distinct from what kind of situation is involved, then it may turn out that conflicts relating to sexuality are by no means *unique* in the sense of constituting the sole class of crippling influences. From the perspective of a person-oriented theory of object relations, in contrast, conflicts with important others may or may not include sexual elements, but if the others are important persons, such as parents, the potential for serious conflict must necessarily be of a high order whether or not sexual factors are present.

What is plain to see is the mixed nature of Freud's legacy. Try as he will, his theory of sexual motivation (as distinct from his theory of sexual development) never manages to divorce sexual impulses from objects more than momentarily, and analytically—in the root sense of the word (from *analyein*, to "break up"). It therefore becomes reasonable to say that in addition to a drive-oriented motivational theory he bequeaths elements of a person-oriented theory of object relations, especially if one thinks about the relative weight of object-relational factors in the oedipus complex. The same point holds true a fortiori with regard to the transference, which is nothing if not a replication of variants of earlier object relations. Also worth mentioning here, if only in passing, is the object-relational orientation of the mental processes known as incorporation, introjection, and identification, particularly where Freud talks about the internalization of aspects of an object relation, as in the case of the development of superego functions, and the introjection of an object in the instance of mourning. While it is true that Freud conceptualizes the "introjection of the object into the ego" as "a substitute for a libidinal object-tie" (1921, 108), one has only to replace "libidinal" by "emotional" for such a passage to be harmonious with a person-oriented perspective.

CONTRIBUTIONS TO OBJECT RELATIONS THEORY

The task of identifying various contributions, other than Freud's, to the development of a person-oriented position in psychoanalysis begins with Melanie Klein. She may be thought of as an amphibian, a creature who swims in the great sea of Freudian instinct theory but travels as well on the solid land of object relations. She accepts libido theory without reservation. She does more than merely accept the idea of a death instinct. She embraces it, thinking of it as innate in infants and as giving rise to fears of annihilation and persecutory anxiety (1952a, 198). Her views of the importance of human sexuality parallel Freud's and often take the form of comparably extreme statements, such as her claim that behind every [!] type of play activity of children "lies a process of discharge of masturbatory phantasies" (1932, 31). Grosskurth, writing in connection with the case of Richard, quotes E. R. Geleerd as remarking, "Klein's random way of interpreting does not reflect the material [of the Richard case] but, rather, her preconceived theoretical assumptions regarding childhood development" (1986, 270). Grosskurth then quotes from her own interview with Richard:

> The only toys I can remember were the battleships. I mentioned to you this morning that I remember going on about the fact that we were going to bomb the Germans, and seize Berlin, and so on and so on and then Brest. Melanie seized on b-r-e-a-s-t, which of course was very much her angle. She would often talk about the "big Mummy genital" and the "big Daddy genital," or the "good Mummy genital" or the "bad Daddy genital" . . . a strong interest in genitalia. (273)

In Klein's defense it is only fair to say that her preoccupation with aggression balances her interest in sexuality. As Dr. David Slight, another of her analysands, put it, "Freud made sex respectable, and Klein made aggression respectable" (Grosskurth 1986, 189).

In contrast to her reliance on instinct theory, on the other hand, Klein's work has been celebrated for its conceptualization of a personal world of internalized objects, "a world of figures formed on the pattern of the persons we first loved and hated in life, who also represent aspects of ourselves" (Riviere 1955, 346). In its early stages, this is a terrifying world: "The idea of an infant of from six to twelve months trying to destroy its mother by every method at the disposal of its sadistic tendencies—with its teeth, nails and excreta and with the whole of its body, transformed in imagination into all kinds of dangerous weapons—presents a horrifying, not to say unbelievable, picture to our minds" (Klein 1932, 187). Before they become whole ones, the objects of this world are "part objects" by virtue of the process of splitting: "The good breast—external and internal—becomes the prototype of all helpful and gratifying objects, the bad breast the prototype of all external and internal persecutory objects" (1952a, 200). Worth noting is the frequency with which Klein broadens sexuality and aggression into experience-near terms like "love" and "guilt": "Synthesis between feelings of love and destructive impulses towards one and the same object—the breast—give rise to depressive anxiety, guilt, and the urge to make reparation to the injured love object, the good breast" (1952a, 203). The objects of this inner world follow law-like mental processes, among them, introjection, projection, and projective-identification. Most important for its implications for a person-oriented theory of object relations, Klein envisions a world of internalized objects in which sexual aims and sexual objects are not, as in Freud, isolated from each other: "There is no instinctual urge, no anxiety situation, no mental process which does not involve objects, external or internal; in other words, object-relations are at the *centre* of emotional life" (1952b, 53).

Because of the extent to which he repudiated instinct theory in favor of an object-relations orientation, Fairbairn's role was even more pivotal than Klein's. Fairbairn did away with the death instinct, and with the id. He states the relevant positions succinctly in his synopsis (1963): "There is no death instinct; and aggression is a reaction to frustration or deprivation" (224). "Since libido is a function of the ego and aggression is a reaction to frustration or deprivation, there is no such thing as an 'id' " (224). He almost, but not quite, did away with libido as well, his most revolutionary statement in this regard being, "The ego, and therefore libido, is fundamentally object-seeking" (224). Fairbairn launched what looked like a frontal, all-out attack on libido theory in his 1941 paper, where he devoted an early section of the paper to "the inherent limitations of the libido theory," arguing that the time has come for classic libido theory to be transformed into a theory of object relations, that "the great limitation of the present libido theory as an explanatory system resides in the fact that it confers the status of libidinal attitudes upon various manifestations which turn out to be merely *techniques for regulating the object-relationships of the ego,*" and that "*the ultimate goal of libido is the object*" (1952, 31; italics Fairbairn's). Although Fairbairn did not fully and officially liberate himself from the concept of libido, he may be said to have done so in a *virtual* way. One sees this change, for example, in the case he mentions of a female patient so desperate for attention and affection from her father, a detached and unapproachable man, that the thought occurs to her one day, "Surely it would appeal to him if I offered to go to bed with him!" (1952, 37). Fairbairn's "take" on this thought is that it constitutes a kind of pseudo-incest: "Her incestuous wish thus represented a desperate attempt to make an *emotional contact* with her object" (37; italics added). Later he adds, "What emerges as clearly as anything else from the analysis of such a case is that the greatest need of a child is to obtain conclusive assurance (a) that he is genuinely loved as a person by his parents, and (b) that his parents genuinely accept his love" (39). The frustration of not being loved, and not having his love accepted, "is the greatest trauma that a child can experience," writes Fairbairn (40), who, in contrast to Freud's tendency to think in terms of quantities of excitation, stresses "the quality of dependence upon the object" (40) and, by implication, the quality of treatment by the object.

Fairbairn needs to be recognized as an important forerunner of attachment theory, especially in connection with his remarks on wartime neurosis and psychosis. His experience of military cases leaves him in no doubt that "the chief predisposing factor in determining the breakdown of a soldier . . . is infantile dependence upon his objects," the most distinctive feature of military breakdowns being "separation-anxiety" (1952, 79–80). He discusses several cases (256–88). The drift of the problems is that those who seem to need to go home because they are ill in actuality become psychologically ill because they need to go home! In line with what Fairbairn has in common with attachment theory (though in a different context), Greenberg and Mitchell remark that for Fairbairn "the essential striving of the child is not for pleasure but for contact. He *needs* the other. If the other is available for gratifying, pleasurable exchange, the child will enter into pleasurable activities." But if the parent offers only painful or unfulfilling contacts, they add, "the child does not abandon the parent to search for more pleasurable opportunities. The child needs the parent, so he integrates his relations with him on a suffering, masochistic basis" (1983, 173).

The work of Winnicott is so well known and so uncontroversial as to warrant summarizing his contributions to person-oriented object relations theory with a brevity disproportionate to his influence. Not being a systematic theorist may have made it easier for him to retain his official allegiance to traditional instinct theory while in practice he sustained a decidedly person-oriented position, with only occasional lapses, such as the Kleinian tenor of his technique with the so-called Piggle case mentioned earlier. Winnicott's contributions to person-oriented theory take many forms, one of them being his enlargement of the psychoanalytic scene by paying at least as much attention to children's actual relationships with their real mothers as he did to their internalized (m)others. He regarded Klein as giving lip service to environmental factors but as being temperamentally incapable of giving them their due (1962, 177). Winnicott's concepts of transitional objects and transitional phenomena continue to be influential, as does the attention he paid to object-relational aspects of the location of cultural experience and the nature of the creative process (1971). He also helped to survey the location of the origin of madness by pinning it down, essentially, to the experience of separation anxiety (1971, 97), a position consonant with Fairbairn's assumptions about the development of wartime psychosis. Characteristic of the fundamental soundness of Winnicott's ideas about object relations, and perhaps representative of other things that might be included among his contributions, is his understanding of the importance of the possibility of self-object differentiation taking place without triggering unbearable feelings of interpersonal isolation. He understood the paradox that only in the *presence* of their mothers can children develop the capacity to be alone (1958, 29–36), and the further paradox that separateness (in the sense of being alone but not lonely) can be experienced without the loss of a sense of relatedness by virtue of the possibility of the benign internalization of the good object, and by virtue of what Winnicott refers to as the "use" of an object (1971, 86–94).

Guntrip, who enjoyed the distinct advantage of being analyzed by both Fairbairn and Winnicott (see Guntrip 1975), makes his own contribution in the form of integrating the views of others. "The history of psychoanalysis is the history of the struggle for emancipation, and the slow emergence, of personal theory or object-relational thinking" he writes in his last book (1971, 46), where he records these developments. After criticizing Freud's libido theory as mechanistic and nonpsychological (31–34), Guntrip classifies sexuality as an "appetite," like hunger, thirst, excretion, and other bodily needs, and remarks, "The appetites *can* all be endowed with personal-relationship significance" (35). "I have never yet met any patient," he adds, "whose overintense sexuality and/or aggression could not be understood in object-relational terms, as resulting from too great and too early deprivations of mothering and general frustration of healthy development in his childhood" (40). In praise of Klein's contribution he writes, "She arrived at the fundamental truth that human nature is object-relational in its very essence, at its innermost heart" (58). Guntrip also pays tribute to the strength of the social elements in the work of figures like Sullivan and Erikson. What seems most distinctive about Guntrip's achievement in the context of the present discussion is his adoption of a definitive position, one fully embracing a person-oriented theory of object relations while rejecting drive-oriented explanations. At the same time, Guntrip contrives to be reality oriented (in the sense of external, interpersonal relationships) without obliterating, as attachment theory tends to do, the equally real realm of internalized object-relational processes.

While not all contributions to the development of a person-oriented theory of object relations lend themselves to easy categorization, the group of figures Greenberg and Mitchell devote a chapter to under the heading of "Interpersonal Psychoanalysis" can scarcely be overlooked. Greenberg and Mitchell maintain that interpersonal psychoanalysis, unlike classical Freudian drive theory, does not qualify as an integrated theory. "It is instead a set of different approaches to theory and clinical practice held together by shared underlying assumptions and premises, drawing in common on what we have characterized as the relational/structural model" (1983, 79). The key figures of the group, Harry Stack Sullivan, Erich Fromm, Karen Horney, Clara Thompson, and Frieda Fromm-Reichmann, began with a common starting point, "a conviction that classical drive theory was fundamentally wrong in its basic premises concerning human motivation," and shared in common the belief "that classical Freudian theory underemphasized the larger social and cultural context" (80). Greenberg and Mitchell mention Sullivan's claim that every major aspect of Freudian drive theory can be understood better in the context of interpersonal and social processes (87), in which connection they quote this passage: "A personality can never be isolated from the complex of interpersonal relations in which the person lives and has his being" (90). Sullivan's pair of theorems concerning what he refers to as "the tension of anxiety," which I quote because of their parallel to the assumptions of attachment theory, constitute an illustration of his interpersonal emphasis. The first theorem reads, "The observed activity of the infant arising from the tension of needs induces tension in the mothering one, which tension is experienced as tenderness and as an impulsion to

activities toward the relief of the infant's needs" (1953, 39). The second
one reads, "The tension of anxiety, when present in the mothering one,
induces anxiety in the infant" (41).

The enlargement of a person-oriented theory of object relations so as
to include attachment theory is so substantial a task that discussion of the
work of Bowlby and his followers will be reserved until chapter 2, except
to say in passing that the concept of attachment provides a broad, fundamentally sound, empirically well-substantiated explanation of a realm of
behavior crucial to the concerns of psychoanalysis.

Still to be considered are two important figures on the American scene:
Margaret Mahler and Heinz Kohut. The work of both figures leans in the
direction of person-oriented object relations while harking back, in various ways and to differing degrees, to a drive-oriented position. Greenberg and Mitchell shrewdly point in this connection to the dual referents
of Mahler's concept of symbiosis, which denotes an actual relationship,
that between infant and mother, and an intrapsychic event, a fantasy: "It
is at once a description of the behavior of two people and a metapsychological explanation of the behavior of one of them" (1983, 286). Thus
Mahler creates "an interface between a developmental theory of object
relations and a drive-model metapsychology" (286)—or at least tries to.
Greenberg and Mitchell call into question "the extent to which she has
integrated her observations into the explanatory framework of drive theory" (294). For his part, Eagle believes that Mahler's concepts of "symbiotic gratification and particularly separation-individuation are most
meaningfully understood, not in terms of (sexual and aggressive) drive
gratification, but in terms of attachment behavior" (1984, 25). As for
Kohut, his early work utilizes libido theory pervasively. He refers, for
example, to the self itself as a structure "cathected with instinctual energy"
(1971, xv), and speaks of "idealizing narcissistic libido" as "the main
source of libidinal fuel" (40) for culturally valued activity (Freud's concept
of sublimation, in essence). Kohut's later work (1977) radically qualifies
his reliance on drive theory in a way that makes many of his formulations
seem not all that different from British object relations theory (which he
seldom refers to; he employs the term "self-object" in those situations in
which non-Kohutians would simply use "object"). Kohut writes that
drive experiences are "*subordinated to* the child's experience of the relation
between the self and the self-objects" (1977, 80; italics added). "The
infantile sexual drive in isolation is not the primary psychological configuration. . . . The primary psychological configuration (of which the drive

is only a constituent) is the experience of the relation between the self and the empathic self-object" (1977, 122). Yet the incidence of Kohut's references to drive theory remains high in his later work. Another complication lies in the way Freud's concept of narcissism, itself born of libido theory, constitutes the cornerstone of Kohut's self psychology. Mahler and Kohut may both be read, if one is so inclined, as important figures in the inexorable advance of person-oriented object relations theory, even though their loyalties to drive-oriented theory proved more than mildly intractable.

DRIVE THEORY: CRITIQUES AND DEFENSES

Most of the discussion in the previous section concerning the relative merits of drive-oriented and person-oriented object relations theories proceeded without the benefit of considering various frontal attacks on drive theory that have been launched during recent decades from within the pale of psychoanalysis. Critiques by Holt, Rubinstein, G. S. Klein, Bowlby, Rosenblatt and Thickstun, Peterfreund, and Breger will be treated as representative. These figures belong to no easily definable psychoanalytic school. With the notable exception of Bowlby, their critiques do not arise in the immediate context of object relations theory. Because of the length and complexity of these studies, only a sampling of the views put forth can be mentioned here.

Holt (1965) examines the biological assumptions of Freud's theory deriving from his teachers (all of the school of Helmholtz: against vitalism and preaching the doctrine of physicalistic physiology), in particular Freud's adoption of Brucke's reflex-arc model of brain activity. At one point Holt lists a number of "biological facts" Freud would have deemed significant had he known them: the fact that "the nervous system is perpetually *active*"; the fact that "the effect of stimulation is primarily to *modulate* the activity of the nervous system"; the fact that "the nervous system does not *transmit* energy" but *propagates* it instead; and the fact that "the tiny energies of the nerves bear encoded information and are *quantitatively negligible*" (108–9). One of the most interesting points Holt makes concerns the inadequacy of Freud's drive-discharge theory in accounting for "*enduring* object-relations" (118). In a later, less guarded paper, Holt says that the theory of instinctual drives "is so riddled with philosophical and factual errors and fallacies that nothing less than discarding the concept of drive or instinct will do" (1976, 159). He proposes, in lieu of it, to focus on Freud's concept of wish. In his paper on the psychoanalytic theory of motivation, Rubinstein proposes that the explanatory purpose of psychic energy can be taken over by the concept of information: "In current descriptions of nervous functioning the concept of information plays a much more prominent role than the concept of energy" (1967, 73). In G. S. Klein's analysis of what he refers to as Freud's two theories of sexuality (metapsychological and clinical), he denounces libido theory but does not make a clean break with Freud's emphasis on the importance of sexuality. He regards it as more important than other sources of motivation. He writes, in particular, of "the unique conflict-inducing potential of sexual experience compared with other motivational sources" (1976, 114). Eagle remarks in this connection, "Klein believed he could separate libido theory from the general Freudian position regarding the centrality of sexuality in behavior, but, in fact, they are too intimately linked for that to be easily accomplished" (1984, 89).

The next four figures, all influenced by general systems theory, have in common a strong commitment to the perspectives of science. In his critique of libido theory, Bowlby claims that the model of psychical energy is unrelated, logically, to the concepts that psychoanalysts since Freud regard as central to psychoanalysis: "the role of unconscious mental processes, repression as a process actively keeping them unconscious, transference as a main determinant of behaviour, the origin of neurosis in childhood trauma" (1969, 16). What multiplies the power of Bowlby's critique is the cogency of what he substitutes for drive theory, namely, attachment theory, a theory of object-relational behavior that he grounds on empirical data and elaborates on within a framework of general systems theory, especially the branch known as cybernetics. Independently and at about the same time Peterfreund (1971) reconceptualized virtually all aspects of psychoanalysis along similar lines, paying particular attention, among other things, to the deficiencies of Freud's theory of psychic energy. Also at about the same time Rosenblatt and Thickstun (1970) published a critique of the concept of psychic energy, criticizing it, among other reasons, for its mind-body dualism and for its inability to explain the phenomenon of pleasurable tension. "It is our belief," they conclude, "that the theory of psychic energy should be abandoned, and that the elements for substitute paradigms are now available" (272). In *Modern Psychoanalytic Concepts in a General Psychology* (1977) they elaborate those paradigms.

Breger's critique of Freud's theory of sexuality contends that the meta-psychology brings together "two powerful, conventional trends: the belief that theory should have a physicalist-mechanist form and the belief that sexuality is basically a harmful activity" (1981, 67). This contention is an extension of Breger's thesis that sexuality gets treated within psychoanalytic theory in inconsistent ways, reflecting Freud's "unfinished journey, the incomplete transition from a conventional to a critical world view" (51). Breger, who addresses the problems of Freud's theory of sexuality as a whole as distinct from just libido theory, concludes that "a theory which attempts to explain so many human actions and feelings solely in terms of sexuality creates more problems than it solves" (65). The real question, of course, lies not in the degree of Freud's reductionism, that is, the comparative economy of his explanation of so many things in terms of one principle; the more pressing question has to do with whether he latched onto the right explanatory principle in the first place.

One measure of the bankruptcy of Freudian drive theory may be taken in terms of the presumed efficacy of orthodox sexual (usually oedipal) interpretations in psychoanalysis. If Guntrip can bear witness, Winnicott's empathic, person-oriented responses were far more helpful than Fairbairn's detached, oedipal-libidinal interpretations (1975). At one point in the record he kept of his first training analysis, Guntrip wrote,

> This is one of the points at which I now feel that Fairbairn's constant reiteration of interpretations in terms of penises was a survival of classic Freudian sexology that his theory had moved beyond. I feel that kept me stationary, whereas interpretations in which mother did her best to restrict and dominate would have felt to me much more realistic. In effect, his analysis was a "penis-analysis," not an "ego-analysis." (in J. Hughes 1989, 111)

A rather similar instance of comparisons between the conventional sexual interpretations of one analyst and the person-oriented interpretations of another can be found in Margaret Little's account of her treatment (1985), first and superficially with a Jungian, then from 1940–47 with Ella Freeman Sharpe, and finally for seven years with Winnicott. Little, who characterizes her anxieties as psychotic, pictures her analysis with Sharpe as one of constant struggle between them, Sharpe "insisting on interpreting what I said as due to intrapsychic conflict [having] to do with infantile sexuality, and I trying to convey to her that my real problems were matters of existence and identity" (15). Little continues: "I did not know what 'myself' was; sexuality (even if known) was totally irrelevant and meaningless unless existence and survival could be taken for granted, and personal identity established" (15). Little explains her dilemma this way: "Whenever I spoke of either of my parents, what I said was, for her, phantasy, and any reference to the realities was taking refuge from it. So I was doubly caught in the 'spider's web'; *I* was the crazy one, not my mother; *she* [Sharpe] was the one who 'knew,' as my mother, not I, had always known; while *my* recognition of my own and my mother's psychosis was dismissed as phantasy" (16). After an interim period with Marion Milner, Little began an analysis with Winnicott. He was able to provide a long-term, empathic environment that allowed Little to "work" at her own pace. He evidently succeeded in providing for Little the kind of potential space she required in order to become a person in her own right—with a corresponding relief from her psychotic anxieties. "In the words of an old friend from before analysis, I was 'not recognizable as the same person' " (37). While Little's experiences do not provide a perfectly clear-cut, uncomplicated illustration because of the presence of other issues, such as the differing developmental levels Sharpe and Winnicott chose to address, plus the fact that Little's work with Sharpe was by no means without object relational elements, certainly not without very early ones, Little's account may nevertheless be regarded as highlighting some of the differences between drive-oriented and person-oriented approaches. Extensive case material in chapters 3 and 4 will serve as further illustration of such differences.

Given the amount and seriousness of the criticism of drive theory in psychoanalysis, the comparative absence of significant countering responses, and the extent to which so many figures important in the history of object relations psychology have shifted toward a person-oriented position, the amount of profession-wide reluctance to give up drive theory is surprising. One instance can be located in the fence-straddling position, mentioned earlier, of Greenberg and Mitchell: their claim that we shall have to live with two incompatible theories of human behavior, one drive oriented and one person oriented. Late in their book—an extraordinarily valuable compendium of information about object relations theory remarkable for the degree of attentiveness, discrimination, and detachment they exhibit in describing, usually with great fidelity and thoroughness, the differing viewpoints at issue—they speak of the two object relational orientations as being based on incompatible but equally meaningful philosophical positions, one being that humans are inescapably individual creatures and the other that they are unavoidably social creatures (1983, 403). Claiming further that "model mixing is unstable" (403), they argue that "it is neither useful nor appropriate to question whether either psychoanalytic model is 'right' or 'wrong.' Each is complex, elegant, and resilient enough to account for all phenomena" (404). They even go so far as to declare that "the evaluation of psychoanalytic theories is a matter of personal choice" (407)! Yet Greenberg and Mitchell appear to drop their stance of rhetorical neutrality at that point in the book where they associate themselves with Jacobson's position: "Jacobson's work overall constitutes *what we consider* the most satisfying drive/ structure model theory after Freud's" (306; italics added). Here they seem to associate themselves with her position even though they recognize her accommodations to an object-relational view to be an instance of model mixing, a practice they elsewhere decry. If the position they adopt here constitutes a departure from their customary neutrality, perhaps it accounts for why they fail to do justice to the critiques of drive theory by Guntrip, G. S. Klein, Gill, Holt, and Schafer which they cite. One cannot, after all, take these critiques seriously while at the same time maintaining that explanatory parity exists between the drive-oriented and person-oriented positions. An alternative possibility is that the appearance of fence-straddling created by the pose of detached objectivity in Greenberg and Mitchell does not mask any lingering allegiance to drive theory but, on the contrary, disguises their unfettered commitment to more progressive views, views they may have avoided espousing directly as a way of circumventing the arousal of counter productive antagonism that might further polarize the opposing camps instead of encouraging a potentially productive exchange of ideas. Whatever his strategy in 1983, five years later Mitchell unequivocally endorses "a purely *relational* mode perspective, unmixed with drive-model premises" (1988, 54). He also says that work in preparation by Greenberg takes a similar position (135). It matters little whether the radical shift in their position was real or virtual; what I am calling attention to is the fact that in giving the appearance of countenancing drive-oriented object relations theory as still being intellectually respectable in 1983, the enormously influential, authoritative study of Greenberg and Mitchell may have had the effect of deterring rather than spurring a desirable evolution of views in the profession.

Another and more obvious instance of the present unsatisfactory state of affairs in psychoanalysis appears in the form of the polemical aggressiveness of Edelson's recent book, *Psychoanalysis: A Theory in Crisis* (1988), especially that portion of the work focusing on the theory of sexuality.

We have but to weed the garden of psychoanalysis of its stagnating, choking overgrowth, believes Edelson, for the distinctive contributions of psychoanalysis to emerge "sharp, clear, in bold relief" (xvi). For him this means giving primacy, among other things, to "the causal force of the quest for sexual pleasure over that of the quest for the object . . . and the causal force of sexual wishes over that of aggressive (and non-sexual) wishes" (xxi). Edelson believes the psychoanalytic theory of sexuality "to be in danger of dilution and displacement to the periphery by current preoccupation with 'the self,' 'identity,' 'object-relations,' 'interpersonal interactions,' 'the importance of the mother-infant relation and the pre-oedipal experiences of the very young infant,' and 'aggression' " (xxvii). What he wants to do is to restore sexuality to the glory of its former centrality in psychoanalysis. He asks, "Do object-relations theories involve rather a redefinition of just what phenomena are of interest to psycho-analysis?" (224) He admits, "I don't know," yet that admission of igno-rance does not deter him for a moment from asserting that "the inevitable slide away from the mind's workings to interpersonal interactions directly contradicts"—as far as he is concerned—"what is most distinctive about psychoanalysis" (225). If he believes "the slide" to be "inevitable," one wonders why Edelson insists on adopting the heroic posture of fighting fate by positioning himself directly in opposition to it. The point of mentioning Edelson's position on drive theory, one that many may find starkly reactionary, is that his viewpoint—that of a psychoanalyst of some eminence—is far from being unshared by others, and must be taken seriously, if only for the distinctness with which it describes a perspective currently in question.

The position espoused in this chapter, and further discussed in chapter 2, amounts very nearly to a mirror-opposite of the one defended by Edelson. It assumes that attachment behavior, which will be treated as a special branch of object relations behavior, is instinctive, like sexual be-havior, at least in its beginnings. It further assumes that sexual behavior needs to be regarded, especially in terms of its potential for producing conflict, as intermingled with, but subordinate to, object-relations behav-ior. The concept of psychic energy has no place in this explanatory framework. Sexual behavior, whatever its degree of instinctiveness, re-flects but one of many human needs whose priority at any given moment varies according to circumstances, that is, to the urgency of other priori-ties, but which over long periods of time does not ordinarily take prece-dence over the need of human beings for emotionally significant personal

attachments, including not only the initial and highly instinctive attachment of child to parent but also those taking the form of endless possible
permutations of the primal one such as those we encounter in the form of
fantasy in the realm of art. The problem of the relationship of self to other
in this scheme of things constitutes a separate but related issue.

2.

TOWARD A UNIFIED THEORY
OF OBJECT RELATIONS

One of the tasks facing anyone discussing object relations theory is that of mapping the terrain. What is to be included in the territory? To what extent is the field of object relations congruent with the domain of psychoanalysis as a whole? Pine treats object relations as just one of what he calls the four psychologies of psychoanalysis: "the psychologies of drive, ego, object relations, and self" (1988, 571). Pine's discussion of these realms of theory makes no effort to reconcile their incompatibilities. He ignores the massive case against drive theory. He also ignores the possibility that ego psychology, self psychology, and object relations have much in common, whatever their differences. Pine's uncritical eclecticism may be contrasted to Gedo's cautious holism. Gedo, who laments the failure of psychoanalysis "to produce a theoretical consensus with regard to the proper place of object relations in our conceptual armamentarium" (1979, 362), questions Kohut's claim that scientific disciplines may legitimately utilize uncoordinated fragments of theory: "If we have a choice, a unitary theory is preferable to a patchwork, the components of which bear no discernible relation to each other" (364).

According to the perspective assumed in this chapter, the deficiencies of drive theory and ego psychology have long since overwhelmed their former usefulness. The functions they sought to explain, such as unconscious motivation and conflict, can be better understood along different lines. As for what is left of Pine's four psychologies, object relations theory and what I call *self theory* (as distinguished from Kohut's self psychology) overlap so much as to make their concerns virtually inseparable *within the territory of psychoanalysis,* provided, of course, that one assumes that psychoanalysis is a special psychology, limited in scope, which entertains no ambitions to be a general psychology. When I say that the concerns of self theory and object relations theory are virtually inseparable, I naturally do not mean they are indistinguishable from each other as fields of investigation. As definable areas of knowledge they reflect different perspectives and priorities. The crucial task is to explore the overlap of these distinguishable realms of attention without becoming confused by the differences. One aspect of the problem is terminological. For example, use of the terms "self" and "object" propagates a measure of confusion by tending to reify abstract categories in a way that blurs the existential inseparability of self and other, a conceptual problem addressed by Winnicott's famous dictum (1952, 97–100) that there is no such thing as a baby (in that babies never appear except as parts of the "nursing couple" dyad). Mitchell speaks to the same issue, the impossibility of dealing with self and other separately, when he writes, "To assign priority to sense of self, object ties, or patterns of interaction is like trying to decide whether it is the skin, the bones, or the musculature that preserves the body form. . . . The intrapsychic and the interpersonal are continually interpenetrating realms, each with its own set of processes, mechanisms, and concerns" (1988, 35).

For the practical purposes of ordinary discussion, therefore, the present work handles self theory as an aspect of object relations theory, object relations theory as an aspect of self theory, and attachment theory as a special branch of both. The possibilities for consolidation seem endless. One has only to think, for instance, of Bowlby's emphasis on children's sense of security in the presence of attachment figures in conjunction with the attention Winnicott and Mahler give to children's ability to play in the presence of their mothers to get a sense of how much attachment theory has in common with object relations theory. An instructive instance of a particular analyst whose work successfully utilizes the combined perspectives of classical psychoanalysis, object relations theory, attachment theory, interactionalist views (Bower, Brazelton), and self theory without ignoring the differences can be found in V. Hamilton's *Narcissus and Oedipus* (1982). Stern speaks of his version of self theory as having much in common with psychoanalysis and attachment theory, though it differs from them in treating a subjective sense of self as its primary organizing principle (1985, 25). Eagle (1984) aligns his views of object relations theory with attachment theory. Though other examples of partial integration of these theories could be mentioned, the task of systematically combining the most meaningful parts of the various perspectives in question (in a way that would meet Gedo's standards for a unitary theory) remains so formidable as to be far beyond the scope of the present chapter, which aspires to do no more than peek through certain windows of opportunity in order to see what a unified theory of object relations might look like when seen from a contemporary vantage point.

POSITIONING ATTACHMENT THEORY

What should be the place of attachment theory in a person-oriented theory of object relations? The beginning of an answer can be glimpsed in the anecdote Guntrip relates concerning a question Fairbairn poses to a child whose mother has cruelly thrashed her: "Would you like me to find you a new, kind Mummy?" The child answers, "No. I want my own Mummy" (Guntrip 1975, 146). In the context of attachment theory, one can say that the strength of the child's tie to a particular mother—however harsh she may be—infinitely outweighs the possible desirability of any substitute figure. As Guntrip glosses the situation, "The devil you know is better than the devil you do not, and better than no devil at all." One can also say of this tie that it is instinctive, primary (not based on any secondary drive, such as the need for food), and, in Bowlby's cybernetic terminology, the child's behavior (in this instance, her answer to Fairbairn) "is a product of the activity of a number of behavioural systems that have proximity to mother as a predictable outcome" (1969, 179), so that in the presence of anxiety or difficulty (being thrashed) the child paradoxically needs the attacking object more than ever!

Attachment theory can be regarded as the cornerstone of a person-oriented theory of object relations in part because it provides a meaningful substitute, as Bowlby intended it should, for the drive theory of human motivation. It has the potential for modeling both conflictful and harmonious (growth-inducing) relationships. It does not pretend to be a universal theory explaining all forms of human behavior, such as the kind denominated by Lichtenberg (1989) as "exploratory-assertive," but it does offer a suitable framework for understanding the range of behavior normally understood to be subsumed under the heading of object relations. As Rosenblatt and Thickstun remark, speaking of attachment theory, "The central importance of social relationships (in psychoanalytic terms, 'object relations') in shaping the person's emotional and cognitive growth is the clinical essence of psychoanalysis" (1977, 122). Or as Greenberg and Mitchell put it, in person-oriented object relations theory "the unit of study of psychoanalysis is not the individual, but the relational matrix constituted by the individual in interaction with significant others" (1983, 220).

Bowlby himself rarely puts into play the conceptual vocabulary of object relations. Why is that, one may ask, and whatever happened, intellectually and emotionally, to Bowlby's own analyst, Joan Riviere, and to Melanie Klein, one of Bowlby's supervisors? Bowlby does not neglect to acknowledge his debt to them "for grounding me in the object-relations approach to psychoanalysis, with its emphasis on early relationships and the pathogenic potential of loss" (1969, xvii), yet most of his work departs radically from Klein's. The necessary inference for those familiar with Bowlby's methodology and cognitive style is that in rebelling against certain features of contemporary British object relations theory Bowlby bent over backwards to avoid any inferences not based on solid, empirical evidence. Yet his subject matter, as distinguished from his methodology, is entirely object relational. He himself declares that his most "central concepts" are "object relations, separation anxiety, mourning, defence, trauma, [and] sensitive periods in early life" (xv), a group of categories that can be lumped together without any distortion as "object relations." Bowlby specifies that attachment theory *derives* from object relations theory and has much in common with the work of Melanie Klein, Fairbairn, Balint, and Winnicott (17).

Positioning attachment theory vis-à-vis object relations theory necessitates supplying what attachment theory leaves out, such as attention to particular individuals, and to internalized representations and their processing, while emphasizing those features of object relations theory, collectively considered, with which attachment theory is correlative and compatible, such as psychological responses to loss. When I say "object relations theory, collectively considered," I refer as well to ideas deriving from self theory not hitherto part of earlier versions of object relations theory, such as the concept of intersubjectivity and the process Stern calls "affect attunement." Within an expanded framework of self theory and object relations theory, attachment theory as we find it in Bowlby constitutes a special branch, one that continues to grow through his followers' contributions.

After relating the anecdote about Fairbairn's question to the abused child, Guntrip mentions that the story illustrates Fairbairn's concern about the *quality* of parent-child relations. As a rule, Bowlby pays little direct attention to the quality of parenting. He speaks instead, along quantitative lines, of the presence, or temporary absence (separation), or permanent absence (loss) of parenting figures. Since his method is prospective rather than retrospective, he does not rely on case histories of adult individuals for illustration. He limits his attention to pathology pretty much to the directly observable consequences of separation and loss— such as those mentioned in experiments with animals, especially Harlow's. Yet even though Bowlby does not talk much about pathological object relations directly, he does do so on occasion, one of them being when he approvingly cites Bateson's double-bind theory of the origin of schizophrenia (Bowlby 1973, 317–19). Another instance that comes to mind is when Bowlby mentions two cases of matricide: "One, an adolescent who murdered his mother, exclaimed afterwards [presumably without irony], 'I couldn't stand to have her leave me.' " In the other case, "a youth who placed a bomb in his mother's luggage as she boarded an airliner explained, 'I decided that she would never leave me again' " (1973, 251). The point to be registered is that although Bowlby keeps neurosis and psychosis in the background of his discussion in the *Attachment and Loss* trilogy (1969, 1973, 1980), and although he does not spend much time focusing on separation as a source of crippling emotional conflict or behavioral maladaption except when discussing experiments with animals, a comprehensive theory of object-relational conflict cannot possibly avoid attending to the themes of attachment, separation, and loss, particularly insofar as the effects of pathological parenting can be regarded as comparable to those of separation and loss. The beginnings of such an expansion of attachment theory have already been initiated by such figures as Ainsworth, Main and Weston, Henderson, Brown, Adam, and Parkes (all in Parkes and Stevenson-Hinde, 1982), and Bowlby's later work (1979, 1988) addresses the issues of etiology and psychopathology more directly than the *Attachment and Loss* trilogy.

Guntrip's anecdote concerning Fairbairn's question to the little girl implies the presence of a sexual factor when Guntrip remarks (presumably paraphrasing Fairbairn) that the girl's response reflects "the intensity of the libidinal tie to the bad object" (1975, 146). Is this just another instance of "libidinal" being used loosely as a synonym for "emotional," or are such ties erotic? Attachment theory assumes they are not erotic, the need for attachment itself being the primary instinct in operation. What, then, may be said concerning the relation of attachment behavior to sexual behavior, especially when Bowlby expressly declares attachment theory to be an alternative to libido theory (1969, 17)? The answer is that while Bowlby jettisons the theory of psychical energy, and while he tends to exclude sexual behavior from the areas of his attention, he does not in fact deny the existence or even the importance of sexual behavior. He treats sexual behavior (1969, 230–34) as a separate system of activity that has "close linkages" to attachment behavior. These otherwise separate systems of behavior may "impinge" upon and "overlap" each other, the examples he gives of sharing behavioral components being adult clinging and kissing. Presumably only King Solomon could separate erotic factors from attachment factors in lovers' kisses—or in their sexual intercourse, for that matter. For Freud, even thumb sucking is an erotic activity. But Fairbairn believes babies suck their thumbs because there is no breast to suck, so that thumb sucking "represents a technique for dealing with an unsatisfactory object-relationship" (1952, 33). And for Winnicott also, thumb sucking, a transitional phenomenon, clearly pertains as much to other as to self (1971). What matters in this connection is not to locate particular instances of unmixed instinctive behavior but to recognize the high degree of ambiguity often prevailing in human action with respect to the kind, and proportion, of instincts involved. Granting the presence of that ambiguity makes it understandable that what has usually been interpreted as sexual behavior under the aegis of Freud may in fact have been primarily or essentially motivated by attachment needs, a proposition that will be illustrated at length in the reading of Freud's cases in chapter 3.

A factor to consider in the task of positioning attachment theory in a broader theory of object relations concerns the common practice of using the term "attachment" in a literal and very circumscribed manner, often with a sharp distinction between "attachment" and "attachment behavior" (Bowlby, 1982, 371; 1988, 28). Used in this way, the child's answer to Fairbairn, "I want my own Mummy," denotes a fairly literal tie, or emotional bond, to what is by definition the child's primary attachment figure. Although Bowlby generally limits his discussion of attachment behavior to such instances in early childhood, he recognizes that "attachment behaviour does not disappear with childhood but persists throughout life" (1969, 350). He also clearly links transference activity to attachment behavior (1969, 17; 1973, 206, 271). A particularly good instance of Bowlby's use of "presence" and "absence" in a non-literal way occurs when he writes, "A mother can be physically present but 'emotionally' absent. What this means, of course, is that although present in body, a mother may be unresponsive to her child's desire for mothering" (1973, 23). The point being led up to is this: if attachment theory is to be part of a broader theory of object relations instead of being confined for the most part to developmental psychology, then the concept of attachment must be deliteralized and broadened in a way that recognizes its endless permutations. Freud remarks that "the finding of an object is in fact a refinding of it" (1905b, 222). By the same token, one can say that subsequent attachments to some extent replicate earlier ones. All major attachments in adult life constitute versions, or permutations, of earlier attachments, which is tantamount to saying that adult interpersonal relationships reflect the object-relational history of the individuals concerned. Such, at least, will be the position adopted in the pages to come, which will treat all object relations as involving the element, or process, of attachment—even conflicted ones. Normally, of course, the term "attachment," when unmodified by such words as "anxious," has only positive connotations—unlike "object relations," an affectively neutral phrase. Thus expanded, the concept of attachment behavior—roughly the equivalent of Fairbairn's "object-seeking"—functions as the motivational foundation of the entire spectrum of object-relational behavior, including mentational activity such as fantasy. Even masochistic behavior makes a kind of sense within this explanatory framework. It becomes a compromised form of attachment behavior—the perpetuation, or recreation, of the modality of an important earlier relationship—rather than a perverse search for unpleasure, sexual or otherwise.

WHERE, IN REALITY, ARE SELF AND OTHER?

One of the issues that persists in psychoanalysis has to do with the comparative reality of what goes on inside and outside of the domain of mental processing. Where, in this connection, can self and other be said to be located? In defiance of common sense, object relations theory situates others both outside, in "real" space, and inside, in the equally real yet imaginary space of the mind, in the form of residues, or internalizations, of outside others. In similar defiance of common sense, aspects of the self may seem to reside within but may unconsciously be projected onto outside others, or invested, by identification, in some outside per-

son, such as a religious or political leader (Freud 1921). And, to compli-
cate the situation, what was once outside, the other, may, after internalization, be temporarily relocated in outside others (transference), such as
one's analyst. Yet as Schafer reminds us, there are no mental places (1976,
158). A solution to the problem of avoiding the dangers of the convenient fiction of "mental places" is to locate representations of self and
other systemically, as stored information, that is, as conceptual and behavioral programs: "All long-term relationships—including mother-and-child,
husband-and-wife, and patient-and-analyst relationships—can be profitably studied as feedback-regulated, information-processing systems"
(Peterfreund 1971, 159).

Then where does reality come in? Are real events involving real, outside others more real, or more important psychologically, than the undeniably real (really occurring) inner events involving the imagined others
of fantasy? This issue has been troublesome for psychoanalysis. Bowlby,
in the course of criticizing Klein's position that anxiety derives from the
operation of the death instinct, argues that this position has led to clinical
practice that tends to ignore "a person's real experiences, past or present,"
and to treat him "almost as though he were a closed system little influenced by his environment" (1973, 173). Bowlby himself has gone to the
opposite extreme of virtually ignoring fantasy activity in the process of
favoring conventionally observable behavior, a practice suiting his methodology but disenfranchising denizens of the inner world of memory and
desire. Stern addresses the issue of fantasy versus reality by reminding us
that Freud's conception of fantasy as experience distorted by defenses and
wishes "resulted in an ontogenetic theory of experience as fantasy, not of
experience as reality" (1985, 254). Arguing that "current findings from
infancy studies fly against the notion that the pleasure principle develop-
mentally precedes the reality principle," (254–55) Stern contends that
what infants experience, from the very beginning, is mainly reality, and
that subjective experiences involving distortions of reality derive from
later stages of development: "This position is far closer to Kohut's and
Bowlby's contention that pre-Oedipal pathology is due to deficits or
reality-based events—rather than to conflicts, in the psychodynamic sense"
(255). In contrast, Laplanche and Pontalis speak of the danger of regarding real relations with others "as the chief determining factor. This is a
deviation that must be rejected by every analyst for whom the object-
relationship has to be studied essentially in terms of phantasy (though of

course phantasies can modify the apprehension of reality and actions directed towards reality)" (1973, 280).

What I always wonder about while reading Klein's interpretations of the fantasies of her patients' in-session play is not the reality of the fantasies as reported but rather the extent to which these fantasies may be joint productions of analyst and patient, sometimes with more input from analyst than patient, especially in the matter of cueing the patient about the value of sexual elements. Here again is the fantasy, quoted in chapter 1, of an infant attacking its mother (presented in *generalized* form, with Klein's comment): "The idea of an infant of from six to twelve months trying to destroy its mother by every method at the disposal of its sadistic tendencies—with its teeth, nails, and excreta and with the whole of its body, transformed in imagination into all kinds of dangerous weapons— presents a horrifying, not to say unbelievable, picture to our minds" (Klein 1932, 187). Yet even if one elects to argue, siding with Stern, that the evidence of infant research does not corroborate the likelihood that an infant (of six to twelve months) could have experienced such a fantasy, one can nevertheless scarcely deny the extraordinary resemblance of this fantasy to the one depicted in Ted Hughes's poem called "Crow and Mama":

> When Crow cried his mother's ear
> Scorched to a stump.
>
> When he laughed she wept
> Blood her breasts her palms her brow all wept blood.
>
> He tried a step, then a step, and again a step—
> Every one scarred her face forever.
>
> When he burst out in rage
> She fell back with an awful gash and a fearful cry.
>
> When he stopped she closed on him like a book
> On a bookmark, he had to get going.

Then, after futile attempts by Crow to escape from his mother's clutches by jumping successively into a car and a plane,

> He jumped into the rocket and its trajectory
> Drilled clean through her heart he kept on

And it was cosy in the rocket, he could not see much
But he peered out through the portholes at Creation

And saw the stars millions of miles away
And saw the future and the universe

Opening and opening
And kept on and slept and at last

Crashed on the moon awoke and crawled out

Under his mother's buttocks.

                                                            (T. Hughes 1971, 5)

In the words of a discussion on the nature of fantasy, what we may be said to have in hand "is not an *object* [of desire] that the subject imagines and aims at, so to speak, but rather a *sequence* in which the subject has his own part to play and in which permutations of roles and attributions are possible" (Laplanche and Pontalis 1973, 318). Infants may not have such fantasies, but adult poets obviously can, and do, and it is equally obvious that in reading such a poem adult readers can re-experience elements of their own infantile omnipotent rage—as well as a certain Winnicottian satisfaction at the indestructibility of the subjective object. What we may also be said to witness in such a poem, beyond all controversy, is the essential innerness of all literary fantasy, and the emotional reality of it, so that even if Klein's theory and clinical practice may have contaminated the evidence she presents, we can look to the fantasies of literature and other forms of art with at least as much confidence as Freud looked to dreams for wondrous instances of the workings of the mind, especially in the field of object relations.

As for the location of self and other, it will be assumed throughout the present study that figures in a text may be treated as temporary introjects by readers. When I read that Crow's catastrophic mother—to borrow a phrase from Rheingold (1967)—closes in on him "like a book / On a bookmark," I, too, have to get going. And when Crow's activity scars his mother's face forever, I, as reader, may be said to have momentarily internalized Crow-hero's behavior according to the model of the Intro-jecting Reader (Holland 1968). Presumably an elaborate matching takes place during the reading process in which, hypothetically, a perceived or imagined aspect of Hughes's real mother becomes internalized by Hughes, then eventually projected onto Crow's Mama, an attribution that I as reader subsequently introject, match with internalizations of my own, and then respond to—or not, as the case may be—cognitively and affectively, at both conscious and unconscious levels.

CONCEPTUALIZING SELFHOOD

The nature of selfhood is at least as problematic as its location. While the word *self* does not accumulate much resonance in Freud's works, the latent importance of the term can easily be seen reflected in such concepts as the ego (a specialized aspect of self), the superego (the internalized other as part of self-structure), narcissism (self-love), guilt (self-reproach), and self-observation in dreams (Freud's dream censor). The rise of ego psychology and identity theory, and the reactivation of the theory of narcissism in self psychology, may be regarded in some respects as precursors of the development of self theory. Self theory as represented by (but not confined to) Peterfreund (1971), Rosenblatt and Thickstun (1977), Stern (1985), Basch (1988), and Lichtenberg (1989) should probably be regarded as far from fully developed. Even so, and even granting the difficulty of defining selfhood, viable models of self—and the relation of self to other—are now available.

Freud worked with at least three models of selfhood: the layered, or topographical, model (conscious, preconscious, unconscious), a developmental model (oral, anal, phallic, oedipal, etc.), and the structural model (id, ego, superego). Various post-Freudian models of self, in the order of increasing capacity to reflect complexity, treat the self as a container of forces (libido, aggression), a container of representations (e.g., memories, wishes, fantasies), a structure of representations (id, ego, superego; internalized others), and a system of systems (including such systemic functions as were hitherto attributed to the Freudian ego).

Aspects of these ways of modeling self may be glimpsed in the following selection of observations and definitions. Hartmann makes a point of distinguishing ego from self (1964, 127). Jacobson follows Hartmann in using "self" to refer to the whole person (including the individual, his body, body parts, psychic organization). She remarks, "The self. . . points to the person as a subject in distinction from the surrounding world of objects" (1964, 6). Greenberg and Mitchell observe that for Hartmann the self is an *object* as distinct from the *subject* of experience (1983, 299) and that for Mahler the self is "less a functional unit than a critical developmental achievement" (300). Winnicott postulates the existence of a spectrum of selfhood integrity. He represents this spectrum in the form of dichotomous selves: the spontaneous True Self and the compliant False Self (1960, 140–52). Erikson's (1950) identity theory, drawing heavily on Freud's structural and epigenetic models, presents us with a picture of the self functioning to provide continuity through change. Lichtenstein, who postulates that identity maintenance "has priority over any other principle determining human behavior" (1961, 189), offers a transformational model of self as "the sum total of all transformations which are *possible* functions of an early-formed invariant correlation of the various basic elements of the mental apparatus" (1977, 241). For Bettelheim (1967, 56) self "is not an isolated entity. It is a totality of inner processes that develops slowly." Searles (1966) discusses identity as a perceptual organ. In this connection he tells about a schizophrenic patient who repetitively knits "eyes," which are "saucer-like structures with an aperture in the center" (26). When Searles asks if these "eyes" signify "I's", the patient confirms his intuition and makes a drawing of the world as she perceives it: "three large mountain peaks in the center, the head of an Indian prince on the left and a submarine on the right." In essence, says Searles, "she conveyed to me how crazy is the worldview of one who has no reliable 'I' with which to see" (27).

George S. Klein, in conceptualizing self, speaks of beginning "with the assumption of a single apparatus of control which exhibits a variety of dynamic tendencies, the focus of which is either an integration experienced in terms of a sense of continuity, coherence, and integrity, or its impairment, as cleavages or dissonance. I call this central apparatus the 'self' " (1976, 8). Klein views self as effecting control, sustaining identity (a person-oriented element), and resolving conflict. Eagle goes so far as to claim that "without expressly stating it, Klein (1976) essentially reformulates psychoanalytic theory as a psychology of self" (1984, 87). As for Kohut, he writes confusingly of *the* self as a *content* ("a content of the mental apparatus"), as a *structure* of the mind rather than an agency (a structure "cathected with instinctual energy"), and as a *location* (a psychic location) of self representations (1971, xv). Later he stresses the need for what he regards as complementary approaches: "a psychology in which the self is seen as the center of the psychological universe, and a psychology in which the self is seen as a content of a mental apparatus" (1977, xv). Astonishingly, the author of self psychology eventually confesses, "My investigation contains hundreds of pages dealing with the psychology of the self—yet it never assigns an inflexible meaning to the term self, it never explains how the essence of the self should be defined" (310). A less biased observer might contend that Kohut simply fails to treat the topic with reasonable consistency.

Schafer, who emphasizes the wholeness and integrity of individuals as *agents* who must learn to take responsibility for their actions, including their thoughts and feelings, has proved to be one of the most incisive critics of ego psychology, identity theory, and self psychology in his efforts to avoid semantic confusion resulting from models involving split selves, anthropomorphism, reification, and various related errors he encounters in psychoanalytic writing. Schafer criticizes Kohut's conceptualization of self as suffering from an attempt "to mix a phenomenological, experiential, representational concept with the traditional structural-energic metapsychological entities [such as narcissism]" (1976, 116). Schafer even attacks the term "self" itself because of the multiplicity of meanings attributed to it. Worse, the nominative phrase, "the self," tends to reify the concept of self: "Like the thingness and agency attributed to identity, '*the* self' concretizes or substantializes a term whose referents are primarily subjective or experiential and whose force is primarily adverbial and adjectival" (117). Moreover, he adds, "in some of its usages, such as 'self-actualization,' '*the* self' is set up not only as the existential referent of behavior but as, all at once, the motor, the fuel, the driver, and the end point of the journey of existence" (117). Elsewhere Schafer remarks, with commendable clarity, "Self and identity are not things with boundaries, contents, locations, sizes, forces, and degrees of brittleness" (1973, 51). He mentions that individuals' representations of themselves vary enormously in scope, time, origin, and objectivity: "Many are maintained unconsciously (for example, self as phallus and self as turd), and many remain forever uncoordinated, if not contradictory" (52). Schafer distrusts the term *self* because of its protean meanings: it can signify "my body, my personality, my actions, my competence, my continuity, my needs, my agency, and my subjective space. Self is thus a diffuse, multipurpose word" (53). When Schafer addresses the concept of self-control he asks, "But just what does *self-control* refer to? Does it refer to a self that controls, and if so what is the nature of that self? Does it refer to a self that is to be controlled, and if so what is its nature and how does it stand in relation to the exerciser of control . . .?" (1978, 78). As far as Schafer is concerned, "To say that the self controls the self is to commit a category mistake in that controlling anything is one of the constitutive features, or one of the referents, of what we mean by self. We would not say that a thermostat controls a thermostat. . . . When someone is admonished, 'Control yourself,' a logical mistake is being committed" (79).

As it happens, there are models of selfhood that render moot such issues as the multiplicity of function attributed to self and the problem of the location of control. These may be referred to collectively as the systemic model. According to this model, self can be conceptualized as a set or system of indwelling interrelated governing *functions* of the whole person, a superordinate system incorporating innumerable subsystems, both physical ones with bodily organs such as lungs (the respiratory system), and others with less palpable, ponderable elements, such as memory systems, value systems, and sets of self-and-object representations. There is no need for any homunculus-like ego, a regulatory self within the self. Regulation can be thought of, metaphorically, as built in, or wired in. From a cybernetics point of view, the system is self-regulating, the function of control being systemically located, feedback-operated, and subject to the heirarchical constraints of a range of well-established priorities. A systemic view of selfhood conceptualizes awareness in terms of systemic monitoring, and lack of awareness (unconsciousness) as absence of access to specific behavioral programs. Inherently dynamic in conception (process-oriented), the systemic model accounts for both normal and neurotic conflict, the latter (less than optimal self-regulation) resulting from the activation of incompatible programs (see Schafer 1983, 82–95 regarding conflict as paradoxical action). A systemic model accounts for motivation as goal-oriented behavior (not necessarily conscious), the categorization of principal goals in the version of Rosenblatt and Thickstun (1977, 298–99) being the maintenance of positive affective relationships with significant others (attachment behavior), the satisfaction of basic (mostly physical) needs, and the goal of defending against the threat of any form of injury.

Though Stern remarks with plausible common sense that "no one can agree on exactly what the self is" (1985, 5), he himself may be numbered among the many psychoanalysts whose theory is compatible with a systemic view of self. (The extent to which analysts explicitly subscribe to a systemic model appears to be a function of the degree of their familiarity with general systems theory.) Well before the advent of systems theory, Sullivan wrote about what he called "the self system," which for him is essentially "an organization of educative experience called into being by the necessity to avoid or to minimize incidents of anxiety" (1953, 165). The father of systems theory, Ludwig von Bertalanffy, insists that modern views of man have in common the principle "to take man not as a reactive automaton or robot but as an active personality system" (1968, 207), meaning, among other things, an open (as distinguished from closed), information-processing, dynamically self-regulating system. Peterfreund, whose application of systems theory to psychoanalysis remains the most comprehensive and valuable treatment, writes that "self, object, and superego representations are highly interrelated and interdependent; they form a vast system, and each part constantly feeds back information to every other part" (1971, 159). Rosenblatt and Thickstun say that the self system "can be conceptualized as the superordinate system, or the organism itself, encompassing *all* of the systems operating within the organism" (1977, 300). Bowlby, who embraces systems theory, tends to think in terms of groups of individuals rather than isolated ones, and he seems to be uncomfortable with person-oriented terms. He discusses the concept of self (1980, 59–64), yet makes little use of it; there is, nevertheless, little or nothing in his writing that conflicts with a systemic view of selfhood. Although Stern's book on self theory (1985) does not explicitly refer to systems theory, nothing in his focus on epigenesis appears to be at odds with the systems model. Lichtenberg (1989), whose work derives partly from Stern and partly from self psychology, makes extensive use of the concept of system even though, methodologically, he does not appear to rely much on general systems theory as such. Lichtenberg, who defines "the self as an independent center for initiating, organizing, and integrating" (12), generates a schema of five distinct yet interactive motivational systems: a system regulating physiological requirements, an attachment-affiliation system, and exploratory-assertive system, an aversive system, and a sensual-sexual system. "As each system self-organizes and self-stabilizes, the needs that constitute the system's core are met or fail to be met" (275). Basch represents the case for a systemic view of selfhood well when he writes, "The modern term *psychodynamics* can be understood as referring to the movement of goal-directed systems toward decisions. The process is measured by and expressed in terms of information. Thus is the once-mysterious psyche taken out of the realm of the supernatural to join science, the search for order in nature" (1988, 58).

While alternative models of self will doubtless continue to be formulated, it seems almost inevitable that the more valuable ones will incorporate systemic perspectives. If systems models of self become increasingly accepted in psychoanalysis, one consequence will be the total abandonment of libido theory and ego psychology, and sexuality will probably play a more modest role, as in Lichtenberg's formulation. To a considerable extent the systemic model renders null the criticism, emanating from people like Lacan, of the idea of a highly coherent, specialized, centered self. For Lacan, self, at the mirror stage, is but the reflection of an alienated other (1977, 2–6); at a later stage (the Symbolic) self, or "subject," is a subjectivity dispersed in language and culture. In contrast, the systemic model, which represents selfhood as *an operational whole* in spite of the number and diversity of its systemically located "parts," preserves the possibility of *virtual unity* in functioning individuals without delimiting the complexity with which larger environments (culture) can be represented within the self system. Barratt (1984), who quotes Adorno as saying that identity is the primal form of ideology (251), mocks the notion of "a unified, albeit multifaceted, subject," (139), or self, or ego, especially as favored by neo-Freudians and object relations theorists, but his own ur-Freudian model of man as fundamentally alienated and irreparably conflicted refuses recognition of the possibility of functionally unified selfhood such as may be said to be epitomized, in the vision of W. B. Yeats, by the dancer who cannot be distinguished from the dance. In any case, one can claim the existence of room in the systemic model for virtually unlimited complexity of the representation of self, other, and culture.

One can also claim that the systemic model accommodates both self-oriented and other-oriented perspectives on object relations theory. Stern declares that he places sense of self at the center of his inquiry (1985, 5), yet he manages to pursue his study with full recognition of the extent to which the other (mother) influences the development of selfhood in infants. In contrast to Stern, Lichtenstein's other-oriented version of object relations theory may be thought to undersell infant individuality and potential for autonomy by defining identity strictly in terms of instrumentality (self as an instrument of an all-influential other). He writes, "Even as an adult, I believe, man cannot ever experience his identity except in terms of an organic instrumentality within the variations of a symbiotically structured *Umwelt*" (1961, 202), identity being experienced unconsciously by adults as variations on themes "imprinted" on them as infants by their mothers (208). In point of fact, Lichtenstein's theory of selfhood, as *identity* theory, focuses as much on self as on other. As for the implication that self theory appears by its very name to favor self over other, what matters in the present context is that self theory models not foreclose in any way on the representation of other.

As a general rule, the idea that the development of self results in large part, though not exclusively, from the interaction of self with other appears to be beyond controversy. Object relations theorists have always been interested in what has come to be referred to as "intersubjectivity" (Atwood and Stolorow, 1984). Winnicott explains in a famous passage how a mother's face, functioning as a mirror, allows the child to begin to experience itself as a self (1971, 111–18), and throughout his discussion of transitional phenomena he emphasizes that transitional objects are *subjective objects*. Kohut may be thought of as having extended the concept of the subjectivity of the object through his use of the term *selfobject*. Stern (1985) throws an abundance of light on the topic of intersubjectivity. As part of his articulation of the dynamics of the infant-mother dialogue, Stern speaks of attachment as self-experience (102); he illuminates the importance of "peek-a-boo" and "I'm-gonna-getcha" as games constituting "we-experience," a self-other phenomenon (101–2); and he points to the way in which being with others promotes the beginnings of psychological self-regulation (75). In keeping with his declaration that "the sharing of affective states is the most pervasive and clinically germaine feature of intersubjective relatedness" (138), Stern develops at length the concept of "affect attunement," which he defines as "the performance of [complex interactional] behaviors that express the quality of feeling of a shared affect state without imitating the exact behavioral expression of the inner state" (142). Rich and detailed, the rigorous accounts of the observation of infant-mother interaction of Stern, Beebe (1986), and others hold forth great promise for the better understanding of adult object-relations behavior.

INTERNALIZATION

In a footnote Schafer remarks that when he was writing *Aspects of Internalization* (1968) he had not yet realized "the extent to which the very idea of internalization was part of a major problem in psychoanalytic theorizing" (1976, 177). For Schafer the problem concerns what he regards as the illicit use of pseudospatial terms such as "internal objects." When analysts employ the term *internalization*, he writes, "we refer not to a fantasy but to a psychological process, and we are saying that a shift of event, action, or situation in an inward direction or to an inner locale has occurred" (155). The question is, he asks, "inside what?" He then proceeds to develop his perfectly legitimate claim, mentioned earlier, that there are no mental places, or spaces. Apart from what we now know about the localization of various functions in the brain, Schafer's claim seems undeniable except that in his efforts to get the language of psychoanalysis straightened out he has forgotten that people think as-ifly, with models, and express themselves as-thoughly, through language, especially when they speak of matters, such as relationships, that cannot be weighed, measured, or located in space. In language, mental places do exist. Even unicorns exist in language! Schafer, who appreciates the danger of reifying abstractions, fails to realize the pointlessness of deliberately literalizing conceptual metaphors, that is, of setting metaphoric models up as straw men by attributing literal reality to what, in context, are consensually understood to be conceptual abstractions expressed through more or less concrete metaphoric language—as in the phrase "internal objects."

For Meissner "the issue of internalization lies at the very heart of contemporary psychoanalytic concerns" (1981, ix). He makes this statement in the context of the emergence of "a more articulated theory of object relations," one that "emphasizes the importance of relationships with significant objects both in development and in current adaptive functioning," on the one hand, and the rise of "a psychology of self" on the other (ix). It does not require much of an argument, says Meissner, to show that the concept of internalization "is central to the dialectic between object and self, and that it provides the conceptual bridge between an object relations theory and a concept of self" (ix). For Meissner, then, what is at stake is not the legitimacy but the centrality of the concept of internalization.

One of the things Meissner tries to accomplish is to codify terminology pertaining to internalization. Such terms as "incorporation," "introjection," "identification," and "projective identification," among others, have been used with so much variation in meaning that standardization proves difficult. Certainly there is a serious danger posed by unrestrained multiplication of taxonomic designations of internalized objects such as Grotstein (1982) exhibits in his discussion of object relations theory. He himself refers, with something less than full awareness, to what he calls "a warehouse of internal objects" (84). On display in this warehouse, in addition to a series of six selfobjects, the first of which he calls the

"Background Subject-Object of Primary Identification," the bedazzled reader encounters—successively—the nutrative object, the poisonous or starving object, the stimulating object, the defective boundary object, the collusive internal object, the scavenger object, the corrupt object, the protective object, the "object with tenure," the Albatross or defective frontier object, the obstructive object, the corrupt background object, the autistic object, the symbiotic object, the ultimate containing object, the nuclear object, and the orbital object. One need not question the potentially infinite variety of forms internalizations may take in order to doubt the wisdom of attempting to categorize as many types as possible by giving them names.

To say so is not to deny the potential usefulness of typology. Stern calls one of the more interesting types of internalized object the "evoked companion": "Whenever a RIG [a representation of an interaction that has been internalized] of being with someone (who has changed self-experience) is activated, the infant encounters an evoked companion" (1985, 111). According to Stern, "the evoked companion functions to evaluate the specific ongoing interactive episode" (113), thus serving as an internalized reference orienting response. The seemingly unaccountable experience by an adult of strong emotion, such as love or anger, as a response to a relatively trivial situation involving a comparative stranger might be accounted for by assuming that an "evoked companion" has suddenly been mobilized, however unconsciously. Where else could all that affect come from? What Bollas calls "the transformational object," an object "experientially identified by the infant with processes that alter self experience" (1987, 14), closely resembles Stern's evoked companion, the emphasis in both instances being on the reexperience of a pattern of transformative interaction as distinct from a naked, unmediated encounter with a familiar figure. Interesting in this connection is the fact that Hadley speaks of the neurophysiology of attachment not in terms of connections and bonds but in terms of *process:* "Attachment is the internalized representation of repetitive interactions with caregivers" (1989, 358). In similar fashion, Beebe emphasizes internalization as a process by stressing action schemes (interactional patterns) as precursors of self and object representations: what is internalized in the earliest representations "is not simply the infant's own action, nor the environment's response, but rather the dynamic interplay between the two. To expand upon Piaget, representation of the self and the human object is conceptualized as interiorized *inter*action, rather than unilateral action per se" (1986, 28).

One topic of immense significance for object relations theory is the internalization of personal meaning. Guntrip comments, "The significance of human living lies in object-relationships, and only in such terms can our life be said to have a meaning, for without object relations the ego itself cannot develop" (1969, 19–20). Marris writes about the element of uniqueness in human attachment in contrast to the comparative inter-changeability of objects implied by Freud's libido theory:

> The relationships that matter most to us are characteristically to particular people whom we love—husband or wife, parents, children, dearest friend —and sometimes to particular places—a home or personal territory—that we invest with the same loving qualities. These specific relationships, which we experience as unique and irreplaceable, seem to embody most crucially the meaning of our lives. We grow up to look for such relationships. If we do not find them, our lives seem empty; pleasures, ambitions, ideals, career tend to lose their interest or their purpose without this context of unique personal bonds. If we lose these bonds, we suffer grief; and in the depth of grieving, the bereaved cannot be consoled by any substitute relationship. Even the idea of such consolation is abhorrent, because it seems to deny the unique value and meaning of what has been lost. (1982, 185)

Although Marris suggests that "meaning is inherently emotional" (192), he does not speak of the meaningfulness of object relations simply in the sense that they are emotionally important; he asserts that attachments structure meaning in a larger way, allowing us "to make sense of our experience and to direct our lives" (191).

Because attachments structure meaning, says Marris, the loss of key attachment figures tends to precipitate confusion: "When people are be-reft of a crucial relationship, nothing seems to make sense any longer. The world seems meaningless" (194). Elizabethans were keenly sensitive to images of global disorder. Shakespeare uses the word *chaos* in a context both personal and global when he has Othello say of Desdemona:

> Excellent wretch! Perdition catch my soul
> But I do love thee! and when I love thee not,
> Chaos is come again.
>
> (3.3.91–93)

As Marris describes it, the experience of "losing someone you love is less like losing a very valuable and irreplaceable possession than like finding the law of gravity to be invalid" (195). The rational course of giving up the lost object at the behest of reality is not available because "grief is a

reaction to the disintegration of the whole structure of meaning dependent on this relationship rather than to the absence of the person lost"
(195). By way of supplementing the explanation of Marris, it might be
said that the disorientation resulting from some instances of loss involves
a loss of self, not just a loss of other. Loss disorients precisely to the
extent that the structure of selfhood has been invested in an ongoing
relationship with a living other. In those instances, such as the gradual
loss of an aging parent, where the bereft person experiences anticipatory
mourning, and where the internalization process has been more nearly
completed, the death of an attachment figure is less likely to be so disorienting, however painful.

Other psychoanalytic commentators have clarified the fact that meaning is not internalized exclusively in the form of representations of, and
feelings about, *persons*. As Hadley remarks, "We may 'attach' to many
things, to ideas and ideals, to the self as well as other people" (1985,
547). The emotional investment people make in ideology would be a
good example. Faber writes about how the world of culture incorporates
internalized attitudes and beliefs that function defensively to provide
psychological security for the group comparable to that afforded by the
mothering figure in early development of the individual (1989, 33).
Riviere remarks that internalization of objects "persists throughout life in
more developed forms as a main feature of our mental functioning. . . . In
later life, moreover, these objects, external or internal, no longer need to
be exclusively persons, but may be represented by non-human, inanimate,
or abstract interests" (1955, 351). The object-relational dimension of
interests has been discussed at length by Eagle. He argues that "interests
are most meaningfully understood as object relations that involve cognitive and affective links to objects in the world and serve some of the same
psychological functions [such as orientation] served by more traditionally
viewed object relations" (1981, 161). Eagle uses the term "interests" in
the broad sense of any focus of attention or activity with deep emotional
correlatives, such as a pastime or a profession. He notes that in clinical
work absence of the development of important interests in a patient
constitutes "a negative prognostic indicator" (6). In contrast, "the evidence supports the idea of a strong relationship between security of
attachment and independent exploratory behavior" (1982, 169) of the
kind that develops into areas of interest in the (superficially) nonpersonal
world.

* * *

REORIENTING PSYCHOANALYTIC THEORY

Whereas Pine (1988) speaks with uncritical syncretism about "the four psychologies of psychoanalysis," Holt (1989)—who is nothing if not critical—writes about the current status of psychoanalytic theory in a mood verging on despair. After identifying the major trends of the mid-1980's as, first, the death of metapsychology, second, the debate about whether psychoanalysis is a scientific or a hermeneutic discipline, and third, "the rise into increasing prominence of object relations theory and self psychology" (324), Holt goes so far as to label the third trend as a fad (338). Without bothering to justify the casualness of his linking of object relations theory with self psychology, Holt goes on, not without some justice, to claim that

> despite certain attractive features of both object relations theory and self psychology, they fail to make any serious or searching critique of metapsychology, and—like ego psychology—they retain a good deal of it. As rebellions, they are much too limited to accomplish the needed radical (indeed, revolutionary) change. . . . Fairbairn (1952), Guntrip (1969), and Winnicott (1958), however, all incorporate far too many of the defective parts of psychoanalytic theory to make their corrections much more than cosmetic. (338)

It will be noticed that Holt makes no attempt at this point to distinguish, as I do, between self psychology and the emerging presence of a science-oriented self theory, nor does he appear to be sufficiently aware of the possibility of wresting a sound and healthy person-oriented theory of object relations from the decaying womb of Freud's drive-oriented theory. There is one exception, however. What Holt most notably does do, in a sentence I have purposely omitted from the quotation above, is to say that his remarks do not apply to attachment theory considered as, in his phrasing, "a member of the object relations school" (338).

Part of the problem, of course, is that at present there is no coherent group identifiable as "the object relations school" of psychoanalysis. But perhaps—as I contend—a unified theory of object relations may now be glimpsed on the horizon of possibility. As envisioned in this chapter—however incompletely—such a theory of object relations will be person oriented. It will have dispensed with the assumptions of libido theory and the metapsychological trappings of ego psychology. It will build a theory of motivation and conflict on the foundation provided by an attachment theory expanded to include all *meaningful* features of object relations theory, classical and contemporary. This expanded theory of object relations will be interdependent with self theory insofar as the two realms of theory share the same concerns about human motivation and conflict. Selfhood will be conceptualized in terms of a systemic model for both branches of theory. And whatever other features it may possess, the systemic model in question will exhibit virtually unlimited capacity to register and process internalized representations of itself, of other, and of the nonhuman environment as it regulates itself and its organism's personal interaction with the outside world.

II

STORIES OF REAL PERSONS

3.

FREUD'S CASES REREAD

By early in the last decade of the nineteenth century Freud had become preoccupied with sexual pathology and the possibility that it serves as a causative factor in neurasthenia and psychoneurosis. Writing to Wilhelm Fliess in October of 1893, Freud remarks, "Meanwhile things have grown livelier. The sexual business attracts people; they all go away impressed and convinced, after exclaiming, 'No one has ever asked me that before!' " (1954,78). His letter to Fliess the following month contains this passage: "The sexual business is becoming more and more firmly consolidated, and the contradictions are fading away" (80). Before long, Freud ascribes the cause of hysteria to sexual conflict: "hysteria is conditioned by a primary sexual experience (before puberty) accompanied by revulsion and fright" (129). By the time of the paper on the role of sexuality in the etiology of the neuroses, Freud's consolidation of "the sexual business" is complete: "The unique significance of sexual experiences in the aetiology of the psychoneuroses seemed to be established beyond a doubt; and this fact [!] remains to this day one of the corner-stones of my theory" (1906, 273).

During the next two decades or so Freud makes innumerable efforts to document this hypothesis in his case histories, sporadically in the *Studies on Hysteria* (1893–1895) and insistently in the other cases being considered in this chapter. The main question to be considered is this: To what extent do Freud's clinical hypotheses reflect his data in a comparatively detached, objective manner and to what extent do they exhibit motivated conceptualizations, that is, theory-driven positions he *wants* to find evidence for in his case material? A critical rereading of Freud's cases shows that his explanations along libidinal lines do not hold up, being

variously ancillary, forced, inconsistent, irrelevant, exaggerated, supposi-
tious, and sometimes downright wishful—not always, of course, but with
damaging frequency. These cases nevertheless still constitute meaningful
documents in the context of a revised theory of object relations—a person-oriented as distinguished from a drive-oriented one. They remain
meaningful to a significant degree for various reasons, among them the
high quality of most of Freud's observations, the merits of his method of
investigation, the shrewdness of his insights, and because the semantic
richness of these clinical texts is such that they contain the data needed to
substantiate *alternative* readings at odds with the interpretations Freud
tries to impose on them.

A crucial aspect of the residual significance of this case material lies in
the fact that Freud insists on the importance of conflict in the etiology of
neurotic behavior. In a passage designed to discriminate between obsessional neurosis and hysteria, he remarks in a letter to Fliess that "at the
root of hysteria is always *conflict* (sexual pleasure versus an accompanying
unpleasure)" (1954, 139). Naturally Freud conceptualizes conflict along
sexual lines in keeping with his fateful decision to regard all objects as
sexual objects. Had Freud chosen instead to situate the origins of neurotic
behavior in *object relational conflict,* without insisting on the presence or
primacy of sexual factors, and above all without invoking his metapsychological deus ex machina of libidinal hydraulics, who would say him
nay? Again and again in the case material to follow, emotional conflict
concerning self and other will be seen to occupy the center of the stage,
while sexual conflict—when present at all—remains in the background.

STUDIES ON HYSTERIA

The first of the cases in *Studies on Hysteria,* that of Anna O., was handled
by Breuer, but Freud knew it intimately, learned from it, and commented
on it. For purposes of the present discussion, it may be treated almost as
if it were one of Freud's cases. Anna O., who appears to have had a
normal childhood, develops a variety of symptoms, chiefly conversion
symptoms and some dissociative behavior. The symptoms begin to emerge
after Anna has been nursing her dying father for several months, although
she takes to *her* bed well before he dies. During what appears to be the
most representative of several traumatic scenes, Anna envisions, during
the night at her father's bedside, a waking dream (hallucination) of being

unable to prevent a menacing black snake from approaching her father's bed (for the purpose of biting him). The fingers of her paralyzed right hand turn into "little snakes with death's heads (the nails)" (1893–1895, 38). Although Breuer succeeds, with the aid of hypnosis, in exhuming this and other forgotten scenes of conflict, which results in a cure, his case history remains oddly silent concerning the exact nature of the conflict in Anna's mind. Content to focus on traumatic, seemingly exterior events, Breuer fails to comment on the presence of a fairly blatant death wish directed, for obvious reasons, by the overstressed Anna toward her burdensome but otherwise beloved father. Breuer makes no explicit mention of any tormenting guilt resulting from this wish, though he may have intuited its existence. Freud, commenting on the case in his *Five Lectures* (1910), accurately represents the symptoms as deriving from "emotional" traumas (10) and " 'strangulated' affects" (18) without specifying what these were. He makes no direct reference to specific sexual elements in the case itself, yet he feels at liberty to generalize about the strangulated affects in terms of "somatic innervations" and "cathected mental processes" in a manner that can be said indiscriminately to lump together emotions, psychic energy, sexual energy, "mental" processes, and physiological processes of the brain.

Guilt appears to be a factor in the case of Frau Emmy von N. Frau Emmy consciously hates her younger daughter for three years, she says, because she believes—quite unrealistically—that she would have been able "to nurse her husband back to health if she had not been in bed [ill] on account of her child" (1893–1895, 63). Anxiety is an obvious feature of the case. Frau Emmy has an endless series of bad dreams. She remembers—with Freud's help—a series of fearful experiences from her youth, and continues, at the age of forty, to be afraid of innumerable innocuous situations. At an unspecified period in Frau Emmy's childhood, her mother was committed to an asylum, a situation that may or may not have produced the anxious behavior that in attachment theory would be attributable to extended separation of child from mother at a vulnerable age, but of course Freud does not explore such a possibility. Instead he *infers* the presence of a "neurotic factor" due to "the fact that the patient had been living [as a widow] for years in a state of sexual abstinence" (88). "Such circumstances," he adds, "are among the most frequent causes of a tendency to anxiety." He maintains this position despite his later admission of "a complete absence of the sexual element" in "all the intimate information given me by the patient" (103). Freud simply *assumes* she has emended her life story in this regard into "a bowdlerized edition." He freely concedes that he feels uncertain about his diagnosis of the problem (85) and admits that the help he has been able to give his patient with her pains and phobias proves to be only temporary (101).

In the case of the governess, Miss Lucy R., the patient experiences persistent olfactory delusions, specifically the odors of burnt pudding and cigar smoke, subsequent to being cured of an actual nasal infection. Through the treatment process, Freud discovers that these symptoms relate to emotional conflict Lucy suffers having to do with her promises to her charges' dead mother, ill treatment by the domestic help, her unacknowledged love for her employer, whom she unrealistically hopes to marry, and her shock at her employer's displays of anger. Lucy's nose knows. Her sense of smell functions as a kind of memory bank—a nasal palimpsest. Her tormenting olfactory delusions serve as markers; they are like gravestones indicating the sites of buried memories of painful scenes, such as the employer's rage when his accountant kisses the children (in Lucy's charge) on the lips. These markers are metonymic signs, arbitrary in their relation to the events in question except for their coincidence in point of time (that is, the smells occur in temporal conjunction with the painful scenes). Other than the possibility of choosing to look at the romantic element of Lucy's story in sexual terms, which Freud refrains from doing, one can see that all of the conflict in this case reflects the "mnemonic repression," as it were, of emotional disturbances in the sphere of object relations. Deeper conflicts, if present, remain unrecorded. The treatment, intermittent and covering only nine weeks, helps Lucy to adjust to her emotional problem and removes her delusional symptoms.

In the case of Katharina, a simple mountain girl about twenty years old, Freud immediately recognizes that her physical symptoms reflect anxiety attacks. Katharina has no idea where they come from. By questioning her Freud learns she was exposed to the sexual advances of her uncle at the age of fourteen, and that she caught a glimpse of a scene she did not fully comprehend at the time: her uncle having intercourse with Katharina's cousin. Freud concludes, "The case of Katharina is typical. In every analysis of a case of hysteria based on sexual traumas we find that impressions from the pre-sexual period which produced no effect on the child attain traumatic power at a later date as memories." (133). What Freud does not admit until nearly thirty years after the publication of this case, in the form of a footnote, is that the man who made the sexual advances was not Katharina's uncle but her father! While admitting that this "distortion" was a mistake, Freud neglects to elaborate in any way on the implications of this new information for understanding the case. One way of rereading it, in object-relational terms, is to perceive that Katharina was traumatized not by sexuality itself but by the conflict generated in her by her father's incestuous behavior. Had he chosen to pursue the issue in this case, Freud might have been inclined to view this conflict as involving the threat of tapping the daughter's unconscious, tabooed desire. Victims of such advances will themselves no doubt elect to see them rather as emotionally devastating breaches of the sanctity of a natural bond entirely different in kind from Freud's understanding of it as a fundamentally incestuous attachment. But even if allowance be made for the possibility of an element of deep-seated sexual conflict, unconscious on Katharina's part, between desire and taboo, what emerges from consideration of this case, a fortiori, is that psychological conflict has the greatest potential for development in an object-relational context, especially when the objects in question are primary attachment figures. Not surprisingly, the most conflictful scenes of Greek tragedy are usually family scenes. Aristotle recognizes that the most terrible, pitiful events portrayable in tragedy occur when "suffering is inflicted upon each other by people whose relationship implies affection, as when a brother kills, or intends to kill, his brother, a son his father, a mother her son, a son his mother" (1958, 27).

In the last of the studies on hysteria, Fräulein Elisabeth von R. suffers hysterical pains in her legs. After a normal, happy childhood, during which she is "tenderly attached to her parents" (Freud, 1893–1895, 139), she experiences these pains for the first time after she has been devotedly nursing her father for a period of some twelve months. She identifies with her father in various ways. She unconsciously identifies with *the pain he has in his leg* because of his heart trouble. She eventually realizes, with Freud's help, that the particular location of pain in her right thigh must have something to do with the fact that her father rested his own badly swollen leg on hers when she changed the bandage on it (148). Ramifications of her symptom ensue when she experiences pain in her legs in a way that is unconsciously associated with the pleasure of taking a walk with her sister's husband (156), with whom Elisabeth von R. has fallen in love unawares. The psychological plot thickens when this sister dies not long thereafter. Fräulein Elisabeth feels unbearably guilty when, in the midst of mourning the death of her sister, this thought flashes through her mind concerning her sister's husband: "Now he is free again and I can be his wife" (156). As part of his overview of the case, Freud concludes that the hysterical pain in her thigh occurs "at a moment when the circle of ideas embracing her duties to her sick father came into conflict with the content of the erotic desire she was feeling at the time. Under the pressure of lively self-reproaches she decided in favour of the former, and in doing so brought about the hysterical pain" (164). What happened, continues Freud, is that "she repressed her erotic idea from consciousness and transformed the amount of its affect into physical sensations of pain" (164). By the phrases "erotic desire" and "erotic idea" Freud refers to Fräulein Elisabeth's attachment to, or love for, her sister's husband. But Freud makes no reference to any explicitly lustful thoughts or impulses. The point is that Freud often blurs the differences existing between attachment behavior and sexual behavior in favor of attending to what they may have in common, this practice being in contrast to his attempt, notably in the *Three Essays on the Theory of Sexuality,* to keep sexual aims and sexual objects conceptually isolated from each other. Even if Elisabeth von R. did in fact experience what we would today describe as "erotic desires," readers of the case never become privy to any details about them. Here, as so often, a gap exists between sexual experiences *attributed* by Freud to his patients and the memories of actual feelings and events *elicited* by Freud during the analytic process.

DORA

There cannot of course be any question concerning the presence of sexual impulses in the case of Dora ("Fragment of an Analysis of a Case of Hysteria," 1905a), only many, if not most, of these sexual impulses belong to other people! Be that as it may, my concern is not to defend Dora against Freud, which a number of legitimately angry feminists have already undertaken to do in recent years (Bernheimer and Kahane, 1985), or to attempt a thorough sorting out of the tangled skein of interpersonal relationships in this case. I confine my attention to matters concerning the relative weight and pertinence of sexual factors in Dora's case, especially as they come into play within the framework of Dora's oedipal relationships.

Beginning with Dora's case, conducted late in 1900 and written up, for the most part, early in 1901, the relative weight of Freud's attention to sexual matters increases exponentially as compared to *Studies on Hys-*

teria. "Sexuality is the key," he trumpets in his finale to the case. "Sexuality provides the motive power for every single symptom," he says. "I can only repeat over and over again—for I never find it otherwise—that sexuality is the key to the problem of psychoneuroses. . . . No one who disdains the key will ever be able to unlock the door" (1905a, 115). Apart from the sexual impulses belonging to other persons, exemplified by the long-standing affair of Dora's father with Frau K. and Herr K.'s attempted seductions of Dora and a governess, the door into which Freud inserts his analytical key opens up a Pandora's box of what he regards as perverse infantile sexuality. It should be noticed that Freud *attributes* the experience of a primal scene to Dora as distinct from eliciting fragments of the memory of one. He then uses this *construction* to explain Dora's breathing difficulties by *assuming* that what she heard was lots of heavy breathing (accentuated in her father's case because of his tuberculosis). Freud further *attributes* Dora's vaginal discharge to masturbation, with a great show of authority and in spite of Dora's claim that she cannot recall engaging in this practice. Still worse, at least as far as symptom formation goes, is the oral eroticism of Dora's infantile sucking. Freud discusses thumb sucking in connection with his *attribution* of a fellatio fantasy to Dora, largely on the basis of the fact that Dora believes her father to be impotent and responds to Freud's query about how her father can, under the circumstances, be having an ordinary love affair by saying that "she knew . . . that there was more than one way of obtaining sexual gratification" (47). Freud *infers*, without really demonstrating, that this "unconscious phantasy" gives rise to Dora's hysterical coughing (51). Last but not least, Freud *attributes* a "homosexual current" (60) to Dora's affection for and loyalty to Frau K.; in fact, he asserts in a letter to Fliess that in this case "the principal part in the conflicting mental processes is played by the opposition between an attraction towards men and one towards women" (4). A possibility that does not enter into Freud's calculations is that Dora may be capable of being attracted to Herr K., as a man, in a way that is not incompatible with experiencing fondness for a woman like Frau K., whose children she has taken care of, whom she looks up to, and who in all likelihood serves as an unconscious substitute for the maternal support figure Dora's mother can no longer be because of her emotionally crippling "housewife psychosis"—as Freud calls it.

Even if one grants, in theory, the persistence in Dora of remnants of polymorphous sexuality deriving from childhood that constitute, insofar as they become synthesized, her adult, genitally oriented sexuality, these questions remain: To what extent do sexual factors affect her adult object relations and to what extent do her symptoms derive from object-relational conflict as distinct from sexual conflict? Looking at what Freud writes about Dora in an oedipal context suggests an alternative reading to the one he proposes—not a totally different but a significantly qualified one. The premise underlying this view of the oedipus complex, applicable to other cases as well, and perhaps generally to everyone, is that sexual issues, such as incest and castration anxiety, do not constitute the essence of oedipal conflict—contrary to what Freud has for so long persuaded so many. An appropriate perspective on oedipal object-relations *in childhood* should focus on attachment behavior, not sexual behavior, because the latter elements derive primarily *from adulthood* by way of a process Freud himself named and discussed, that of deferred action (*Nachträglichkeit*). Given this perspective on Dora's oedipal experience, her childhood rivalry with her mother can be seen to take the form of possessiveness, or greedy attachment to her father, as distinguished from the inner excitation of lust for her father's body.

Freud launches his own oedipal "hypothesis" this way: Dora's "preoccupation with her father's relations to Frau K. owed its obsessive character to the fact that its root was unknown to her and lay in the unconscious. . . . She felt and acted more like a jealous wife—in a way which would have been comprehensible in her mother. By her ultimatum to her father ('either her or me'). . . she was clearly putting herself in her mother's place" (56). Except for his casual reference in the next sentence to the "sexual" nature of Dora's cough (the fellatio connection), one cannot take exception to the object-relational cast of Freud's remarks here or in what immediately follows: "She was therefore identifying herself both with the woman her father had once *loved* and with the woman he *loved* now. The inference is obvious that her affection for her father was a much stronger one than she knew or than she would have cared to admit: in fact, that she was *in love* with him" [meaning "in love with him in an inappropriate, incestuous way"] (56; italics added). Freud tends to use words like "affection" and "love" ambiguously in a manner similar to what he calls "switch-words" (65n), words that can track on different sets of rails. But Freud's mention in the subsequent paragraph of Oedipus, and his reference to "the forces of the libido," leave no doubt as to which track he has taken.

Nevertheless, in this same paragraph, and the following one, Freud speaks of matters allowing today's readers to switch to the object-relational track instead. Freud writes of the probability that the traces of oedipal feeling in all of us "must be assumed to be more intense from the very first in the case of those children [like Dora, presumably] whose constitution [or early development] marks them down for a neurosis," these being children "who develop prematurely and have a craving for love" that leads to "a fixation of this rudimentary feeling of love" (56). From the perspective of attachment theory, all children need love, contact, and security, but those who exhibit excessively anxious, clinging behavior do so because they have experienced either some form of traumatic separation, or flawed intersubjectivity, which they may carry over into adult relationships. Since Freud elsewhere mentions how "tenderly attached" Dora was to her father (18), and he to her (56), and since we know about the emotional unavailability of Dora's mother (both to her husband and daughter), we can allow for the likelihood of the derivation from her childhood of a certain turbulence in Dora's adult emotional life, yet we need not assume this turbulence to be strictly sexual in nature. As for her emotional conflict taking the form of hysterical symptoms, Dora has an abundance of neurotic models to imitate, including her mother, her aunt, and Frau K.

When Freud confronts Dora by contending that her childhood affection for her father "must at a very early moment have amounted to her being completely in love with him," meaning incestuously, Dora says she does not remember anything like that but then goes on to tell an anecdote about a seven-year-old girl she knew. Freud construes this anecdote as confirming Dora's implicit acceptance of *his version* of her oedipus complex. The little girl, after witnessing a heated altercation between her parents, later whispers into Dora's ear: " 'You can't think how I hate that person!' (pointing to her mother), 'and when she's dead I shall marry Daddy' " (57). Parsimoniously construed, all the anecdote confirms is the person-oriented object-relational view that childhood attachments, especially possessive ones, are often regarded by children as involving competitions with adults and may be represented as taking on, in a child's eye, the *form* of the attachments of the adults with whom the child identifies. Marriage, in this instance, serves as a metaphor for the kind of emotional intimacy the child sees her parents' relationship as partaking of. "Marriage" is a metaphor, a representational model, that does not necessarily include any sexual baggage as far as a child is concerned.

By the same token, if the quality of deep attachments of children to parental figures must be regarded as founded on physical closeness, emotional responsiveness, security, a sense of self-worth, and above all on what Erikson calls *basic trust,* then Dora's anger at her father, and at Herr K., are perfectly understandable in object-relational terms. Dora may love her father (such attachments being, as Henry James once said of one's bond to one's native land, prior to choice) but she nevertheless knows him to be "insincere," manipulative, and inappropriately self-centered (34). As for her father's unspoken collusion with Herr K., Freud understands that she feels embittered "by the idea that she had been handed over to Herr K. as the price of his tolerating the relations between her father and his wife," and he adds, "Her rage at her father's making such a use of her was visible behind her affection for him" (34). Similarly, if Dora does love Herr K., as Freud insists and as Dora ultimately does not continue to deny, she may love him in the sense that she secretly wishes she could marry him rather than because she welcomes his erotic attentions (the abrupt kiss and furtive embrace when she is fourteen), as Freud believes she ought to. She may love him even though she does not welcome the blunt erotic proposition by the lake when she is older, a proposition the more unwelcome because she recognizes it as being couched in the same language Herr K. uses to proposition his children's governess, a scene Dora already knows about.

HANS

Maintaining clear and appropriate distinctions between sexual behavior and attachment behavior in the case of Little Hans ("Analysis of a Phobia in a Five-Year-Old Boy," 1909a) becomes more difficult than in the case of Dora because of the way the boy's father, in cahoots with Freud, endeavors to impose sexual interpretations on everything he does, and thinks, and dreams, thereby precipitating iatrogenic conflicts in him in the process. Another complication derives from the functional ambiguity of Hans's penis, which eliminates waste products from his body, which gives him pleasure when touched, and which furthermore represents gender differentiation and the potential for sexual reproduction, topics Little Hans does not understand very well and about which no one gives him timely, appropriate, accurate information.

Poor Little Hans: he gets reprimanded for touching his "widdler" (*Wiwimacher,* in the original), so how can he make wee-wee without conflict? When he is three and a half years old, his mother, seeing his hand on his penis, spontaneously performs her official Freudian function by threatening him: "If you do that, I shall send for Dr. A. to cut off your widdler. And then what'll you widdle with?" (1909a, 7–8). When he is four and three-quarters, Hans wakes up one morning in tears from a bad dream. He tells it to his mother: "When I was asleep I thought you were gone and I had no Mummy to coax [cuddle] with" (23). When, shortly thereafter, Hans develops a phobia about going out into the street because he is "afraid that a horse will bite him," the father, one of Freud's adherents, thinks the ground may have been prepared by "sexual over-excitation due to his mother's tenderness," and he thinks the fear seems "somehow" related to being frightened by a horse's penis: "He had noticed at a very early age what large penises horses have, and at the time he inferred that as his mother was so large she must have a widdler like a horse" (22). Freud needs no prompting to convince himself that Hans's fear of losing his mother must coincide with an "enormously intensified," age-specific (oedipal), erotic attraction to his mother. So Freud arranges for Hans's father to tell his son "that all this business about horses was a piece of nonsense and nothing more. The truth was, his father was to say, that he was very fond of his mother and wanted to be taken into her bed. The reason he was afraid of horses now was that he had taken so much interest in their widdlers" (28). Freud believes, in sum, that Hans's animal phobia reflects castration anxiety stemming from his oedipal desires and fears.

During his early years Hans's impressionable mind is subjected to a staggering amount of misinformation ranging from mild distortion to outright lies—some of them whoppers—by Freud and the boy's parents. No wonder he gets confused. Sometimes the parents tell fibs: babies are brought by the stork, and naughty children get arrested by the policeman at the Schönbrunn. Often distortions take the form of neglecting to correct faulty impressions, such as Hans's perception that his new baby sister has a widdler that is "quite small" (11), but "so lovely" (21), and his bizarre but understandable inference that his large mother has a large widdler, like a large male horse. Hans gets no error-correction feedback to help him deal with his misconceptions. Sometimes his parents furnish him with information that is simply misleading or inaccurate, for example, that babies are pressed out "like *lumf*" (feces) during the birth process. Horses do not bite, Freud tells Hans, though Hans knows better and tells Freud about a white horse at Gmunden that bites. When Hans mentions what Lizzi's father said to her as she was departing,—"Don't put your finger to the white horse or it'll bite you"—Freud responds to this undistorted report of a real event (remark) by telling Hans he cannot mean what he says: "I say, it strikes me that it isn't a horse you mean, but a widdler, that one mustn't put one's hand to" (29). How, one might ask, is Hans supposed to understand that this communication is designed to be an interpretation rather than a flat contradiction of his perfectly good memory? Hans responds with imperturbable logic: "But a widdler doesn't bite." And what does Freud say to that? He says, "Perhaps it does, though" (30). Such distortions amount to small fry compared to others mentioned in the text. Twice, for instance, Hans's mother assures him that she does have a widdler, knowing full well that the term "widdler" means "penis" to Hans. Can Hans possibly understand what Freud is driving at when he tells him that "he was afraid of his father precisely because he was so fond of his mother" (42)? Later, a thoroughly mystified Little Hans complains to his father, "Why did you tell me I'm fond of *Mummy* and that's why I'm frightened, when I'm fond of *you?*" (44). And can Hans possibly fail to become even more confused when confronted by the interpretation of Freud quoted earlier: (1) that his fear of horses is "nonsense"; (2) that the "truth" is that "he was very fond of his mother and wanted to be taken into her bed"—which is true enough, but how can the horse business be meaningless (nonsense) if there's an underlying truth to it?; and (3) that "the reason he was afraid of horses [contradicting the nonsense-explanation of (1)] was that he had taken so much interest in their widdlers," which must also contradict explanation (2)—not for Freud, of course, but for Hans. One may be permitted to doubt that Hans eventually outgrew his phobia any faster by virtue of the quality of the information he was receiving.

Be that as it may, a fundamentally different interpretation of the animal phobia of Little Hans can be found in Bowlby's reading of it (1973, 283–87). If ever there were a case designed to set up a contrast between the interpretation of object relations along orthodox, Freudian, drive-oriented lines as compared to the person-oriented lines of attachment theory, this is the one! Bowlby does not, in this instance, attack Freud's theory of sexuality directly. He does so indirectly by suggesting a more plausible explanation of Hans's situation, one more in line with the facts of the case and more in line also with what is now known about comparable instances of animal phobias in children. Bowlby concentrates on separation anxiety as distinct from castration anxiety. What he sees through the lens of attachment theory is the evidence the case provides that Hans's anxiety about leaving home *precedes* the form it later takes of an animal phobia, and that the phobia signifies fear not so much of leaving home as fear of being separated from his mother. The anxiety dream about his mother being gone also precedes the horse phobia. Bowlby notes that in Hans's mind there exists a link between being bitten by horses and the theme of the departure of someone he likes (Lizzi's father warns her as she departs not to stick out her finger or the white horse will bite it). Bowlby observes that Hans's father himself realizes that Hans's "present anxiety, which prevents him from leaving the neighborhood of the house, is in reality the longing for [his mother]," though the father later falls in with Freud's libidinal interpretation. Bowlby points out that Hans's fear of leaving the house arises subsequent to Hans's having been kept away from his mother during the birth of Hanna when Hans was three and one-half, a prime age for the experience of separation anxiety. Bowlby stresses that the case records the mother as having threatened Hans with not coming back home (Freud, 1909a, 44–45), and he speculates that Hans may have had a premonition of eventually being separated from his mother by the divorce of his parents. One of the key differences between the two interpretations is that Freud reads Hans's eagerness to cuddle with his mother and his desire to climb into bed with both parents as reflecting an increase of libidinal excitation and an expression of oedipal rivalry whereas Bowlby recognizes the eagerness as an increase of the need for closeness and love by a child experiencing separation anxiety—and dreaming about it. The dream is ambiguous: "When I was asleep I thought you were gone and I had no Mummy to coax with." Freud reads it one way, and Bowlby quite another.

As for Hans's castration anxiety, what is at issue is not its *reality* but its *origin*. It originates, first of all, as a result of an actual, explicit threat uttered in the context of Hans's taking pleasure in fondling his penis. Though the mother's tone and manner may in part have been playful and teasing ("And then what'll you widdle with?"), and her intentions good, the residual effect of the threat itself seems to have proved harmful in the sense of constituting one of the several factors promoting Hans's clinging behavior later on. The remarks of Freud and his father may also have increased Hans's castration anxiety. Hans's keen interest in anatomy (sharpened, no doubt, by his mother's cutting remark) becomes an anxious one because the theme of things being bitten off (fingers by horses) gets muddled—not by Hans but by his father and Freud! By the time they are through indoctrinating him with their explanations (of things like widdlers that bite), it is no wonder his castration anxiety becomes heightened.

Ironically, it is possible that what Freud terms "masturbation" in this case may be more of an object-relational phenomenon in early years than an erotic one. If the consequence of the manual stimulation of a nerve-rich portion of his anatomy—his penis—is analogous in function to the paradoxically calming effect of self-induced oral stimulation—in the instance of non-nutritive sucking on pacifiers—Hans's so-called masturbation may have served him principally for the purpose of allaying anxiety in the liminal situation of falling asleep (bedtime was his usual time for fondling himself). If Winnicott is right about thumb sucking as a transitional phenomenon, then perhaps genital manipulation *in childhood,* in addition to supplying direct sensory gratification, serves both short-term object-relational needs (the self as object) and long-term object-relational development. Thus what looks like purely erotic behavior may not be.

An amusing instance of adult preoccupation with sexuality in this case occurs when Hans's father insists on his opinion that Hans wants his mother to have a(nother) baby. Hans replies, "But I don't want it to happen" (92). Father: "But you wish for it?" Hans (probably confused): "Oh yes, *wish.*" Father (seeing an opening): "Do you know why you wish for it? It's because you'd like to be Daddy." Hans responds, "Yes. . . . How does it work?" Father: "How does what work?" Hans: "You say Daddies don't have babies; so how does it work, my wanting to be Daddy?" During the ensuing dialogue, Hans's father asserts that if Hans were married to his mother he would "like Mummy to have a baby," clearly meaning, adultomorphically, "make a baby with Mummy." Hans responds by emphasizing that if he were married to his Mummy they wouldn't want any more (baby sisters!). His father, attempting to salvage what he can of the shredded remnants of his oedipal hypothesis, asks, "Would you like to be married to Mummy?" "Oh yes," says Hans, speaking, presumably, in much the same way Dora's little friend speaks when she declares she will marry her father when her mother is dead. Hans's father believes Hans desires his mother as a sexual object whereas Hans himself seems to be thinking along the object-relational lines of possessing his mother, as an attachment figure, and at the same time relating to his beloved father by identifying with his marital status.

RAT MAN

Of all the cases being discussed, that of Rat Man ("Notes Upon a Case of Obsessional Neurosis," 1909b) offers the greatest challenge to the claim that Freud overemphasizes sexual factors in neurosis. It does so partly because of the cogency of Freud's solutions to Rat Man's puzzling thoughts and behavior, and partly because of the brilliance of Freud's discussion of obsessional neurosis. But the most direct challenge lies in the comparative prominence of erotic elements in this case. Mahony's *Freud and the Rat Man* (1986) calls attention to the extent Freud was aware, to a degree remarkable in 1909, of the operation of internalized object relations. Mahony cites this passage: "It seems likely that he [the patient] is also identifying himself with his mother in his criticisms of his father and is thus continuing the differences between his parents within himself" (43). At the same time, Mahony points out, "Not recognizing the *full* importance of early object relations at the time, Freud put predominant weight on the father's role as interferer of instinctual gratification" (43). Mahony himself, while he does tend to pay more attention than Freud to object-relational factors, nevertheless unquestioningly goes along with most of Freud's sexual formulations. In that respect, Mahony's study resembles the otherwise very different one by Sherwood (1969). Focusing on the explanatory process itself as distinguished from the merit of the terms (or premises) of Freud's explanation of the case, Sherwood remains locked into Freud's assumptions about the sexual etiology of neurotic conflict. The following discussion will slight the considerable complexity of detail regarding Rat Man's "rat complex" and the intricacies of his obsessional thinking in order to attend to the issue of the relative importance of sexual factors in Freud's explanation.

Freud gives not one but many explanations, that is, many distinguishable but overlapping lines of explanation. To begin with, Freud explains Rat Man's problem as neurotic conflict between "an erotic instinct and a revolt against it" (1909b, 162), Freud's specific formulation of Rat Man's situation being: "If I have this wish to see a woman naked, my father will be bound to die" (162). The presence of noxious experiences early in life constitutes another explanatory line, instances being Rat Man's precocious sexual experience of crawling under the skirt of his governess and fingering her genitals, and the episode of rage against his father at the age of three when, innocent of swear words, he hurls such terms of abuse at his father as "You lamp! You towel! You plate!" (205). Another explanatory line takes the form of hypothecating Rat Man's "disintegration into three personalities," one unconscious and two preconscious ones, between which consciousness oscillates. His unconscious one is comprised of "passionate and evil impulses." "In his normal state he was kind, cheerful, and sensible—an enlightened and superior kind of person—while in his third psychological organization he paid homage to superstition and asceticism" (248). This formulation, foreshadowing Freud's "structural" triumvirate of id, ego, superego, fits only too well in the sense that it may be said to fit everyone, not just Rat Man. Still another explanatory line takes the nosological form of designating Rat Man as an obsessional neurotic. The shoe fits well enough in this case except that Freud's reasoning tends to be circular: Rat Man behaves like an obsessional neurotic, and an obsessional neurotic behaves like Rat Man. This approach has the unquestionable value of matching an individual with a class of behavior, yet it is the special merit of psychoanalytic case histories that at their best they deal with the particularities of individual life history.

What succeeds best in this case is Freud's holistic-biographical approach, which constitutes not only another line of explanation but perhaps the most powerful one because of its semantic richness and specificity. This line of explanation operates by situating a piece of puzzling behavior—mysterious when isolated from the appropriate contexts—within a larger biographical matrix. Freud's explanations of such puzzling episodes as the strange business of Rat Man's futile attempts to pay for the pince-nez glasses, and the bizarre behavior of playing with his penis in front of the mirror at midnight instead of studying, just when his *dead* father might be expected to check on his work habits, make sense precisely because they fit, congruently, with other information we have about Rat Man's object-relational history.

This question remains: To what extent are Rat Man's problems sexual in nature, that is, problems resulting —to a significant degree—from factors and experiences exhibiting conflict over sexuality itself as distinguished from object-relational conflict that on occasion takes on the *appearance* of sexual behavior? A representative instance crops up when Freud ventures to "put forward" one of his theory-driven "constructions" to the effect that in childhood Rat Man may have been "guilty" of the "sexual misdemeanor" of masturbation. To Freud's initial delight, Rat Man remembers being told by his mother that there was "an occurrence of this kind" in early childhood, only, as it turns out when Rat Man interrogates his mother, what he had done at the age of three was to *bite* someone. This was the occasion when he attempted to swear at his father because his father spanked him. Freud admits that in the mother's account "there was no suggestion of his misdeed having been of a sexual nature," (206), yet at this point Freud appends a leviathan footnote, probably defensive, the drift of which is to deny the force of the mother's recollection of the nonsexual nature of the event. Since Rat Man's biting was hostile, and his verbal abuse of his father was certainly angry, and since the problem of handling anger bulks so large in this and other cases of obsessional neurosis, it may be asked, rhetorically at this point, if Rat Man's unconscious guilt (conflict) does not lie more in the sphere of hostile impulses than that of sexual ones.

Rat Man, who is familiar with Freud's theories before he begins analysis, happily brings up various anecdotes about his early sexual life: how he used to experience erections at the age of six, how he crept under Fräulein Peter's skirt and fingered her genitals at the age of four, an experience leaving him with "a tormenting curiosity to see the female body" (169), and his exploits at the age of seven with Fräulein Lina: "When I got into her bed I used to uncover her and touch her, and she made no objections" (161). Freud infers that Rat Man as a child was "under the domination of a component of the sexual instinct, the desire to look" (162). What Freud fails to do is to establish beyond reasonable doubt that such episodes had any lasting, negative effect on Rat Man's development, though he implies that they did.

Apropos of his wish to see females naked, Rat Man tells Freud that an uncanny feeling, "as though something must happen if I thought such things, and as though I must do all sorts of things to prevent it," accompanies this wish to see females naked. Asked for an example of what might happen, he responds: "For instance, *that my father might die*" (162), this in spite of the fact that Rat Man's father has been dead for several years. Recognizing such thinking as involving what Freud later calls "distortion by ellipsis" (227), and applying the heuristic strategy of filling-in-the-gaps that Freud uses to explain the thought, "If I marry the lady, some misfortune will befall my father" (226), allows us to reconstruct Rat Man's thought along the following lines. "Something must happen." What? In the context of the cultural taboo on sexuality, especially as it obtained at the beginning of this century, what must happen is punishment for the crime. Since the father is the conventional repository of moral authority in the nuclear family, he will carry out punishment for *any* misbehavior, just as he presumably did in the biting episode. "Something must happen" includes both the fear of experiencing the punishment deserved (for dirty thoughts as well as dirty deeds) together with Rat Man's equally guilt-inducing fear that he will be tempted to *retaliate* against the punisher— as he later retaliates against Freud in the transference. In such a conflict-inducing sequence, *which is emotionally conflictful primarily because of the child's attachment to the punitive parent,* the sequence of desire (seeing girls naked) leading to fear (of punishment) leading in turn to anticipation of his own hostility toward an attachment figure may relate to any behavior, not just sexual behavior. As Freud explains Rat Man's obsessional train of thought in the instance of "If I marry the lady, some misfortune will befall my father [in the next world]," it means, with the gaps filled in, "If my father were alive, he would be as furious over my design of marrying the lady as he was in the scene of my childhood; so that I should fly into a rage with him once more and wish him every possible evil" (226). *Ira furor brevis est.* If anger is brief madness, anger toward a loved person is madness multiplied. The more important the object, the sharper the conflict.

Part of Freud's explanation of the case in sexual terms involves his assumptions about Rat Man's "anal erotism" (213). So phrased, the term fuses sexuality with anality, just as the term "sexual object" tends to define all objects as sexual ones. If we were to accept Freud's claims in *Three Essays* about orality and anality being component instincts, then the sexual elements of Rat Man's pregenital sexual organization would loom larger than otherwise because of the manifest pervasiveness of anality in the case. Freud assumes, for example, that sadism is a psycho*sexual* phenomenon; in contrast, I assume that sadism may more profitably be regarded as a form of object relations that sometimes includes sexual behavior. But even if one were to agree with Freud in regarding Rat Man as an anal erotic instead of seeing him, as I prefer, as exhibiting an anal-obsessional person-ality whose behavioral style, including ways of thinking, can extend to and modify his sexual activity, the question remains as to the priority of sexual over object-relational factors in the case.

Rat Man's playfully hostile transference fantasies reek with anality. There is no doubt of that! They usually contain sexual elements—but not always. What they *always* reflect is hostility. Once Rat Man dreams that he makes the "mistake" of mocking Freud instead of condoling with him after his mother dies. Another time he imagines, in session, that Freud's mother stands in despair as all her children are being hanged (284).

Distinct from such nonsexual, nonanal fantasies are the following ones. Rat Man thinks about Frau Professor Freud licking his (Rat Man's) anus (293). Another one, which Freud the archeologist describes as "a most wonderful anal phantasy," is this little gem: "He was lying on his back on a girl (my daughter) and was copulating with her by means of the stool hanging from his anus" (287). What seems to be happening is that in the process of uncorking his hostility in the transference Rat Man raises the emotional ante by discharging insults, as the Yahoos dump theirs on Gulliver, in the shittiest form imaginable, with a twist of erotica for accent. That Rat Man's hostile attacks on his father via the transference often include sexual elements by no means establishes the primacy of these elements.

Many of the scenes of conflict referred to in Rat Man's history partake of no sexual element whatsoever. Illustrative examples are when Rat Man bites someone at the age of three and then "curses" his father after being spanked; when he attempts to shoot his younger brother in the eye with the ramrod of his toy gun; and when he commits the "crime" of failing to be at his father's bedside when he dies because he has misunderstood the answer to the question he asks the doctor concerning when the danger would be over. All of these instances involve conscious or unconscious hostility toward important others, and hence conflict, but not sexual conflict, unless, of course, one reads all hostile behavior as sadistic, and all sadistic behavior as reflecting anal eroticism, as Freud is wont to do. All of these instances reflect ambivalence. Other conflictual episodes marked by ambivalence but lacking overt sexual elements occur when Rat Man thinks Gisela might be more kind to him if a misfortune occurred to him, like the death of his father, and when the idea comes to him that he will be rich enough to marry Gisela if his father dies. In the case of his practice of masturbating in front of the mirror when he should be studying, where the sexual element appears to be inescapable, Freud himself recognizes the operation of ambivalence in Rat Man's wishful fantasy that his father will return from the dead, and—more important—he realizes that Rat Man's violation of a prohibition requires the *defiance* of a command. The object-relational element of defiance presumably weighs far more in this episode than the sexual form the resistance to studying takes. Rat Man's defiance of his father also operates, as Freud understands, in the matter of his wanting to marry Gisela, which he eventually does after the treatment is over (Mahony 1986), rather than the girl his family picks out for him to marry. Even Gisela comes in for her share of Rat Man's ambivalence.

Once, when she lies ill in bed, Rat Man suddenly wishes "she might lie like that forever" (1909b, 194), and he admits to Freud that he experiences occasional impulses "to do some mischief to the lady he admired" (195). At one point he is horrified by the thought, which crosses his mind, that "she is a whore" (301), a thought thoroughly at odds with his customary deep respect for her.

The points being made, in short, are that the essence of Rat Man's conflict is object relational rather than sexual, and that the essence of his object-relational conflict lies in his ambivalence toward important others, stemming from childhood and carrying on into adulthood. The essence of what Freud achieves in treating Rat Man is to enable him to come to terms with that ambivalence.

DR. SCHREBER

Sexual factors appear to play a substantial part in the case of Dr. Schreber ("Psycho-Analytic Notes on an Autobiographical Account of a Case of Paranoia [Dementia Paranoides]," 1911). Schreber believes, among other things, that it is his mission "to redeem the world and to restore it to its lost state of bliss" by being transformed into a woman and impregnated by God (16–17). Freud notes that prior to his second prolonged illness he had the idea, as a kind of reverie, "that after all it really must be very nice to be a woman submitting to the act of copulation" (13). According to Freud, Schreber's delusions about sexual abuse and gender change, persecutory for the most part, reveal that "what lies at the core of the conflict in cases of paranoia among males is a homosexual wishful phantasy of *loving a man*" (62). Freud claims this to be the common finding in every one of "a number of cases" coming "under observation" by Freud, Jung, and Ferenczi (59).

Libido theory plays a prominent role in Freud's formulation of the case. "The exciting cause of his illness, then, was an outburst of homosexual libido" (43), this outburst being conjunctive with a four-day absence of Frau Schreber. The concept of libido becomes a universal explanatory principle, accounting for Schreber's withdrawal from reality (a "detachment of the libido from people—and things—that were previously loved," 71), his delusions of grandeur ("fixation at the stage of narcissism," 72), and the form of his delusions of persecution (the extent to which they are sexual in nature). Freud even goes so far as to venture this startling

comparison: "Schreber's 'rays of God,' which are made up of a condensation of the sun's rays, of nerve-fibres, and of spermatozoa, are in reality
nothing else than a concrete representation and projection outwards of
libidinal cathexes; and they thus lend his delusions a striking similarity
with our theory" (78).

Freud's difficulty is threefold. His use of libido theory and his insistence on sexual conflict in the etiology of neurosis—and here, psychosis
—constitute two aspects of the problem. The third aspect consists of his
claim that in the instance of paranoia the real villain is not just the
repression of sexual drive in general but the repression of homosexual
impulses in particular. Freud's reiterated claims concerning the etiological
significance of latent homosexual desire in paranoia seem problematic
today. For one thing, Freud implicitly hypothecates an intrinsic conflict
between homosexual and heterosexual orientations (165) in a way that
does not tally with what we know today about "core gender identity," the
concept designating the "conviction that the assignment of one's sex was
anatomically, and ultimately psychologically correct" (Stoller 1985, 11).
Except for his delusions, which technically speaking are not homosexual but
transsexual, with Schreber playing the role of a female engaging in heterosexual intercourse, the outward facts of Schreber's life (his childhood,
marriage, desire for children, and social and professional identity in a
markedly patriarchal society) indicate Schreber's core sexual identity to be
heterosexual. Another difficulty with Freud's position lies in the fact that
modern surveys regarding the incidence of homosexuality in paranoia
weigh heavily against his claim (Meissner 1978, 19; Ovesey 1969, 53).

In Part 3 of the case, a large portion of which has nothing directly to
do with Schreber, Freud presents a remarkable series of defensive transformations as being typical of paranoia. He claims that "the familiar
principal forms of paranoia can all be represented as contradictions of the
single proposition: 'I (a man) *love him* (a man).' " One contradiction is: "I
do not *love* him—I *hate* him." But another contradiction is that "I hate
him" becomes transformed by *projection* into: "*He hates* (persecutes) *me,*
which will justify me in hating him." In short, "I do not *love* him—I *hate*
him, because HE PERSECUTES ME." Freud shrewdly adds that there is no
doubt "that the persecutor is some one who was once loved" (1911, 63).
(Two other sets of transformations in this passage I omit from discussion
here because they have no bearing on the case of Dr. Schreber. One
involves the theme of sexual jealousy, and one the transformation of a
male object into a female object.) Freud shows, of course, that the "he" is

God, and also Dr. Flechsig, and by extension the psychological father, though Freud explicitly discriminates the psychological father in this case from Schreber's biological father. What we now have more information about, in the light of the research of Niederland (1984) and others, is what kind of a god God was in this case, the gist of the situation being that Schreber's delusions of persecution undeniably reflect, in however bizarre and exaggerated a manner, the very real physical and psychological "persecution" (or what looks like persecution) visited upon Schreber as a child by his father. What this information makes possible is the generation of another transformation in the emotional grammar of Schreber's soul—one which Freud has overlooked. Side by side with Freud's "I do not *love* him—I *hate* him, because HE PERSECUTES ME" we can inscribe, "Because he persecutes me, I hate him whom I love." If we examine this emended version in the light of attachment theory and at the same time discard Freud's benighted notion that children's love of parents of the same sex must necessarily be erotic and therefore homosexual, what precipitates out of the propositional calculus is a poignant sense of the emotional double-binding to which Schreber had been subject as a child. We gain a firmer grasp of the object-relational elements of the case as distinct from the allegedly libidinal ones. We realize that because of what seemed like persecution, Schreber could not help hating the father he loved.

What remain to be mentioned are the factors that may have led the fifty-one-year-old Schreber to *represent* the delusional form of his submissive relationship to his father as a sexual one. In the circumstances, these factors will have to be largely conjectural—though because some are conjectural does not mean they cannot be correct. We do know that the various impulse-restraining mechanical contraptions invented by Schreber's authoritarian father to condition children and deracinate all signs of "self-will," represented by Schreber in his delusions as "soul-murder," were designed to effectuate *bodily control*. Thus part of the basis of the delusions lies in the intense involvement of the emotionally beloved same-sex parent with his son's body in a way that created pain and shame, not pleasure. What we may also be seeing in the delusional representation of nonsexual love between parent and child as a sexual one is the kind of adultomorphization of childhood behavior by Schreber that leads to the confusion of innocent physical intimacy in childhood with what, in adulthood, especially in Schreber's society, would be largely confined to conjugal relationships. Quite apart from the question of adultomorphization, how, in so patriarchical a society, would the highly stratified power relationships of father and son be represented metaphorically when those relationships were loving ones characterized by domination on one side and submission on the other? The schema of master and slave comes to mind, of course, though that of husband and wife more nearly corresponds to an intense emotional relationship characterized, according to the conventions of the day, by dominance and submission. However his ideas came to take such a form, what Schreber gives us is an omnipotent God on one side and on the other a castrated redeemer transformed, at a later date, into God's wife and sexual slave.

Virtually all of the delusional material Schreber presents in his memoirs needs to be read as metaphorical rather than literal. But Freud elects to read the gender change and other sexual business literally. In contrast, a contemporary clinician makes a distinction between true homosexuality and what he calls "pseudohomosexuality" (Ovesey 1969), the latter being a form of conflict developing (according to Meissner's summation, 1978, 20) "in men who fail to meet the standards of society for masculine performance," as Schreber may have felt he failed to do when he was defeated as a candidate for the Reichstag, just before his first illness, and as he may have feared to fail after being promoted to the high office of presiding judge in the Court of Appeals, just before his second illness. "The equation of failure with castration, feminine inadequacy, and homosexuality underlies the pseudohomosexual conflict" (Meissner 1978, 20). Although Ovesey does not discuss the Schreber case at length, he offers "an adaptional revision of the Freudian theory of paranoia" demonstrating "that paranoid phenomena can stem from nonsexual adaptions to societal stimuli, and motivationally need have nothing to do with homosexuality whatsoever" (1969, 54).

Many interesting features of the dynamics of Schreber's psychosis fall outside the scope of the present discussion, among them his depression (he was suicidal at the beginning of his first two periods of illness) and the vicissitudes of his self-esteem. But a few words more need to be devoted to some of the object-relational elements of his story. To begin with, the period of stress precipitating Schreber's illnesses, described in terms of "mental overstrain" and the "burden" of his professional duties, may be likened to exposure to an external danger triggering attachment behavior in children. On the occasion of the commencement of his second illness, Schreber's principal support figure, his wife, was absent, the presumption being that the operative factor was stress-plus-separation as distinct from what Freud claims, namely that "the mere presence of his wife must have acted as a protection against the attractive power of the men about him" (1911, 45). In this connection it is worth noting that Schreber's final flight into insanity occurred not long after his mother's death in 1907, that is, after the loss of his original primary support figure. Given the absence of adequate interpersonal support, and lacking inner resources of character—which can be conceptualized as fully assimilated internalizations of beneficent others sufficient to sustain him in his hour of need—Schreber may be regarded as having sought help internally in the form of a massive regression to the time of his greatest closeness to his all-powerful father, represented in psychotic fantasy as God. For someone with Schreber's childhood experiences, to plug into this omnipotent source of power was like making a pact with the devil. God became his ally only at the price of becoming his adversary: "God Himself was on my side in His fight against me" (Schatzman, 1973, 75). Schreber also tells us that "when the work of creation was finished, God withdrew to an immense distance" (Freud 1911, 22). This distance is the inner equivalent of separation from his biological parents. The enormity of the hostility experienced by Schreber as a consequence of the demands made upon him by God, such as "in the matter of the urge to evacuate" (25) and the devastating (though voluptuous) effect of the divine rays of God, was such that Schreber felt "entitled to sh— upon the whole world" (26). The fundamental power of God in Schreber's delusions may be compared to the elemental power of any primary attachment figure, the power to threaten withdrawal of love: "God Himself demands that He shall be able to find voluptuousness in him, and threatens him with the withdrawal of His rays if he neglects to cultivate voluptuousness and cannot offer God what He demands" (30).

Freud recognized the metaphoric nature of the religious elements of Schreber's delusions readily enough. Had he not been so preoccupied with his metapsychological assumptions, Freud might have understood the sexual elements to be metaphoric as well.

WOLF MAN

As for Wolf Man ("From the History of an Infantile Neurosis," 1918), Sherwood, in commenting on the difficulties presented by this case, believes there is "good reason to doubt whether Freud ever satisfactorily understood this patient" (1969, 262). True or not, the case does pose

many problems, Freud's apologies notwithstanding. One problem arises
because Freud decided to write—instead of a true case history—the
distillation of an account of a (hypothetical) infantile (childhood) neurosis, said to be implied by the case as a whole, with the unhappy
consequence that this material becomes factually and conceptually isolated
from the case proper and from the transference. Another problem turns
on the question of the severity of Wolf Man's adult and childhood illnesses. Freud introduces him as being "entirely incapacitated and completely dependent upon other people" (1918, 7) at the beginning of
treatment, a description lacking in specifics and radically at variance with
Wolf Man's situation as we learn about it from his memoirs. Freud also
asserts that Wolf Man's early years were "dominated by a severe neurotic
disturbance" (8), an assessment that more nearly characterizes Freud's
perception of the endopsychic drama he "reconstructs" than it conforms
to the actualities of Wolf Man's outward life. These actualities are such as
to make Wolf Man's childhood sexual experiences seem unremarkable and
his "phobias" more like the normal fears of childhood. What cannot be
overlooked, though the problem cannot be resolved in the present discussion, is the overall disparity between the accounts provided by Freud and
by Ruth Mack Brunswick, on the one hand, and those furnished by
Muriel Gardiner and the Wolf Man himself (all except Freud in Gardiner,
1971). The discussion to follow will be confined to raising certain questions with respect to the force and plausibility of Freud's claims concerning sexual factors in the case.

Freud often succeeds in handling childhood sexuality with a light,
comic touch, as in the anecdote he records about the three-year-old girl
who asks her friend, as she and her friend and her little brother go to the
toilet together: "Have you got a purse too? Walter's got a little sausage;
I've got a purse" (1900, 373). In contrast, the sexual scenes of the Wolf
Man case are serious to the point of qualifying as psychic melodrama.
Many of them are scenes of "seduction," a term redolent with overtones
of adult sexuality. During the first one mentioned, Wolf Man's sister, a
couple of years older, "had seduced him into sexual practices" by propos-
ing, "Let's show our bottoms" (1918, 20). Wolf Man is three and a
quarter years old at the time. As their mother works in an adjoining
room, "his sister had taken hold of his penis and played with it, at the
same time telling him incomprehensible stories about his Nanya [nanny]"
and the gardener: "She used to stand him on his head, and then take hold
of his genitals." Far from regarding this episode as comical and harmless,

Freud holds this "seduction" responsible for inducing sexual passivity in the boy and for stimulating him to compensatory fantasies (dreams) in which he plays an aggressive sexual role toward his sister, the dates being unspecified and the text of the dreams unrecorded (19–20). The lack of specificity regarding the timing and content of these fantasies leave their connection to the "seduction" of Wolf Man open to question.

As for the second "seduction," Freud would have us believe that young Wolf Man rejects "the allurements" of his sister and tries to "win" his nurse instead. Supposedly acting on the hint provided by his sister concerning Nanya and the gardener, "He therefore began to play with his penis in his Nanya's presence, and this . . . must be regarded as an attempt at seduction" (24). Nanya responds by making "a serious face" and telling her little charge that children who play with their privates get a "wound" in that place, a response Freud reasonably enough construes as a veiled threat of castration.

According to Freud, this scene of frustrated seduction, and the psychic scars left by the first one, lead to a third seduction. After Nanya's rejection of his advances, Wolf Man "began to contemplate another person as a sexual object": his father. Asked as a boy what he wants to become, he replies, "a gentleman like [my] father" (27). "This object of identification of his active current [of libido]," says Freud, homing in on libidinal hydraulics while ignoring object-relational factors of a nonsexual kind, "became the sexual object of a passive current in his present anal-sadistic phase. *It looks as though* his seduction by his sister had forced him into a passive role, and had given him a passive sexual aim" (27; italics added). This reasoning leads Freud to construe Wolf Man's naughtiness—yet to be discussed—as a masochistic attempt to provoke physical punishment ("beatings") from his father in order to obtain the masochistic "sexual satisfaction that he desired. His screaming fits were therefore simply attempts at seduction" (28). Elsewhere Freud links what he chooses to regard as passive behavior, seeing it as homosexual and therefore automatically passive, to Wolf Man's identification *with his mother* as she purportedly engages in anal intercourse with his father in the primal scene (age one and a half) constituting part of the background for the later dream of the wolves in the tree that becomes the centerpiece of the case history.

Freud's presentation of a fourth seduction scene, so remarkable for its artistry and ingenuity that one almost neglects to be concerned about veridicality, depicts the recovery by Wolf Man of the recollection of anxiety he experiences as a child at seeing a butterfly he had been chasing land on a flower, a scene associated in his mind with the image of a kneeling nurserymaid named Grusha: "When he saw the girl scrubbing the floor he had urinated in the room and she had rejoined, no doubt jokingly, with a threat of castration" (92). Freud hypothesizes that when Wolf Man saw the nurserymaid on her knees, scrubbing the floor, with her buttocks projecting, "he was faced once again with the posture which his mother had assumed in the copulation scene" (92), the one dated by Freud as occurring when Wolf Man was one and a half years old. "She became his mother to him; he was seized with sexual excitement. . . . and, *like his father* (whose action he can only have regarded at the time as micturation), he behaved in a masculine way towards her. [Happily, in this instance, Wolf Man identifies with his father rather than his mother.] His micturation on the floor was in reality an attempt at a seduction, and the girl replied to it with a threat of castration, just as though she had understood what he meant" (93). Besides failing to explain why the girl would respond to a child's sexual advances by threatening castration, Freud overlooks two alternative possible scenarios. First, Wolf Man's remembrance of things past may have been confused with regard to sequence. The nurserymaid may have been doing what nurserymaids do, namely cleaning up messes. Even if little Wolf Man were precociously stimulated by Grusha's alluring rump, that vista in all likelihood *followed* rather than preceded the scene of his urinary incontinence. Second, this particular peasant girl may well have been cranky at the moment (tired of cleaning up messes), so that her playful threat to cut off his little hose may well have been designed to frighten him into continence.

According to Freud's oedipal script, "it would seem palpably obvious [not just "obvious" but "palpably obvious"] that the repression and the formation of the neurosis [meaning the obsessional neurosis of Wolf Man's childhood] must have originated out of the conflict between masculine and feminine tendencies, that is, out of bisexuality" (110). Freud finds this conclusion uncontradicted by Wolf Man's eventual development of normal, heterosexual, genital organization during puberty, that is, prior to his analysis. This somewhat unexpected revelation invites the following question. If Wolf Man functioned normally as an adult in the sexual realm, in spite of his childhood situation (obsessional conflicts, a negative oedipus complex, a traumatic primal scene, the "seduction" by his sister), what did he need analysis for?

This question leads to a brief consideration of some of the object-relational features of the case, beginning with the ambiguity surrounding the events and circumstances that precipitated Wolf Man's fears and his "naughtiness" as a child. "He seems at first to have been a very good-natured, tractable, and even quiet child" (14–15), we are told, "but once, *when his parents came back from their summer holiday,* they found him transformed [age three and a half]. He had become discontented, irritable, and violent, took offense at every possible occasion, and then flew into a rage and screamed like a savage" (15; italics added). The possibility that the heretofore secure boy may have experienced separation anxiety and as a consequence bitterly resented his parents' absence never comes up for discussion. We do know Wolf Man loved his Nanya, so he may not have resented the absence of his parents. Freud relates that in his earliest years Wolf Man's relation with his father was "a very affectionate one" (17). But we know that attacks of depression led to his father's absences from home, and also that as a consequence of the mother's "weak health" "she had relatively little to do with the children" (13). Wolf Man's attachment to his parents may or may not have been muted and compensated for by attachments to his Nanya and his sister. Freud ascribes the boy's angry behavior to the disruptive presence of an eccentric English governess who stayed on that summer and who quarrelled with Wolf Man's Nanya, calling her a "witch" (15). In contrast, I am inclined to attribute the sudden emergence of Wolf Man's angry behavior, and the obsessional defenses with which he attempts to cope with his anger later on, to disappointment by or conflict with primary attachment figures, whoever they may have been.

Freud asserts that Wolf Man told him he felt scarcely a trace of grief at the sudden, unexpected news (when he was nineteen) that his sister had committed suicide. Perhaps this response had reference only to an initial numbness. In any case, Wolf Man writes in his memoirs about the depth of his loss: "After the death of Anna, with whom I had had a very deep, personal, inner relationship, and whom I had always considered as *my only comrade,* I fell into a state of deepest depression" (Gardiner 1971, 25; italics added). Further on he remarks, "I had fallen into such a state of melancholy after Anna's death that there seemed to be no sense or purpose in living, and nothing in the world seemed worth striving for" (50). These feelings hamper his studies and cause him to sample the usual wares of the sanatoria of the day. Then, at a sanatorium in Munich, he falls in love at first sight with the beautiful woman who eventually becomes his wife: Therese. Regarding the depression he had been suffering at the school in St. Petersburg, Wolf Man says that whereas "the main symptom of my condition had been the 'lack of relationships' and the spiritual vacuum which this created, I now felt [after meeting Therese] the exact opposite. Then I had found life empty, everything had seemed 'unreal,' to the extent that people seemed to me like wax figures or wound-up marionettes with whom I could not establish any contact. Now I embraced life fully and it seemed to me highly rewarding, but only on condition that Therese would be willing to enter into a love affair with me" (50). Their relationship lasted for thirty years, until the suicide of Therese in 1938. Emotionally, it lasted much longer than that. Wolf Man's sense of loss continues undiminished, as he notes in a letter to Muriel Gardiner in 1960: "As regards myself, also, I am aware over and over again that I shall never really recover from the loss of my wife. And I often think how lonely the evening of my life will be" (339). Looked at in retrospect, the attachments to others and subsequent experiences of loss, including the temporary loss as a child of his parents during the summer of his discontent, appear to be more credible sources of major conflicts in Wolf Man than the alleged sexual sources Freud points to.

The cases discussed in this chapter differ from each other so much that they almost defy consideration as a group. But there are some common elements. A thread running through most of them, as case histories, is what Freud refers to as the sexual business. That thread now seems frayed beyond usefulness, and beknotted beyond untangling. In spite of so grave a limitation, the cases themselves, as independent wholes, retain their object-relational significance. What seems reasonable to say at this point is that all of the individuals analyzed were *conflicted,* to a greater or lesser degree, and that their conflicts developed within interpersonal contexts. The principal source of the conflicts lay in the experience of painful encounters with, or losses of, emotionally important others.

4.

GABRIELLE, ANNA, RENEE, JOEY: FOUR CASE HISTORIES

The cases discussed in this chapter have been selected primarily for the purpose of further exploring the merits of a person-oriented approach to object relations. In those instances where the analysts involved present their material in a way that is consistent with a drive-oriented theory of object relations, I provide alternative readings of the same material from a person-oriented perspective.

The case of Mrs. A. will serve as a brief introduction to the issues at stake. In this particular instance the analyst (Peterfreund 1983) demonstrates a flexible responsiveness to object-relational factors as distinguished from dealing, in a stereotyped way, with sexual factors assumed by others (his supervisor and discussants at a case conference) to underlie the patient's symptoms. Peterfreund intends this case, and the others in *The Process of Psychoanalytic Therapy,* to illustrate two possible approaches to the psychoanalytic process. One he designates as "stereotyped" and the other as "heuristic." The former approach tends to be weighted down by a rigid set of self-confirming presuppositions whereas the much more flexible, open, heuristic approach lends itself better to genuine discovery. Peterfreund's agenda differs from mine. He uses the case of Mrs. A. (and others) to contrast barren and productive modalities of the psychoanalytic process. Peterfreund devotes particular attention to technique and comparatively little attention to the nature of the analyst's theoretical presuppositions. I take the liberty of using a portion of his material for a different purpose because it seems to me that what the group of analysts whose approach he criticizes have in common conforms to the drive-oriented approach, whereas Peterfreund's own assumptions reflect the person-oriented approach to object relations—even though he does not talk about that orientation as such.

Mrs. A's presenting symptoms include hypochondriacal preoccupations, fears of death, intense anxiety, depression, agoraphobia, and episodes of tachycardia in which her pulse rate often exceeds 160 beats per minute. She feels "friendless, alone, ugly, and unloved" (all quotations pp. 7–15). Peterfreund remarks that in all the years of his experience he has "rarely seen, outside of a hospital setting, a patient so anxious, so constantly in terror, so unable to find a moment of peace." Peterfreund's supervisor, critical of his early transference interventions, contends that the patient should be talking about her husband "since he, according to the supervisor, was probably the cause of the patient's difficulties. The supervisor told me she had a hunch that the patient was ill because her husband was making her do a perversion." In the "Rashomon situation" of the case conference, one discussant insists that the patient is only trying to "seduce" Peterfreund through her anxiety, and another believes, on the basis of mouth and throat symptoms, that the patient is "obviously struggling with fantasies of devouring her father's phallus." He wants to know why oedipal issues are not discussed in the case report. The ideas of a third discussant are consistent with the overview Peterfreund provides of the case: "It seemed probable that at age 4 the patient had been struggling with violent aggressive feelings toward her very ill, psychotic, depressed, silent mother."

Although Peterfreund makes no effort to place the relevant biographical facts of the case in a particular theoretical framework, a great many of the details scattered throughout his presentation become especially significant within the perspective of an object relations theory emphasizing attachment deficits. Among them are Mrs. A's anxiety, her depression, and her agoraphobia—especially when considered in the light of Bowlby's view of phobia, discussed in the previous chapter, as a manifestation of separation anxiety. Mrs. A. feels she needs treatment when she becomes unable to leave home alone. "When she first began to work, in her teens, her anxiety was so intense that she had to be accompanied by her mother." She feels "alone" and "unloved." She lives a living nightmare of fear of "death, destruction, cancer, heart disease, *abandonment,* and consequent total *helplessness*" (italics added). She lives in "an unreliable, unstable, unpredictable world, one that could not be trusted." Like the as-if and false-self figures to be discussed in Chapter 6, Mrs. A. feels she must "create a superstructure, a facade to conceal the nothingness. I always copy and become like others. I don't know who the real me is." Specific separations of Mrs. A. from her mother—which may be inferred to be responsible for the patient's developmental deficits—include the mother's depression after the birth of the patient, and one lasting for six months after the birth of a sibling three years her junior, that is, during the critical phase of attachment needs. This mother, described as angry, paranoid, and totally lacking in warmth, is virtually absent even when actually present. "The mother, according to the patient, 'could not hear,' and was intolerant of any opposition. 'Bad' behavior 'killed' her, and she constantly threatened abandonment."

Comparable problems in the realm of attachment needs leading to serious emotional conflicts in later years will be found in all of the following cases. The gravity of the consequences varies considerably. It varies roughly in proportion to the extent of the deprivation, the degree of development achieved prior to the deprivation, and the quality of the emotional support provided by parents and their surrogates after the period of deprivation. Each case is unique, yet all exhibit the consequences of developmental crises involving interpersonal and intrapsychic conflicts stemming from various forms of separation and loss.

GABRIELLE

At the beginning of her sixteen "on demand" sessions with Winnicott (1977), covering a period of nearly three years, Gabrielle, affectionately nicknamed "The Piggle," is only two years and four months of age. This daughter of devoted parents experiences fretfulness, sleeplessness, and scary fantasies about a *black* mummy who "comes in after her at night and says, 'Where are my yams?' " (6). To "yam" is to eat. The term "yams" also designates her mother's breasts. Gabrielle has nightmares about something she calls "the babacar." "Tell me about the babacar, *all* about the babacar," she repeatedly demands of her mother, who understands only that "the black mummy and daddy are often in the babacar together, or some man alone. There is very occasionally a black Piggle in evidence" (7). Though Winnicott does not say so, it becomes apparent to the reader that "babacar" stands for "baby car," a vehicle or container of some kind. Confused at first regarding the meaning of "babacar," Winnicott launches one of his most crucial interpretations when Gabrielle asks him during the second session, "Do you know about the babacar?" After twice asking her to tell him what it is, he risks an interpretation: "I said, 'It's the mother's inside where the baby is born from' " (24). Gabrielle affirms his understanding. "She looked relieved and said: 'Yes, the black inside.' " In spite of this insight, the nightmares about threatening black mummys and ominous babacars continue for a long time. As late as the twelfth session (age 4 years, 1 month) Gabrielle remarks, "The more I go to Dr. Winnicott, the more bad dreams I have" (162). That is scarcely Winnicott's fault—for the most part, at least. The nightmares undoubtedly continue because the related emotional conflict requires further uncovering and working through, and because Gabrielle has need of further maturation—over and above therapy—before she will be able to deal with her problem.

The experience of separation and loss that precipitates Gabrielle's conflict centers around her responses at the age of 21 months to the birth of a sibling, Susan. Prior to this time her behavior was normal, her development optimal. Both the mother and Winnicott recognize that the birth of Susan marks the beginning of Gabrielle's conflict. The mother writes, "She had a little sister . . . when she was twenty-one months old, which I considered too early for her. And both this [event] and (I would think also) *our anxiety about it* seemed to bring about a great change in her" (6; italics added). The mother's sense of guilt derives, we learn, from the fact that she herself experienced (presumably in a negative way) the birth of a sibling at the same age as Gabrielle. How this sense of guilt on the part of the mother affects her handling of Gabrielle does not get explored in the case. There is no mention, either, of the period of time Gabrielle is separated from her mother in connection with the birth of Susan, or how the mother tries to handle Gabrielle's subsequent turmoil other than eventually seeking professional help from Winnicott. We do not learn much about the interactional style of the mother, or whether she attempts to compensate for Gabrielle's sense of loss with extra physical closeness and emotional contact. We do learn about one of Gabrielle's responses to the situation: "When the new baby came she trained herself in a week" [toilet trained] (14). In his notes at the end of the first session, Winnicott writes, "Troubles started with the arrival of a new baby, which forced the Piggle into premature ego development" (17).

Most of Gabrielle's responses to her predicament take the decidedly negative forms of confusion, conflict, guilt, and hostility. She no longer plays "with any concentration now" (7). Identity problems crop up. "She hardly even admits to being herself. She is either the baba, or more often the mummy. 'The Piga [*Piga* = *baba* plus *Piggle?*] gone away, gone to the babacar. The Piga is black. Both Pigas are bad. Mummy, cry about the babacar!' " (7). And Gabrielle no longer allows anyone to call her the Piggle. Throughout the treatment period there are many references to naughty, destructive behavior. Sleeplessness becomes chronic. Thumb sucking begins with the birth of the baby sister (105)! Motor control decreases. "From the age of six months, she adored her father, and at that age said: 'Daddy!' But she soon forgot or ceased to be able to use the word" (14). Her increase of reserve toward her formerly beloved father appears to reflect the emotional distancing that Bowlby (1969, xiii) refers to as "detachment" (resulting from anger toward parents after separation). Gabrielle appears to hold both parents responsible for her troubles —insofar as she understands them. Although Gabrielle verbalizes death wishes toward her "real" mother, saying, rather politely, "I'd like you to be dead" (1977, 87), she directs most of her hostility at fantasied, internalized bad-objects, such as when she dreams of breaking the black mummy into pieces (37), and when she dreams about shooting "the black mummy" (116). At one point she cooks up a truly Kleinian dish: "She had a recurrent dream that her mother and father were cut into little pieces, boiling in some container; whenever she shut her eyes the image returned, so she tried to keep awake" (147). Her fears stem directly and immediately from internalized bad-object and bad-self representations, and only more remotely, in ways beyond her understanding, from actual events connected with the birth and subsequent presence of her sister.

Although Winnicott realizes that Gabrielle's problems *begin* with the birth of her sibling, the frequency of his inclination to shift the focus of his interpretations to sexual matters, along Freudian and Kleinian lines, makes it uncertain that he grasps the extent to which Gabrielle's dreams, her play during the clinical hours, and her other behavior reflect her sense of separation and loss, and her guilt about retaliatory feelings. Many of Winnicott's interpretations are oedipal, often in an explicitly sexual way, in spite of his knowing that the trouble commences in a pre-oedipal phase. When Gabrielle tries to force the toy figure of a little man into the driver's seat of a toy car by pushing it in with a stick, Winnicott responds *during the first session* with "something about man putting something into woman to make a baby" (11). It is as though Winnicott cannot credit the undeniable importance in this case of the theme of birth without insisting simultaneously on the probable relevance, even for a two-year-old, of the mechanics of begetting babies. Susan's mere existence creates the problem for Gabrielle—not how she came into existence. But for Winnicott, rubbing toy carriages together must necessarily symbolize making babies (80). When Winnicott asks Gabrielle what she is thinking about a toy train she is playing with, she says, "It is long, like a snake," and then he asks, "Is it like a big daddy thing?" and she replies (age 3 years, 9 months), "No, a snake. Snakes are poisonous if they bite. If you don't suck the blood out, the man will die" (137). When Winnicott elsewhere addresses the very real possibility that Gabrielle feels guilty because she has her daddy all to herself in the train (the real one she travels to her sessions in), Winnicott says, "You began to be a bit frightened then [when playing with the toy train] to think of having daddy all to yourself in the train, especially when you think of what you want to do to him, because you want to do to daddy the same as you were showing me when you took the stuff[ing] out of the [toy] dog." Then he adds, "When you love me [analyst-daddy] it makes you want to eat my wee-wee" (156).

If Gabrielle wants to eat her parents in the Kleinian stew, it must be out of anger rather than lust. Winnicott notes in one of his lists of session themes, "Guilt because of destructive impulses toward the good object" (131). He also correctly interprets the babacar as an ominous, retaliatory womb. But time and again, at least in this case, Winnicott's otherwise clear perception of the object-relational dynamics becomes overcast with miasmic clouds of sexual interpretation. As I mentioned at the beginning of this book, when Gabrielle puts two stuffed animals together during the sixth session and says, "They are together and are fond of each other," Winnicott feels impelled to remark, "And they are making babies" (77). Gabrielle responds, "No, they are making friends." With the benefit of this corrective feedback Winnicott shortly thereafter recognizes the transference elements of Gabrielle's linking of two toy carriages by saying, "Gabrielle and Winnicott make friends" (78). Functionally speaking, the in-session phrase, "making babies," serves a dual purpose by giving expression to themes in the separate-but-related realms of attachment and sexuality. For Gabrielle, "making babies," to begin with, at least, can only refer to the immediate source of her problem, Susan, and indirectly to the separation she probably experienced at the time, and to the "virtual separation" taking the form of a probable decrease of attention from her mother subsequently. Thus it may be that many of Winnicott's sexually oriented interpretations serve Gabrielle's needs—not because of but in spite of their sexual focus—for the simple reason that the more important, object-relational elements are "co-present" in his constructions.

Gabrielle's condition improves dramatically with the "on demand" support of Winnicott's facilitating environment, the devoted ministrations of a good-enough mother, and the development of such adaptive capacities as learning to tolerate her ambivalence, and learning how (by identifying with mummy, presumably) to tidy things up. She tries to "tidy away" the black mummy (72), though that does not work at first. Before she reaches the age of four she can say (in contrast to her sense of herself as a black Piggle at two), "I am a nice tidy girl; I tidy things up" (148). She internalizes good-mother representations. "She loves cleaning and making things better" (107), writes her mother. In Kleinian terms, "By acquiring habits of cleanliness, the infant's anxieties about his dangerous faeces (i.e., his destructive badness), his bad internalized objects and internal chaos are again and again temporarily diminished" (1952a, 227). Gabrielle learns to mend herself as well as her toys, leading Winnicott to remark in preparation for termination, "You can be a mender, so you don't need me as a mender now" (1977, 166). She has internalized this aspect of his functioning. Above all, Gabrielle learns, directly or indirectly, the answers to many questions, such as "What *is* black, daddy?" (73), and whether witches have breasts (133), and where babies come from, and what it *is* like to be born. "I am just born," she says, playing a game with her daddy, "and it wasn't black inside" (30). "Tell me, tell me," she reiterates, hungry for understanding. "Tell me about the babacar, *all* about the babacar" (7). "*I want to know why* the black mummy and the babacar" (40; italics added). Winnicott often reads her queries as quests for *sexual* knowledge, but I think that is not what she wants to find out about, mainly. She wants to find out about things like badness. Gabrielle has to struggle to comprehend her sense of her own badness, her blackness—as well as the blackness she thinks she encounters in others. She finds her feelings confusing. And why not, if she hates those she loves, including herself?

ANNA

Because the analysand discussed in Lichtenstein's famous paper on "Identity and Sexuality" (1961) was a prostitute, it would seem to be impossible to erase the significance of sexual elements in the case history of Anna, the principal source of evidence supporting Lichtenstein's hypothesis that "human identity is established by a specific use of the non-procreative sexual function" (185). Fortunately, there is no need to erase the sexual elements entirely in order to perceive the extent to which Anna's identity turns out to be much more a function of her early attachment deficits than her early sexual experiences.

When Anna begins treatment at the age of twenty-three, Lichtenstein lists the presenting problems as "prostitution, conflicts arising from homosexual relations, periodic drinking, suicidal impulses and depression" (209). Feelings of despair and loneliness threaten to overwhelm Anna. Lichtenstein particularly concerns himself with the discrepancy between Anna's role as a prostitute and what she calls her "real self." She represents her real self in terms of her interest in the arts, intellectual matters, and self-improvement. "She looked upon herself somewhat like a person who, for some reason outside of himself, has to play a social role disconnected with his original position in life" such as "a forced laborer in a prison camp" who understands he is really a scientist, or musician, or whatever. Anna also has problems in regard to her love affairs. The difficulty, for her, is not that her emotionally important relationships are lesbian, but that these relationships repeatedly follow a disasterous sequence: falling passionately in love with a girl, living with her "as wife and husband" (with Anna seeing herself in the role of wife), feeling possessive and jealous, being unable to maintain the relationship, then falling into depression, excessive drinking, loneliness, and the role of being a prostitute—a role she invariably abandons when her lesbian relationships are stable.

The crucial facts concerning Anna's life circumstances and early object relations are these. She is the illegitimate child of a sixteen-year-old woman who becomes a successful singer in vaudeville. Though she is shown his picture, Anna never meets her father. Her grandmother, "a very religious woman" who cannot accept an illegitimate granddaughter, prays for her grandaughter's early death. In contrast, Anna's grandfather is warm and affectionate. She remembers him as the only person to give her unqualified love during her early years, though she also recalls getting affection from a nursemaid. Her stepfather, who often beats her, makes "sexual advances" on one occasion; no particulars are given about this episode. Anna's relationship with her beautiful, vivacious mother, *who often places her in foster homes while she is on the road,* is profoundly ambivalent, "being at once both passionate and deeply resentful" (213). "For Anna, her mother was the most beautiful woman whose love she constantly was seeking" but "she never knew where she stood with her mother" who "for some reason" she did not understand seemed to be ashamed of her and not to love her (213). The result of all this, says Lichtenstein, is that Anna "became her mother's most ardent lover" and tried her best to arrange for her mother to leave her stepfather so that she and her mother could "live for each other only" (214). When her mother does leave her stepfather, Anna works from the ages of thirteen to fifteen at all kinds of jobs in order to support her mother. When her mother subsequently gets involved with still another man, Anna feels betrayed and decides to run away, at the age of fifteen, shortly thereafter finding a job as a dancer in a nightclub, and not long after that slipping into prostitution as a way of meeting her financial needs.

Lichtenstein's complex discussion of Anna's "sexual identity," on which her prostitution has little bearing, begins by following the lead of Greenacre and Mahler. He quotes Mahler concerning the development of "sexual identity" as follows: "We conceive of the sense of self-identity as arising from [the] alternation of two kinds of experience, namely pleasurable bodily contact with the nursing mother and also pleasurable reunion with her during sleep, alternating with interpolated periods of wakefulness" (190). A gradual "libidinization of the body surface" is assumed to occur. Lichtenstein treats sexuality as an undifferentiated element of identity, as compared, for example, to Lichtenberg's (1989) representation of the sexual system as one of the five more or less separate motivational systems of the self. In Lichtenstein's view, the derivation of the sexual side of identity is essentially twofold, one being the element of *bodily contact* of child with mother and the other being a species of *mental contact* taking the form of fantasied symbiosis (the second kind of experience mentioned by Mahler in the passage above). Thus it is that Anna's devastating experience of loneliness, described as being "of intolerable intensity, undistinguishable from profound anguish, as if, in her words, she would go out of her mind" (219), leads to a reunion fantasy that Lichtenstein regards as fundamentally erotic not because it takes the form of the reunion of adult lovers but because the reunion is symbiotic, symbiotic reunion being intrinsically libidinal from Lichtenstein's perspective.

During periods of loneliness Anna indulges in what Lichtenstein calls her "Mad Lover fantasy." The lover is a madman—or madness itself. "He comes to make love to her, but while doing so, he destroys both her body and her mind," an experience she imagines as one of ecstatic happiness (219). Anna calls the following (written) version of the fantasy "Return":

> Ah, he quiets Sanity, for I hear the sounds of my lover's footsteps.—Is that you beloved, is that you returning to Drown in my madness, to baptise me with the Sweetness of our foolishness? Oh, bring back the strange but happy love.—Bless you, and drink with me my blood to quench our starved thirstiness.—*Farewell, loneliness* of Sanity, for madness has come to save my Soul. Hold my hand, lead me through the gates of Hell where we may rejoice to the Sins of humble men. Embrace me oh madness, let my nakedness and nudity quench thy thirst for madness with love of a longing heart. (219)

A comparable version, untitled, reads in part, "Don't leave me, for with you I am not alone. Keep me safe in your oblivion, safe from the haunting night. . . . Come back, come back, my Sweet love, don't turn me out. . . . Let me drink to our holy madness, to our love of Solitude, Oh madness, I love you, come back to keep me free from Sanity" (219–20). For Lichtenstein, Anna's masochistic fantasy of aggression turned against the self is "obviously a fantasy representing a desire for symbiotic fusion with the lover, expressed in archaic oral concepts of being devoured by the Madman" (220). Lichtenstein goes on to reason that Anna's mother has imprinted upon her an identity theme incompatible with separateness as an individual. He "transcribes" this theme as "being another one's essence" (221).

Assuming identity themes to be "irreversible," yet susceptible of variations, Lichtenstein states that for him the therapeutic problem has to do with whether Anna will become able to experience a less pathological version of the implementation of this theme. In this connection he quotes a letter from Anna, written after termination, that tells about her new relationship with a man called Ray. It reads, in part:

> Never before have I felt peace of mind with anyone, warmth and [a] feeling of wanting to do [things for him?]. I feel so much part of him that when he tells me something that was unpleasant to him, no matter what . . . I hate the thing or person for it. I feel it displeased him and that makes it terrible. If he is very tired, fatigue takes hold of me, and I seem to share his feeling, and usually end up relieving him of it. Does real loving make one feel a part of another? When he makes love to me I really feel that I'm way down deep inside of him, that his arms are my arms, etc. When he laughs, and he does not often, but [when] he really does, I am filled with sheer glee. When he is sad I long to whitewash all that has caused him his miseries and I feel compassion so deep that I usually have indigestion.(229)

For Lichtenstein, the implications of this letter are mixed. Anna's capacity to fall in love with a man rather than a woman implies adaption, but "she loves symbiotically to such a degree" that Lichtenstein doubts that Anna would be able to deal with the loss if this relationship were not a lasting one.

Whatever the scientific status of the concept of symbiosis, there appears to be no reason to quarrel with Lichtenstein's assumption that such themes in Anna's letter (and in her fantasy of the Mad Lover) as union, reunion, fusion, and boundary loss bespeak states of body and mind that might be referred to, if only metaphorically, as "symbiotic." Nor can there be any need to question the value of concepts like "identity" and "identity maintenance"—or even the value of Lichtenstein's claim that identity maintenance takes precedence over all other principles determining human behavior. What one may be permitted to question are Lichtenstein's assertions about "sexual identity," by which he seems to say not that there must be a sexual side or aspect of one's identity but rather than one's identity is intrinsically and inescapably sexual by virtue of one's early bodily contact and "symbiotic" experience of one's mother. One questions, in particular, the conventionally sexual reading Lichtenstein accords various themes in Anna's case. In his phrasing, Anna does not just love her mother; she becomes "her mother's lover," a love characterized, somewhat indirectly, as "incestuous" (217).

Rereading this case history within the framework of attachment theory leads to a quite different understanding of the loneliness theme. Such a reading emphasizes the many traumatic episodes Anna must have experienced when her mother placed her in "foster homes" while she was on the road. It emphasizes Anna's experience of uncertainty in her mother's love even when she was present, a problem presumably stemming from the mother's negative feelings about her daughter's illegitimacy. It emphasizes Anna's craving for intimate relationships, sexual or otherwise, when she becomes an adult. And it assumes that the images of the Mad Lover fantasy Lichtenstein thinks of in terms of symbiosis are after all no more than common expressions of human need for attachment. "Drink with me my blood" may be out of the ordinary, but hardly such passages as "hold my hand" and "embrace me," "don't leave me," "keep me safe," and "come back, come back, my Sweet Love, don't turn me out." These words express Anna's attachment needs, even if she is, in imagination, addressing Madness. Similarly, her depiction of her sense of being at one with Ray, not just in intercourse, metaphorically expresses a virtually universal human need for emotional intimacy. If Anna voices her personal need with a cry that is stronger than ordinary, perhaps that is only because the emotional insecurity of her early life enhances her desire for closeness.

RENEE

If a sense of "self-identity" does arise in part from "pleasurable bodily contact with the nursing mother" (in Lichtenstein 1961, 190), as Mahler assumes, then presumably the absence of sufficient bodily contact with the mother and other parenting figures tends to inhibit the development of functional selfhood. Considerable evidence from cross-cultural studies in social psychiatry shows that the deprivation of bodily contact in child-rearing correlates with disturbed behavior of various kinds, especially violence (Prescott 1979, 67). In the case of Renee, we learn from the extraordinary autobiography she writes after her recovery from paranoid schizophrenia that while she is ill she hates people without knowing why. She expresses the cosmic dimensions of her hostility by constructing—in fantasy—"an electric machine to blow up the earth and everyone with it" (Sechehaye 1951a, 47). She also hates being touched—except by Mme. Sechehaye, her analyst (Sechehaye, 1951b, 38), who institutes innovative modifications in her therapeutic handling of the case *in order to make contact* with her psychotic patient, among them the practice of sitting beside her on the couch instead of behind her on a chair. Renee feels *abandoned* in the traditional format: "When she did not see me, she thought I was not there" (41). So often, and so meaningfully, does the theme of making contact echo and reecho throughout Renee's story—though neither her account nor Sechehaye's make note of the theme as such—that it serves particularly well as a focus for discussing Renee's severe object-relational conflict.

The word *contact* refers variously to *physical contact* with "Mama" (as Renee usually calls her analyst), *emotional contact* with Mama, and *contact with reality*. Renee begins to lose contact with reality at the age of five when she experiences delusional hallucinations, fearing a schoolmate because she suddenly looks like a lion, and seeing a tiny crow's head on everyone's forehead. In spite of incipient depersonalization (people seem like puppets and robots), growing fears, and the loss through regression of certain skills (such as drawing, because she loses her sense of perspective), Renee manages to perform well in school for the most part, and to help take care of her younger siblings until the age of seventeen, when she is diagnosed as lapsing into an irreversible schizophrenia. Her symptoms (initial and subsequent) include deep regression, loss of visual perspective, depersonalization, compulsive masturbation, suicidal and other self-destructive behavior (such as deliberately burning her hand), refusal to eat (for months she had to be tube-fed), mutism, catatonia, visual and auditory hallucinations, delusions of grandeur (believing herself the Queen of Tibet, who is nine centuries old), and delusions of persecution. Renee feels she must annihilate herself at all costs because of the enormity of her guilt: "I was profoundly guilty, a guilt vast and horrible, unbearable, remorseless; of what I knew not, yet deeply, immeasurably guilty" (1951a, 93). Horrible images assail Renee: "It seemed that my mouth was full of birds which I crunched between my teeth, and their feathers, their blood and broken bones were choking me. Or I saw people whom I had entombed in milk bottles, putrefying, and I was consuming their rotting cadavers. Or I was devouring the head of a cat which meanwhile gnawed at my vitals" (59). While Renee does not identify this introject in her autobiography, Sechehaye mentions that Renee compares her mother to "a mysterious cat, the aggressiveness of which she dreaded" (1951b, 27). Complicating the course of her emotional illness are various physical problems, including a kidney infection the consequences of which are so severe that at the age of twenty-two her body weight falls to fifty-three pounds. Analysis commences when Renee is eighteen years old. By the age of twenty-six and a half she has fully recovered from her psychosis.

Among the relevant factors in Renee's childhood contributing to her later troubles, Sechehaye mentions the following pieces of information (1951b, 21–32). These facts, which Sechehaye rarely discusses in direct relation to the contents of the analysis, will readily be seen to involve instances of intimidation, rejection, separation, and loss.

Renee, the first of several children, is unexpected and unwanted by her parents, who had to cancel a wedding trip to Japan because of her. Her mother finds her ugly and is "unable" to breast-feed her. Because her mother puts too much water in the formula, Renee refuses the bottle. She almost starves before her affectionate grandmother begins to spoon-feed her gruel. Perhaps even more important, the grandmother provides loving care and attention—until Renee abruptly loses her grandmother at eleven months. At fourteen months Renee loses a pet—a live, white rabbit— when her father kills it in her presence, after which she refuses to eat. At eighteen months a sibling appears, after which Renee begins to spit at people, including her little sister. At the age of two a servant girl tells her, "Someone must have cut something off of you," implying castration. When Renee is five, her father takes a mistress, leading to serious marital discord. Depressed, the father proposes mutual suicide with Renee, perhaps only jokingly. "When Renee was seven years old, she placed some large stones on a railway track, hoping to derail the train and thereby kill someone; she does not say whom. This train . . . was the one taken regularly by her father. She sucks the rust on fences in order to 'become stiff like iron,' and sucks stones to 'become cold and hard' like them." At nine, her father runs away with his mistress and all the cash, abandoning the family. Renee's mother also talks about mutual suicide with Renee, repeatedly, in which connection it seems worth quoting Bowlby on the subject of threats of abandonment: "Threats to abandon, including suicide threats, play a far larger part in promoting anxious attachment than has usually been assigned to them" (1973, 226). Sechehaye mentions that Renee's mother "frequently threatened that after her death she would return to Renee and pull her by the feet, to punish her for having loved someone other than her mother" (1951b, 27).

In view of the many threatening, anxiety-provoking factors in Renee's early life, it is not surprising that when the positive transference finally becomes established, after much difficulty, Renee feels enormously "relieved" as well as joyful: "She told me later that after leaving the session she would jump up and down in the street shouting, 'I have a mother! I have a mother!' " (1951b, 38). Prior to this time Renee experiences the "indescribable distress" of "absolute solitude"—of being "terrifyingly alone." After Sechehaye becomes Mama, Renee remarks, "Only *near her* I felt *secure,* especially from the time when she began to sit next to me on the couch and put her arm around my shoulders" (1951a, 44, 46; italics added). Yet Renee's selfhood is so fragile, and her hold on reality so precarious, that the slightest disturbance can serve to break off contact, such as when Sechehaye utilizes the pronouns "I" and "you" instead of speaking about "Mama and Renee" (1951a, 52) at a language level consonant with Renee's current level of psychological functioning.

One of the implications of what Renee refers to as "the miracle of the apples" (1951a, 98–108) is that her contact with reality is a function of her emotional contact with Mama. Before the therapeutic breakthrough of the miracle of the apples, Renee allows herself to eat nothing but green apples "still attached to their Mama-tree." When the farmer's wife where she is staying at the time gets angry with her for picking apples that are still green, she feels there is nothing left for her to eat. She flees in rage, shame, and despair, convinced that "an irresistible authority wished me dead." Ordinary food will not serve. Renee refuses the beautiful apples Madame Sechehaye purchases from the store for her, saying, "I want real apples, Mamma's apples, like those," as she points to her analyst's breasts. When Sechehaye responds to this message by holding Renee and feeding her one of the ripe apples after symbolically pressing it against her own breast, Renee is not only able to eat apples, and subsequently to take other food, but she also begins to be relieved of her other symptoms. She no longer risks being changed into a famished cat, "prowling cemeteries, forced to devour the remains of decomposing cadavers." Best of all, she makes contact with reality: "Instead of infinite space, unreal, where everything was cut off, naked and isolated, I saw Reality, marvelous Reality, for the first time. The people whom we encountered were no longer automatons, phantoms, revolving around, gesticulating without meaning." Mama also changes. Before the miracle, Renee experiences her as being like an image, a statue—artificial and unreal. "But from this moment on she became alive, warm, animated, and I cherished her deeply. I had an intense desire to remain *near her, against her,* to preserve this marvelous *contact*" (107; italics added). Renee had detested milk, but now it seems altogether natural to her to drink it. The symbolic apples protect as well as nurture: "On the mantelpiece were always two beautiful apples representing the maternal breasts given me by Mama to protect me. At the least anxiety I ran to them and at once was reassured" (108).

The theme of contact pervades Renee's narrative, directly and indirectly. When she is young Renee experiences one of her friends as unreal, like a statue: "I saw her eyes, her nose, her lips moving, heard her voice and understood what she said perfectly, yet I was in the presence of a stranger. To restore contact between us I made desperate efforts to break through the invisible dividing wall, but the harder I tried, the less successful I was" (1951a, 36). When Sechehaye takes Renee with her to the seashore for three weeks, "I had no contact with her. . . . Apart from the sessions she was a stranger" (88). "It was only when I was near 'Mama,' my analyst, that I felt a little better," she says elsewhere, "but even for this, nearly an hour had to go by. Indeed, it was only toward the end of the hour, and sometimes not until twenty minutes after it, that I made contact with 'Mama' " (49). Renee experiences loss of contact as *abandonment,* such as when the psychiatric nurse serving as Mama's surrogate goes on vacation: "All night long I sobbed in anger and grief; my whole

world had fallen to pieces. Her absence was simply unbearable. . . . I felt
a pervasive sense of abandonment" (112). And she rages against Mama
for allowing it to happen.

Sechehaye's first significant emotional contact with her patient, at the
advent of the positive transference, comes about at the end of three and a
half months of analysis when Renee begins to bring in drawings representing the fantasies of her inner object-relational world. Her presentation
of these drawings relieves Renee and provides her analyst with crucial
insights—much as Milner's patient's paintings do in *The Hands of the
Living God* (Milner 1969). But the most dramatic therapeutic achieve-
ments in Renee's case occur when Sechehaye develops new measures of
achieving contact with her patient through her imaginative utilization of
what Winnicott eventually comes to call transitional objects. (Renee's
analysis concludes in 1938.) The symbolic apples on the mantelpiece
constitute one such set of objects. Many of the most significant objects in
Renee's case are self-surrogates, that is, they represent aspects of her
developing sense of selfhood—like the unnamed cloth monkey Mama
gives Renee, which Renee calls "my first double" (1951a, 95). At first
Renee associates the monkey's raised arms with her own impulse to strike
herself. When she communicates her fear, Mama responds by lowering
the arms and verbally reassuring her. This episode becomes a turning
point in the analysis: "From that moment, the impulse to self harm left
me abruptly" (97) And Renee adds, "I had no more contact with her
except when she took the little monkey in her arms and talked to him, a
thing she did too rarely to suit me" (99). Later on Sechehaye succeeds in
reestablishing contact with Renee by giving her a stuffed tiger: "Then
Mama gave me a beautiful plush tiger, and, taking it from her, I recognized him as my defender which alone, with Mama, could shield me from
harm" (120).

Another critical episode in Renee's redevelopment takes place when
Mama gives her a baby doll whom Renee names Ezekiel. "Taking courage
one day when Ezekiel was in Mama's arms, I pushed his head forward on
her bosom to test whether I had the right to live. At this, Mama pressed
him to her breast and let him nurse. This she did regularly several times a
day so that I awaited the moment in fear of her forgetting. But Mama did
not forget, and I began to dare to live" (123). During a period when
Renee has to be sedated for pain (kidney infection), she experiences the
sedation as being in a green sea "quite like being in Mama's body." When
the pain passes, her greatest joy is to lie peacefully "in the green light, my

hand in Mama's, Ezekiel on her heart. My contact with Mama persisted
without interruption. Her sweet voice alone sufficed now to soothe the
voices [of the persecutorial system] and the impulses [to harm herself].
And more and more, I preferred to be *near* her, rather than *within* her"
(126). At first Sechehaye wisely refuses to allow Renee to eat alone
because Renee dares to feed herself, as distinct from being fed, only if
Mama is close by. "Later Mama gave me a letter in which was noted in
detail what food I was to eat, food she herself had prepared, so that even
in her absence she was near me" (1951a, 126–27). The various transitional objects (the cloth monkey; the doll, Ezekiel) serve as containers of
Renee's externalized self-representations, these being benign constellations of self as distinguished from the more primitive and conflicted ones
(Little Iron Bar; the hostile Famished Cat Self; the grandiose Queen of
Tibet).

Beyond all doubt, Sechehaye's modifications of classical treatment serve
Renee's deepest object-relational needs. Sechehaye's commitments to Freud's
drive and structural theories seem not, in practice, to impede the treatment. When Sechehaye presents a formal interpretation of the case in the
analytical section appended to Renee's autobiography, her language remains locked into libido theory, and into what Bowlby calls the theory of
secondary drive: "Renee could not love herself since her mother had
refused to nourish, hence love, her. When the ego is no longer charged
with libidinal energy produced by the introjection of maternal love, destructive forces soon invade it. As Freud has shown, there is a complication of drives. When the libidinal drives are frustrated, the drives to self-
preservation lose their defensive energy and abandon the ego to self-
destruction" (1951a, 149). In contrast to the many passages referring to
libido theory in the interpretive supplement to the autobiography, Sechehaye expresses her account of the case in *Symbolic Realization,* for the most
part, in ordinary, non-technical language, and rarely resorts to metapsychological formulations. She recognizes more clearly in *Symbolic Realization,* though she does not elaborate on the idea at length, that Renee's
enormous guilt comes from "the aggressiveness against the mother, the
siblings and herself" (1951b, 136). Sechehaye also remarks, in language
perfectly consonant with attachment theory, that "the tragedy of the
situation is that maternal love is indispensable to the baby, and its deprivation leads to hopeless clinging of the child, who does not want to die"
(1951b, 136). In her review of the curative factors in the case, Sechehaye
emphasizes that by "maternal love" she means something like "functional

maternal love," that is, a responsible, loving, and operationally effective response to *all* of the child's needs as distinguished from mere unimplemented or ineffective feelings of affection. As far as Sechehaye is concerned, successful "symbolic realization of the fundamental emotional demands" (1951b, 13) of the child through such enactments as her symbolic care of Ezekiel constitute "proof of maternal love" that encourage Renee to love herself (1951b, 141).

Bowlby's babies are anxious *because mommy has gone away,* or may go away. Klein's babies are anxious *because their hatred may destroy mommy.* Renee's feelings of total abandonment, and her fantasy about a machine to blow up the world, suggest that we need to keep *both* sources of anxiety in mind.

JOEY

Unlike the other cases considered thus far, in which the analysts' perceptions of the material were always, except for Peterfreund, shaped to some degree by a drive-oriented view, the case of Joey exhibits no distortions of this kind. On the contrary, Bettelheim (1967) may be said to present this material, in a book that focuses on infantile autism, in a manner that reflects the basic assumptions of a person-oriented theory of object relations. The person-oriented theory of object relations implicit in Bettelheim's presentation. may furthermore be said to exhibit the elements mentioned in Chapter 2 that characterize a unified theory, one that is informed by attachment theory yet remains fully attentive to the dimension of internalized object relations, and that utilizes self theory as distinguished from ego psychology. Bettelheim contends that self is "stunted" in autism (92) but sufficiently present to initiate defensive withdrawal from others, autism being "an autonomous response" (408) by the child. And as more recent discussions of self do, Bettelheim's commentary stresses the importance of interpersonal mutuality between mother and child for the development of selfhood.

Joey, "the mechanical boy" (as Bettelheim refers to him in the title of his initial publication of the case in the pages of *The Scientific American*), lives in a world where feelings have no place, a world of machines. When he enters Bettelheim's school at the age of nine and one-half years, he is a "talking autistic child," one who has speech but does not communicate. To observers he seems like a robot, devoid of all that is human and childlike. His only play, and all of his fantasies, pertain to machinery. In what looks like a travesty of attachment behavior, Joey feels obliged to plug himself in to sources of electrical energy before he can be empowered to perform basic physiological functions like eating and defecating. He even fabricates a "breathing machine" out of "masking tape, cardboard, pieces of wire, and other odds and ends." Although his observers feel anxious about losing a bit of their own humanity while watching him, he has "the ability to hold the fascinated attention of those who watched him in his vacuum, to seduce them into believing him a machine" (238). When he is one year old, his parents give him an electric fan to play with. After that, all of his transitional objects are inanimate objects—but sometimes highly animated inanimate objects, airplane propellers being his favorite. When he runs around the school grounds he gyrates his hand in front of him, propelling himself with his own propeller—in fact, becoming a propeller. Machines are his protectors and controllers. He must insulate himself from the dangers of the world, such as when eating: "Under no circumstances, now, could he eat unless in touch with the table. He had to sit on a piece of paper, pressed against the table, and his clothing had to be covered with napkins. Otherwise, he later told us, he was not insulated and the electric current would leave him" (244). He refuses to drink except through piping systems built from straws, believing that the liquids are pumped into him. When he masturbates, he moves his penis as if it were the handle of a machine and calls it "cranking up the penis" (304).

What does it take to create a robot boy? Not surprisingly, we learn that at his birth Joey's mother thinks of him as a thing rather than as a person. She refuses to nurse him, not so much out of dislike as out of indifference. During the early months Joey's mother never cuddles him, or plays with him, or even touches him except when necessary. The mother impresses members of Bettelheim's staff as being deeply insecure and as incapable of regarding Joey as a person in his own right. Joey simply never succeeds in penetrating the wall of indifference set up by the mother. After his mother leaves Joey at Bettelheim's school, psychotherapy helps her to understand some of her own emotions: how trapped she feels by the marriage, how rigid she is about maintaining control of her emotions, and how anxious she feels about the possibility of coming "unglued and becoming a mental patient." Bettelheim infers that "Joey must have felt that his emotional demands on his mother were a burden to her, of which he should free her by not asking for affection any more" (260).

Joey exhibits marked detachment from people in general and his parents in particular. When it is time for his parents to depart after they bring him to the school, he gives no sign of feeling. He never (until he improves) refers to anyone by name; instead he refers to them by such phrases as "that person" or "the small person." In a way that is typical of autistic children, he avoids using personal pronouns, especially the word "I." They are too dangerous. For two years he refuses to do any reading unless he may skip the word "father" when it appears on the page. Later, when he develops enough to be able to use personal pronouns, he uncovers his anger: "If my parents were here, I would kill them; it's not the School that's bad; it's my parents' fault. If they were here and I had a fan, I'd put their fingers in it while it's whirling, and I'd cut them to pieces" (258). He is angry at his mother, he says, "because she didn't punish me for my angry feelings I had about her. I had to punish myself" (259). Years more have to pass before Joey can uncover the yearning for emotional contact that lurks beneath the anger. Searles mentions that in his experience with chronic schizophrenics the transference suggests that underlying the hatred and rejection the analyst encounters in his parental role there are always powerful feelings of genuine love: "The schizophrenic illness now becomes basically revealed as representing the child's loving sacrifice of his very individuality for the welfare of the mother who is loved genuinely, altruistically, and with the wholehearted adoration which, in the usual circumstances of human living, only a small child can bestow" (1958, 220). Considered in this context, it would seem that in becoming a machine, Joey only became the "thing" his mother beheld— and perhaps needed him to be.

When Joey draws a portrait of himself, the figure he sketches possesses a head with a jack-o-lantern face and a body formed of nothing except electrical wires. At this stage of his development he expresses anger by way of fantasies concerning tubes about to explode ("That light bulb is going to have a temper tantrum"), and he registers emotional depletion as "not enough power . . . coming in" (Bettelheim 1967, 253, 252). Much later Joey becomes able to risk the passive acceptance of love in the form of allowing his counselors to hold and carry and cuddle him. Much later still, Joey eventually risks actively asserting his own positive feelings toward Lou, his most-favored adult at the time. Initially he does this by putting blankets over himself and Lou, the blankets serving as a safety net to prevent Lou's escape when Joey touches him. "After innumerable experiments at binding the loved person fast," Joey is still so overexcited at the prospect that he has to blow off steam by having what he calls a "rumpus." After he is finally able to touch Lou, "he rushed to the farthest corner of the room shouting wildly, only to approach and reapproach, touching and retouching again. Reaching out for touch on his own was that unbearably exciting" (329).

> Then came many months of a far greater daring when his behavior had less the character of a tantrum and more of a conscious seeking of body closeness. He would put an arm around Lou's shoulder, or sit in his lap for a moment—after which he would rush away. But now the adult was no longer supposed to stay put as when Joey had tied him down. Now he had to rush after Joey and catch him, so that Joey could know that his touch had been welcome. (329)

Once he gets connected to people, Joey no longer needs to remain attached to machines.

Before he achieves this level of development, he must experience a rebirth—and before that, momentous developments take place in the form of evolving self-representations. One of these is Kenrad the Terrible, a destructive alter ego based almost entirely on Joey's projective identification with another boy at the school named Ken. Joey enacts in pantomime the process of pumping or drilling Kenrad's feces out of him so that he will not get constipated. "It was still beyond Joey's comprehension that anyone could possibly move his bowels 'on his own steam.' Only machinery could do that" (300). Another self-representation is Mitchell the Good, similarly based on Joey's projective identification with a boy named Mitchell, healthier than Ken. In this instance, however, Joey recognizes Mitchell as a real person and is able to call him by his name. The theme of rebirth begins when Joey plays at being a "papoose" wrapped up in a blanket. This papoose evolves into an electrical papoose. Then Joey commences a game called "Connecticut papoose," a game in which he is no longer a collection of wires in a glass tube "but a person, though still encased and protected by glass, connected and cut off at the same time (Connect-I-cut)" (304). A great advance in Joey's development occurs when he acquires an imaginary companion named "Valvus," who is a boy "just like me." Valvus is neither all good nor all bad, neither completely helpless nor all-powerful. But like a valve, he can turn himself on or off: "Through Valvus he achieved autonomy, that is, personal contact of his own elimination [processes]" (314). For a period of time Joey enjoys being fed like a baby, using a nursing bottle, with warmed milk, which he takes while lying comfortably in bed. During this period Joey shows a great deal of interest in chickens and eggs. Suddenly one day, after cackling like a hen and flapping his arms like wings he crawls under a table draped with blankets. "There, by his own statement, he gave birth to an egg out of which he pecked his way newborn, into the world. 'I laid myself as an egg, hatched myself, and gave birth to me'" (325). At this point, remarks Bettelheim, "he was no longer a mechanical contrivance but a human child" (325).

Like the clinical texts examined in Chapter 3, the case histories concerning Gabrielle, Anna, Renee, and Joey can be seen to revolve around object-relational issues having little or nothing to do with sexual problems. The essential factor in these cases appears to be the children's need to form psychological bonds that constitute a suitable emotional environment, one that facilitates the natural development of functional selfhood. Winnicott's supportive analysis of Gabrielle's conflict beginning with the appearance of her sibling undoubtedly helps her to adapt to her situation and to overcome emotional deterrents to growth. Although Lichtenstein passes over the transference dimension of his treatment of Anna, her psychological gains suggest that the analytic process in some sense compensates for the severe emotional—as distinct from libidinal—deficits she experienced because of the many separations from her mother. The much greater severity of the emotional problems of Renee and Joey dramatizes how critical are the issues of physical and emotional (but fundamentally nonerotic) contact with parenting figures, and how devastating the guilt-laden rage toward inadequate parents can be.

III

THE IMAGINED SELF
AND OTHER

5.

THE STEPMOTHER WORLD OF *MOBY DICK*

In a chapter called "The Symphony," Ahab muses about the natural beauty of the scene before him: "The pensive air was tranparently pure and soft, with a woman's look, and the robust and man-like sea heaved with long, strong, lingering swells, as Samson's chest in his sleep." A little later we are told, "That glad, happy air, that winsome sky, did at last stroke and caress him; the step-mother world, so long cruel—forbidding —now threw affectionate arms round his stubborn neck, and did seem to joyously sob over him, as if over one, that however wilful and erring, she could yet find it in her heart to save and to bless" (Melville, 1851). The way Melville plays here with the stepmother stereotype echoes a textually remote and seemingly minor reference to Ishmael's memory of a child-hood dream (in "The Counterpane" chapter) that follows an episode when his stepmother, "who somehow or other, was all the time whipping me, or sending me to bed supperless," packs him off to bed at two o'clock on a summer's afternoon. After an agony of restlessness, young Ishmael sleeps, then wakes in terror in a room "now wrapped in outer darkness." He sees nothing, hears nothing, but senses that "a supernatural hand seemed placed in mine," the hand of a "nameless, unimaginable, silent form or phantom" that grasps the hand of his arm hanging over the counterpane. Whose hand it is—his stepmother's, perhaps, or his moth-er's—remains "a mystery." In any case, Ishmael's sensation upon waking up with Queequeg's arm thrown over him "in the most loving and affectionate manner," such that "you had almost thought I had been his wife," reminds him of the uncanny experience of the supernatural hand—

except for the absence of terror—the associative linkage to the childhood event being the resemblance between the patchwork of the quilt and the tattoos on Queequeg's skin.

What Melville refers to as Ahab's "step-mother world" can easily be regarded as relating not only to the immediate physical environment that for the moment manifests balmy air and heaving sea, and to the macro-cosmic universe inscribed in the microcosm of the novel, but perhaps even more directly to the inner world of unconscious fantasy peopled, as Joan Riviere points out in her discussion of Kleinian object relations theory, by "a world of figures formed on the pattern of persons we first loved and hated in life, who also represent aspects of ourselves" (1955, 346). Whatever the correspondence between real persons in his life and the representational figures in the imaginary worlds of his novels, Melville —who had no stepmother—displays in *Moby Dick* an array of relation-ships that resonate with meaning in the context of object relations.

Even as this theoretical vantage point may affect one's reading of literature, so also may literature have implications for the development of psychoanalytic theory—just as works by Sophocles and Shakespeare so notably had for Freud in his formulation of the oedipus complex. Exactly because of the as-if nature of literature, that is, because it is in a special sense not-real—in almost the same way psychoanalytic treatment is as-if and not-real and transferential—literary texts provide a privileged realm of observation comparatively insulated from outer reality by virtue of their fictive, fantastic, imaginary nature. The figures of the worlds of clinic and culture remain forever separate yet forever parallel, as Shakespeare in effect implies when he writes about the similarities of the "shaping fanta-sies" of the "seething brains" of lovers, madmen, and poets in the famous discourse on imagination by Theseus in *A Midsummer Night's Dream.*

Since the experience of relation to an object necessitates the presence, or virtual existence, of an experiencing self, one question to be asked is whether *Moby Dick* delves into the nature of psychological being. There are several passages in the text that appear to address the psychological dimensions of existential problems. Clearly psychological is the quest of Bulkington, whose fearless "deep, earnest thinking" and search after "mortally intolerable truth" Ishmael regards as being "the intrepid effort of the soul to keep the open independence of her sea." Another such passage occurs when, meditating on "the universal cannibalism of the sea," where all creatures prey upon each other in contrast to "the verdant land" of "this green, gentle, and most docile earth," Ishmael declares, "In the soul of man there lies one insular Tahiti, full of peace and joy, but encompassed by all the horrors of the half known life." "Push not off from that isle, thou canst never return," says Ishmael, who does push off, and does return—though when he returns he cannot be quite the same person he was when he left New Bedford. The precariousness of the soul of man engulfed in a cannibal sea, in a novel that has cannibalism as one of its important leitmotifs ("cannibal old me," thinks Ahab of himself), in some sense corresponds to the precariousness of the infantile soul in an intrapsychic world that is charged with fantasies of oral-sadistic, cannibalistic behavior, according to Melanie Klein (1932, 188). Be that as it may, there can be no doubt that Melville portrays the peril of something like psychological fusion, a kind of "oceanic feeling" (as Freud called it) of total dedifferentiation of self and other, or self and world, when he speaks in a comic vein of the risk to a dreamy "sunken-eyed young Platonist" like Ishmael—who has "the problem of the universe revolving" in his mind —of losing his perch on the masthead: "At last he loses his identity; takes the mystic ocean at his feet for the visible image of that deep, blue, bottomless soul, pervading mankind and nature" and plunges into the "Descartian vortices" of what sounds suspiciously like an oceanic version of the Oversoul of American transcendentalism.

Like Bulkington's search for "mortally intolerable truth," Ishmael's "itch for things remote" and his reaching after "the image of the ungraspable phantom of life" amount to exploratory behavior of the same high order as that of the questing adventurer Campbell describes in *The Hero with a Thousand Faces:* "A hero ventures forth from the world of common day into a region of supernatural wonder: fabulous forces are there encountered and a decisive victory is won: the hero comes back from this mysterious adventure with the power to bestow boons on his fellow man" (1949, 30). This exploration, says Melville in the "Cetology" chapter, "is a fearful thing," a groping "down into the bottom of the sea after them [whales]" that is tantamount to having "one's hands among the unspeakable foundations, ribs, and very pelvis of the world." Melville's almost obstetrical phrasing appears to correlate in part with that of Norman O. Brown's Kleinian reading of the hero's task of exploration: "To explore is to penetrate; the world is the insides of mother. . . . Geography is the geography of the mother's body" (1966, 36). Brown also thinks about the hero's progress along genital lines: "The wandering heroes are phallic heroes, in a permanent state of erection, pricking o'er the plain" (50).

Such views of the psychology of questing activity can be placed beside the more person-oriented ideas of Mahler (1975), who sees children's motility in terms of the tasks of separation and individuation, and Bowlby's view of how exploratory behavior complements attachment behavior: "It transforms the novel into the familiar and by this process turns an activating stimulus into a terminating one" (1969, 239). To register Bowlby's point in a broader context, exploration complements attachment by transforming the novel but potentially dangerous environment into a familiar and hence psychologically secure one. Lichtenberg treats the impulse of infants to explore their environment, asserting themselves in regard to it, as a more or less independent motivational system. He says recent experiments indicate that "infants at four months are motivated to explore stimuli that have no direct immediate connection with caregivers and to act assertively [in order] to be the cause of an effect on the nonhuman environment. When they experience themselves as being the initiators of a predictable effect, this experience triggers an affect of pleasure" (1989, 129). But as Lichtenberg recognizes, exploratory-assertive behavior can apply to, and be facilitated by, relations with caregivers. The question asked by Alfred Kazin, "Why does Ishmael feel so alone?" (1956, vii), can be responded to by emphasizing that he does not remain alone. What enables Ishmael's somewhat blind venture into the unknown to become richly meaningful is the *presence* of certain facilitating figures, notably Queequeg, so that the hero's journey can be conceptualized, in part, as the self's assimilation of benign properties and dispositions in some psychological others, and his disengagement from the impediment of destructive impulses represented by other psychological others, notably Ahab.

In a sense, then, Ishmael's voyage outward from New Bedford depicts a voyage inward that maps an evolving psyche. One of the more remarkable expressions of Ishmael's developing selfhood occurs when he and his shipmates witness "Leviathan amours in the deep," as well as the scene of the birth of a baby whale. The spectacle of the Grand Armada of whales fearlessly indulging "in all peaceful concernments," and reveling "in dalliance and delight" even in the midst of being attacked by man, causes Ishmael to remark, "But even so, amid the tornadoed Atlantic of my being, do I myself still for ever centrally disport in mute calm; and while ponderous planets of unwaning woe revolve round me, deep down and deep inland there I still bathe me in eternal mildness of joy." This astonishing assertion of a sense of profound spiritual and psychological stability intimates the existence of something like what Stern refers to, in a rather reifying way, as the "core self" (1985, 11). In contrast, Ishmael refers to this centrality not as a structure but as a state of being represented as a soothing, joyful, self-generated, caretaking process. In any case, Ishmael's bold claim both resembles and contrasts with Ahab's hubristic declaration of psychic invulnerability after having his ivory leg snapped off: "But even with a broken bone, [the soul of] old Ahab is untouched; and I account no living bone of mine one jot more me, than this dead one that's lost. Nor white whale, nor man, nor fiend, can so much as graze old Ahab in his own proper and inaccessible being." In contrast to "his body's part," he says, "Ahab's soul's a centipede that moves upon a hundred legs." Wonderful as Melville's visions may be, the psychological reality probably is that no self, so long as it remains in existence, can ever be totally invulnerable to threatening influences. Such is the implication of Stern's conception of "the sense of self at any moment" as a "network of . . . many forming and dissolving dynamic processes," always in flux (199), which is to say, in terms of the systemic model sketched in Chapter 2, a more or less steady state, or comparatively stable-but-dynamic equilibrium of states, yet one always with the potential for catastrophic change such as we see exhibited by Pip after his "abandonment."

A special complication of the representation of self in literature, one by no means peculiar to *Moby Dick,* appears whenever an author unconsciously portrays a protagonist's self in multiple form, especially when the characters in question seem to be separate and autonomous figures at the narrative level (Rogers 1970). Several critics have commented on the presence of this phenomenon in *Moby Dick.* Newton Arvin hints that Ahab is something less than a whole person when he remarks, "He has ceased to be anything but an Ego; a noble Ego, to be sure; a heroic one; but *that* rather than a Self" (1950, 177). Richard Chase mentions that in Melville's works "Ahab is the one fully objectified character who is both father and son" (1949, 49). Leslie Fiedler contends that "Ishmael is, then, but one part of the split epic hero . . . whose other part is Ahab" (1962, 547). They are secret sharers, psychologically speaking, yet unlike Conrad's presentation of this motif in "The Secret Sharer," Melville provides readers with only furtive hints of what the sailor and his captain have in common. One such hint surfaces when Ishmael contemplates his identification with Ahab's vengeful quest after Ahab orchestrates the ritual vow of drinking to the death of Moby Dick from the "chalice" end of the harpoons: "A wild, mystical, sympathetical feeling was in me; Ahab's quenchless feud seemed mine." When Ishmael declares much earlier, "No more my splintered heart and maddened hand were turned against the wolfish world," he does not mention at whom he was angry. The later passage tells us that he shares Moby Dick with Ahab as an object of hostility.

The topic of being angry leads naturally into a discussion of the portrayal of other in the novel. Ahab is angry at Moby Dick—but who or what does Moby Dick represent? Arvin suggests that, psychologically, "Moby Dick is thus the archetypal Parent; the father, yes, but the mother also" (1950, 173–74). This interpretation depends to a considerable extent on two features of Melville's life that Arvin emphasizes earlier in his biography: the loss of his father at the onset of puberty and his claim, in old age, that his mother had hated him.

Assuming, for heuristic purposes, the validity of Arvin's inference that Moby Dick combines psychological representations of both parents makes room for brief consideration of two passages in the novel that help to delineate certain object-relational features of Moby Dick. One is that he has no features. As Ahab puts it in his jocular comments on the physiognomy of whales, and their habit of showing only their backsides (tails), "If I know not even the tail of this whale, how understand his head? much more, how comprehend his face, when face he has none? Thou shalt see my back parts, my tail, he seems to say, but my face shall not be seen." Melville appears to have in mind what God says to Moses: "I will take away my hand, and thou shalt see my back parts; but my face shall not be seen" (Exodus 33:23). Hence Ahab hates inscrutability:

> All visible objects, man, are but as pasteboard masks. But in each event—in the living act, the undoubted deed—there, some unknown but still reasoning thing puts forth the mouldings of its features from behind the unreasoning mask. If man will strike, strike through the mask! How can the prisoner reach outside except by thrusting through the wall? To me, the white whale is that wall, shoved near to me. Sometimes I think there's naught beyond. But 'tis enough. He tasks me; he heaps me; I see in him outrageous strength, with an inscrutable malice sinewing it. That inscrutable thing is chiefly what I hate. (1851, 139)

In contrast to God's remark to Moses, that his face shall not be seen, good-enough mothers, according to Winnicott, instinctively utilize their own faces as a psychological mirror to reflect back to their infants some sense of what is going on in themselves (1971, 111–12), the point being that Ahab's reverie ("I say again he has no face") implies a significant degree of withholding behavior on the part of the combined parental other. Melville's marked attention elsewhere to the mammalian nature of whales appears to run counter to such withholdingness. Ishmael watches mother whales nursing their infants, and Starbuck sees "long coils of the umbilical cord of Madame Leviathan, by which the young cub seemed still tethered to its dam." Yet the whiteness of Moby Dick (and sometimes that of the sea) becomes associated with milk, frequently in negative, threatening contexts (the "milky sea"; "milk-white fog"). The text may be thought of as responding to this threat of aggression by turning with violence against the maternal other, in a passage positively Kleinian in tenor, when we are told that "when by chance these precious parts [the teats] in a nursing whale are cut by the hunter's lance, the mother's pouring milk and blood rivallingly discolor the sea for rods."

As far as Ahab is concerned, Moby Dick is a persecutory other, threatening annihilation. From a Kleinian point of view, it is the bad breast ("the persecutory breast") that becomes "the prototype of all external and internal persecutory objects" (1952a, 202, 200). In *Moby Dick* psychological threats and attacks against the self take various forms: the "demasting" of Ahab's leg, usually read by Freudians as symbolic castration; the form of oral engulfment ("I saw the opening maw of hell," says Jonah in Father Mapple's hymn); and the form of the perilous enticements of the womb-like head from which Queequeg "delivers" Tashtego: "Had Tashtego perished in that head, it had been a very precious perishing; smothered in the very whitest and daintiest of fragrant spermaceti; coffined, hearsed, and tombed in the secret inner chamber and sanctum sanctorum of the whale." More generally, the sea itself constitutes a threatening environment: "However *baby man* may brag of his science and skill . . . yet for ever and for ever, to the crack of doom, the sea will insult and murder him" (italics added). But unlike Ahab's, Ishmael's collective experience of his stepmother world remains an ambiguous one. His stepmother is not all bad. "She was the best and most conscientious of stepmothers," he tells us, not without some measure of irony. And Ishmael, in keeping with his symbolic name ("God shall hear," Genesis 16:11), survives, just as Jonah survives when, as Father Mapple informs us, "God heard" his plea. An attentive, responsive parental aurality thus seems to mitigate the imagined dangers of a potentially engulfing orality.

* * *

The psychological entities so glibly referred to in object relations theory as *self* and *other* cannot truly be considered apart from each other except for analytical purposes, so that in the strictest sense what are always being dealt with are conditions of intersubjectivity. One kind of intersubjectivity manifested in *Moby Dick* takes the form of oedipal rebellion against authority. Ahab's quarrel with a whale superstitiously rumored by sailors to be not only ubiquitous but also immortal appears to be a version of Melville's never-ending quarrel with God (Thompson 1952). The form of religious worship Ahab preaches and practices is that of defiance. As he addresses the "trinity of flames" of the static electricity illuminating the ship's masts and rigging during a storm, he worships the spirit of fire: "I now know thee, thou clear spirit, and I now know that thy right worship is defiance." As a rebellious, hubristic tragic hero, he will strike through the mask of all existence: "Talk not to me of blasphemy, man; I'd strike the sun if it insulted me." The defiant secret motto of the novel, as Olson reminds us (1947, 53), appears in the scene where Ahab "baptizes" in the name of the devil the harpoon that will eventually strike Moby Dick: "Ego non baptizo te in nomine patris, sed in nomine diaboli!" If religious rebellion symbolizes psychological rebellion of son against father, the appropriate talion punishment for this oedipal crime is castration, symbolized in the story by Ahab's loss of his leg in his first encounter with Moby Dick (Arvin 1950, 172).

At another level in the story, Ahab himself represents the figure of authority against whom others make their oedipal rebellion, as in the contest of "knights" and "squires" like Starbuck and Stubb with that "grand, ungodly, god-like man, Captain Ahab." His lesser soul overmatched by a madman, Starbuck must capitulate to Ahab's commands:"I plainly see my miserable office—to obey, rebelling." Melville dramatizes a comic version of the rebellion theme when Ahab verbally drives Stubb below for daring to hint that he might have the decency to muffle the stomping sound of his midnight pacing with a piece of tow on the ivory leg. Stubb feels mistreated: "He might as well have kicked me, and done with it," a thought leading to the wondrous fantasy of the Queen Mab chapter in which Stubb relates to Flask the crazy dream he had the night before about being kicked by Ahab: ". . . and when I tried to kick back, upon my soul, my little man, I kicked my leg right off! And then, presto! Ahab seemed a pyramid, and I, like a blazing fool, kept kicking at it." Later in the dream "a sort of badger-haired old merman, with a hump on his back" bends over and invites Stubb to kick his rear. To Stubb's dismay, "his stern was stuck full of marlinspikes, with the points out."

In addition to this oedipal grotesquerie, with its suggestion of the futility of a son attacking the armed and impenetrable phallicity of an invincible paternal figure, Melville weaves dozens of other allusions to rebellion into the fabric of his novel, one of them taking the form of the embedded narrative about the quarrel between Radney, the overbearing mate from Martha's Vineyard, and Steelkilt, the "desperado from Buffalo." They have an argument that leads Steelkilt to threaten to murder his captain if he dares to flog him as punishment for fighting with the mate. Later Steelkilt's rebellion against tyranny takes the form of desertion from the ship—as does that of Tommo, the protagonist of *Typee*. In real life, Melville himself deserts from the *Acushnet* in the South Seas.

Because the oedipal aspects of *Moby Dick* have been well attended to by various critics, I pass over much else that might be said along these lines in order to concentrate on preoedipal features of intersubjectivity in the novel, especially issues that need to be considered by a theory of object relations incorporating concepts from attachment theory.

In attachment theory the themes of separation and loss become the essential locus of all anxiety, in contrast to the classic Freudian loci of seduction, incest, castration, and libidinal repression. Given this perspective, the episode of Pip's abandonment takes on as much psychological significance as does the loss of Ahab's leg, especially if Pip be thought of as another double, or aspect, of the venturing hero. Melville meditates in connection with Pip's temporary abandonment about "the awful lonesomeness" of swimming in the open ocean: "The intense concentration of self in the middle of such a heartless immensity, my God! who can tell it?" From the hour of his rescue, adds Melville, "the little negro went about the deck an idiot; such, at least, they said he was. The sea had jeeringly kept his finite body up, but drowned the infinite of his soul." Ahab later attributes this abandonment not to Chance or Fate but to the "frozen heavens." He rails at them: "Ye did beget this luckless child, and have abandoned him." As for the nature of the effect of abandonment on Pip, the psychological realism of it seems perfectly comprehensible in the context of Winnicott's hypothesis about the effect of traumatic separation in childhood: "If the mother is away more than x minutes, then the image fades. . . . The baby is distressed, but this distress is soon *mended* because the mother returns in x plus y minutes. . . . But in x plus y plus z minutes

the baby has become *traumatized*" (1971, 97). In this case the eventual
return of the mother does not repair the alteration resulting from her
absence, "so that primitive defenses now become organized to defend
against a repetition of 'unthinkable anxiety.' " Madness, continues Winnicott, "simply means a break-up of whatever may exist at the time of a
personal continuity of existence."

Abandonment and a cluster of related themes are by no means confined
to the story of Pip. In asking, "Why does Ishmael feel so alone?" Kazin
stresses his isolation and homelessness: "As his name indicates [the Bibli-
cal Ishmael and his mother, Hagar, are outcasts], he is an estranged and
solitary man. . . . Ishmael is not merely an orphan; he is an exile, searching
alone in the wilderness" (Kazin 1956, vii-viii). Kazin sees Ishmael's
"homelessness" as a function of spiritual disbelief, regarding him as "modern man, cut off from the certainty that was once his inner world. Ishmael
no longer has any sure formal belief. All is in doubt, all is in eternal flux,
like the sea" (viii). Arvin, taking a psychobiographical approach, reminds
us that Melville must have felt abandoned by his father, who quickly
slipped from prosperity to financial ruin to insanity and then into death
when Melville was twelve years old, a critical time, presumably, because
of the reawakening of oedipal conflict at the onset of puberty:

> His death was the direst and most decisive event emotionally of Herman
> Melville's early life. Deprived of an idolized father on the very verge of
> adolescence, the boy Melville underwent—can there be any doubt?—an
> emotional crisis from whose effects he was never to be wholly free. In the
> midst of a general insecurity, the most vital embodiment of security, the
> security of fatherhood, was forcibly wrested from him and the frightening
> sense of abandonment, the reproachful sense of desertion, must equally
> have been intense and overwhelming. . . . He was to spend much of his life
> divided between the attempt to retaliate upon his father for this abandon-
> ment and the attempt, a still more passionate one, to recover the closeness
> and the confidence of a happy sonhood. (1950, 23)

A kind of reversal of this situation occurs in the episode concerning the
whaler *Rachel*. The captain of the *Rachel* has lost his own son overboard
while chasing Moby Dick. When he pleads with Ahab for assistance in
the search, Ahab refuses because of his obsession to hunt for the whale
instead. Ironically, the *Rachel* rescues Ishmael in the end: "It was the
devious-cruising *Rachel*, that in her retracing search after her missing
children, only found another orphan."

The innumerable references in the novel to such themes as separation, abandonment, and homelessness may be thought of as constituting an emotional backdrop foregrounded by important relationships. As I pointed out earlier, Ishmael does not remain alone, nor does Pip, because of the crucial bonds they form with Queequeg and Ahab, respectively.

Fiedler and Arvin approach interrelatedness in the novel by treating the relationship of Ishmael and Queequeg in terms of sexuality. Fiedler, who suggests that *Moby Dick* "must be read not only as an account of a whale-hunt, but also as a love story," a story of "the redemptive love of man and man," reads it as depicting "the peculiar American form of innocent homosexuality" (1962; next several references, 531–39). Finding a parallel in Ahab's furtive attachment to Fedallah, Fiedler claims that "the dream of a dark-skinned beloved implies a sense of breaching a taboo, reaching out toward a banned erotic object" as distinct from what some might suppose to be the dream of a humanistic transcending of a social taboo. After quoting the passage "I found Queequeg's arm thrown over me in the most loving and affectionate manner. You had almost thought I had been his wife," Fiedler remarks, "It is worth noting that Ishmael tends to think of himself in the passive, the feminine role." Fiedler associates "the boy's special sin of masturbation" with the hand of "splintered heart and maddened hand," and the hand young Ishmael dares not drag away from the supernatural apparition of his nightmare. Concerning the passage where Ishmael says that Queequeg "pressed his forehead against mine, clasped me around the waist, and said that henceforth we were married," Fiedler discounts Ishmael's quick disclaimer: ". . . meaning, in his country's phrase, that we were bosom friends." Fiedler insists, "This is Platonism without sodomy, which is to say, marriage without copulation: the vain dream of genteel ladies improbably fulfilled in a sailor's rooming-house by two men." Arvin, among others, reads the relationship of Ishmael and Queequeg not only as erotic but also as definitely pathological, specifically as reflecting the same impairment of "capacity for heterosexual love" as Ahab's symbolic castration (1950, 174).

For whatever reason, these otherwise perceptive readers of Melville elect to take rather literally what both immediate and more remote contexts might encourage others to take figuratively. Fiedler and Arvin also read selectively, ignoring such passages as these: the one in which Ishmael comments on his own awareness of "the unbecomingness of his [Queequeg's] hugging a fellow male in that matrimonial style"; the passage immediately following Queequeg's declaration that they were married:

"In a countryman, this sudden flame of friendship would have seemed far too premature, a thing to be much distrusted; but in this simple savage those old rules would not apply"; and this one: "His story being ended with his pipe's last dying puff, Queequeg embraced me, pressed his forehead against mine, and blowing out the light, *we rolled over from each other, this way and that, and very soon were sleeping*" (italics added). One may argue that such passages serve to punctuate Melville's sexual and matrimonial metaphors, semantically marking them in such a way as to heighten (but not confuse) readers' awareness of the measure of their deviance from social norms. One might even go so far as to argue that Melville instinctively and unconsciously mobilizes some measure of reader anxiety about crossing racial and sexual boundary lines the better to call readers' attention to what he has to say about the importance of human attachments in general.

Melville emphasizes this importance throughout the novel by generating numerous images of attachment, especially images of hands grasping and ropes connecting, thereby valorizing the relationship of Ishmael and Queequeg (and Pip and Ahab) in the process. In addition to the umbilical coil of Madame Leviathan, positive images of attachment are notable in the following instances. In one chapter Melville tells us of the "monkey-rope" that connects Ishmael (aboard ship) to Queequeg (on the whale's carcass): "So that for better or worse, we two, for the time, were wedded. . . . An elongated Siamese ligature united us. Queequeg was my own inseparable twin brother; nor could I any way get rid of the dangerous liabilities which the hempen bond entailed." In the emotionally tonic chapter called "A Squeeze of the Hand," where sailors process chunks of fat in tubs of previously boiled whale blubber by squeezing them, Ishmael says that "I squeezed that sperm till a strange sort of insanity came over me; and I found myself unwittingly squeezing my co-laborers' hands in it, mistaking their hands for the gentle globules." "Such an abounding, affectionate, friendly loving feeling did this avocation beget" that Ishmael is moved to declare, "Oh! my dear fellow beings, why should we longer cherish any social acerbities, or know the slightest ill-humor or envy! Come: let us squeeze hands all round; nay, let us all squeeze ourselves into each other; let us squeeze ourselves universally into the very milk and sperm of kindness."

The images of grasping hands and connecting ropes merge in the memorable dialogue between Pip and Ahab. Pip cries, "Ding, dong, ding? Who's seen Pip the coward?" As Ahab responds, "Oh, ye frozen heavens! look down here. Ye did beget this luckless child, and have abandoned him," he offers his hand to lead Pip to his cabin. "Here, boy," he says, "Ahab's cabin shall be Pip's home henceforth, while Ahab lives. Thou touchest my inmost centre, boy; thou art tied to me by cords woven of my heart-strings." And Pip responds, "What's this? here's velvet shark-skin" as he gazes at Ahab's hand. "Ah, now, had poor Pip but felt so kind a thing as this, perhaps he had ne'er been lost! This seems to me, sir, as a man-rope; something that weak souls may hold by. Oh, sir, let old Perth now come and rivet these two hands together; the black one with the white, for I will not let this go." Elsewhere another passage implies that a good grasp has as much meaning for Ahab as for Pip. As the carpenter fashions a new ivory leg for Ahab, the captain remarks, "This is a cogent vice thou hast here, carpenter; let me feel its grip once. So, so; it does pinch some." When the carpenter replies that the vice can break bones as well as hold them, Ahab answers, "No fear; I like a good grip; I like to feel something in this slippery world that can hold."

Images of interpersonal connection such as "cords woven of my heart-strings" and the monkey-rope are not merely decorative metaphors. They have much the same kind of integral significance in the novel that the image of string does in a case described by Winnicott of a very disturbed seven-year-old who attempts to deal with his fear of separation, and to deny it, by using string and related images. The boy's depressed mother cares for him until the birth of a sister when he is three years and three months old: "This was the first separation of importance, the next being at three years eleven months, when the mother had an operation. When the boy was four years nine months the mother went into a mental hospital for two months" (1971, 16). By this time the boy has begun to manifest a lot of anger and regression. When Winnicott engages him in a "squiggle game" (mutual drawing on paper that has diagnostic implica-tions), he realizes that among ten of the drawings there are images of a lasso, a whip, a crop, a yo-yo string, a string in a knot, another crop, and another whip. When Winnicott points out this thematic redundancy to the parents, they mention having noticed that their son has been obsessed with anything and everything having to do with string, and having been worried when he had recently tied a string around his little sister's neck! At Winnicott's suggestion, the mother brings up the theme of string with her son. She finds him to be "eager to talk about his relation to her and his fear of lack of contact with her," and from the time of this conversation, at least for a long while, the boy's play with string ceases and his behavior improves.

Not all the images of cordage and other connectives in *Moby Dick* have positive connotations. Images of perilous and trammeling lines accentuate, by contrast, the possibility of negative or pathological attachments. "All men live enveloped in whale-lines," we are reminded in a passage foreshadowing Pip's momentary entanglement in a whale line—from which Tashtego's knife frees him. "All are born with halters round their necks; but it is only when caught in the swift, sudden turn of death, that mortals realize the silent, subtle, everpresent perils of life." Both Fedallah and Ahab die with whale-line halters round their necks. "Hemp only can kill me!" laughs Ahab in his fury, citing prophetic words in much the same manner as Macbeth repeats the witches' claim he need fear "none of woman born"—and hemp it is that does kill Ahab in the end when he stoops to clear fouled line connected to the harpoon now fast in the flesh of Moby Dick: "The flying turn caught him round the neck, and voicelessly as Turkish mutes bowstring their victim, he was shot out of the boat ere the crew knew he was gone." The death-dealing rope, symbolic of Ahab's monomaniacal obsession with his pathological connection to the object of his hatred, forms a contrast to his comparative absence of positive ties, his distance from important others, and his symbolic isolation. A career of forty years at sea has separated him from home: "When I think of this life I have led; the desolation of solitude it has been; the masoned, walled-town of a Captain's exclusiveness. . . . what a forty years' fool—fool—old fool, has old Ahab been!" And he wonders what has so driven him "against all natural lovings and longings."

At the beginning of the epilogue to *Moby Dick* Melville places this passage from the Book of Job (1:16): "And I only am escaped alone to tell thee." In doing so he once again appears to emphasize the isolated condition of the sole survivor of the *Pequod*, his separation from the others. But Ishmael is no longer strictly alone. The life-sustaining support he finds in Queequeg's buoyant coffin may be taken as representing the support of a now-internalized "good object." Formerly he was attached to Queequeg, the internal bond being represented by such images as the monkey-rope. By the conclusion of the novel the psychological buoyancy of this relationship has been internalized. That internalization may be said to recapitulate an experience mentioned earlier. At the Spouter Inn Queequeg becomes "a bosom friend" whom Ishmael thinks of as a paternal figure: "George Washington, cannibalistically developed." And Ishmael describes the transformation that accompanies the process of attachment this way: "I felt a melting in me. No more my splintered heart and maddened hand were turned against the wolfish world." The "melting in me" mentioned by Ishmael corresponds exactly to what Bollas describes as the infant's experience of "the transformational object," a formulation by which Bollas seeks to emphasize that the intersubjective experience of mothers by infants is a process: *"The mother is less significant and identifiable as an object than as a process* that is identified with cumulative internal and external transformations" (1987, 14). In a sense, then, Ishmael's transformative experience of the effect of Queequeg on his life may be thought to reproduce the benign transformative experience of encounters in real life with inspiring figures such as Jack Chase, the Captain of the maintop of the warship *United States,* to whom Melville dedicated *Billy Budd,* experiences that repeat in turn his experience of his father as a loving person, and of his mother as something other than a demanding stepmother.

Like the mythic hero whose cyclical journey returns him to his home, Ishmael returns home not so much geographically as psychologically. As one critic observes in treating the recurrence of the word *strange* in the text of the novel in the context of Freud's commentary on the uncanny, Ahab is "the casting away castaway who experiences self and world as places of radical, uncanny homelessness," while Ishmael succeeds in domesticating the strangeness of his soul and its travails: "In *Moby Dick* selfhood is defined relationally in terms of homelessness, that is, in terms of jeopardy, of the specter of abandonment or annihilation—of non-relation" (Kimball, 1987, 544–46).

Although no tidy summation of the complex representations of object relations in the world of *Moby Dick* seems possible, a number of related implications may be thought to emerge from this reading. One is that our theory of human motivation may be liberated from the prisonhouse of libido theory without dispensing with sexuality altogether. Another is that, preposterous and unempirical as the suppositions of the Kleinian school of early object relations may seem, they do find some confirmation in the realities of adult fantasy as expressed by a representative literary text. Still another implication is the necessity of giving self parity with other in all formulations concerning human subjectivity. Perhaps not least among the implications of this reading has to do with the merit of an expansion of attachment theory in such a way as to pay greater attention to permutations in adult life of early forms of attachment behavior, and to make room for the meaningfulness of representations of attachment in fantasy—fantasies of authors in their stories and even the fantasies of fantasied characters, such as Ahab's passing, wistful, futile yearning for a stepmother who will throw "affectionate arms round his stubborn neck" and "find it in her heart to save and to bless."

6.

MEURSAULT'S ESTRANGEMENT

Camus' *The Stranger* begins with the right word, "Mother," in precisely the correct context, loss, with exactly the right tone, a mixture of uncertainty and emotional flatness: "Mother died today. Or, maybe, yesterday; I can't be sure. The telegram from the Home says: YOUR MOTHER PASSED AWAY. FUNERAL TOMORROW. DEEP SYMPATHY. Which leaves the matter doubtful; it could have been yesterday" (Camus 1942). From the perspective of attachment theory it would seem that the ontological anxiety attributable to Meursault in this novel might derive from this loss of his primary support figure—except that Meursault is a grown man, no longer dependent on his mother. Besides, they have had little emotional contact for a long time. "For years," he remarks, "she'd never had a word to say to me." When the Judge asks during the trial if the separation from his mother when he sent her to the Home for Aged Persons had caused him any distress, he responds, "Neither Mother nor I expected much of one another—or, for that matter of anyone else." With this statement Meursault gives evidence against himself concerning the heart of his problem, which is a problem of the heart. Meursault, the quintessential stranger, has little emotional contact with anyone at all. This novel, originally entitled *L'Indifférent,* tells us what it means to live without caring in an uncaring universe.

Granting this postulate by no means solves in any detail the many puzzles posed by *The Stranger*. While transparent in some ways, the novel remains opaque in many others. Why does Meursault kill the Arab, for instance? The initial narrative description of the event provides no direct answer to the question. In the courtroom Meursault declares he had no intention of killing the Arab. Pressed for his motives, Meursault responds this way: "I tried to explain that it was because of the sun, but I spoke too quickly and ran my words into each other. I was only too conscious that it sounded nonsensical, and, in fact, people were tittering." Is Meursault insane? The people in the courtroom respond as though he were. Should his action be looked upon, philosophically, as a highly contingent one performed by an existential hero in what is after all an absurd world? Or should the explanation, "because of the sun," be taken more literally in the context of the repeated narrative references to the blinding glare of the sun operating in conjunction with Meursault's headache and his woozy condition after the big meal and the wine and the ensuing commotion on the beach? In other words, should we take Meursault seriously, elsewhere in the novel, when he tries to justify his assumption that death wishes towards loved persons are more or less "normal" by explaining to his lawyer that "my physical condition at any given moment often influenced my feelings"? He refers, in this instance, to tiredness and other forms of physical discomfort he experiences on the day of his mother's funeral. Meursault sees his feelings as a function of his physiological state. Perhaps it would be more accurate to say that in crucial situations his sensations simply supplant emotions that ought to be there—but are not.

Another puzzle has to do with the connection between Meursault's feeling—or lack of feeling—concerning his mother's demise and his lack of feeling when he kills the Arab. As narrative events, they appear to be independent of each other. As textual events, there must necessarily be a meaningful relationship, as the parallel of the physiological malaise on each occasion implies, and as textual wholeness requires. One of the relatively transparent ironies of the novel is that both officials and members of the public insist on trying Meursault not so much for killing an Arab as for not showing grief at his mother's death. Camus doubles the irony by requiring his readers to intuit that, however wrong the public may be on legal grounds, there is some kind of a connection nevertheless.

Any attempt to understand this connection between Meursault's public and private crimes calls for a fairly deliberate examination of the implications of his interpersonal relationships, direct and indirect, past and present, with the personages of the novel, including his mother, his long-dead father, his boss, Marie, Céleste, Raymond, Salamano, Pérez, the examining magistrate, the priest, and even figures so peripheral as the young journalist and the "little robot woman." Such an exploration leads to the inference that what Meursault describes at the end of his story as "the benign indifference of the universe" may be seen as a world view originating in an object-relational matrix.

Consideration of two psychoanalytic interpretations of the novel provides a convenient route for beginning this exploration. The more recent one of Patrick McCarthy adopts a partly biographical orientation: "A simple psychoanalytic reading would lead one to conclude that Camus was torn between an incestuous love for his mother and a hostility towards her coldness" (1988, p. 2)). In McCarthy's Freudian perspective, love for one's mother must necessarily be sexual and oedipal, and he later emphasizes that it is an "incestuous bond" that unites mother and son in *The Stranger* (32). What is not so clear is whether McCarthy intends his readers to take the phrase "hostility towards her coldness" in a sexual sense as well, as an orthodox Freudian might. McCarthy begins the psychological portion of his interpretation by calling attention to biographical aspects of fictionalized passages in Camus' first volume of essays, *L'Envers et l'Endroit*. He says that one essay depicts the mother as emotionally cold: "She never caressed her son because she wouldn't know how to." McCarthy adds, "The denial of affection haunts the narrator who tells a disturbing anecdote about a mother cat eating her kitten. Conversely, the essay depicts an assault on the mother by an intruder, after which the narrator-son spends the night next to her on her bed" (1). Although McCarthy does not elaborate on this episode, which might be read in part simply as an effort of the boy to comfort his mother, what McCarthy implies by it is the boy's identification with the attacker and his lust. If one chooses to deemphasize the oedipal cast of McCarthy's overall interpretation, and if one politely ignores the inconsequential way he toys with stock sexual symbolism (the Arab's knife and the revolver as phallic instruments), one is left with this interpretation: "Hidden away in *The Stranger* lies a psychoanalytic novel where the mother, although dead, continues to strike at her son who strikes back" (41).

A psychologically more sophisticated reading of the novel, but one that makes no use of biography, was originally published in 1947 by an American psychoanalyst, Nathan Leites. This paper pays more attention to personality factors, especially the elements of guilt and defense. Instead of a mother who "continues to strike at her son who strikes back," Leites gives us an unconsciously angry hero who atones for his unconscious guilt concerning his mother's funeral by arranging for his own (263)! Reading the character of Meursault as though he were a real person, but not as an extension of Camus, Leites locates this unconscious anger and guilt not only in the time frame of the narrative present but more especially in the protagonist's early life. After noting the hero's remark that he had never set eyes on his father; that his mother did not speak to him for years; that they didn't expect much from each other; and that the protagonist mentions his sense of the futility of life after being forced to give up his studies, Leites makes this comment: "The child and the adolescent are thus shown as reacting with withdrawal of conscious affect in intrapersonal relations (that is, the relations between various components of the self) and in interpersonal relations. He is thus reacting to the guilty rage induced by the severe deprivations which were imposed by an absent father, an indifferent mother, and a withholding wider environment" (248). What is particularly interesting about the methodology of this relatively early piece of psychoanalytic literary criticism, and what marks its primary difference from McCarthy's sexually oriented interpretation, is that it construes the novel almost entirely in terms of a person-oriented as distinct from a drive-oriented theory of object relations, though a few minor traces of the jargon of libido theory do persist.

There are three aspects of the novel that Leites' paper accounts for particularly well. First, he makes it clear and plausible that Meursault's attack on the Arab represents a *displacement* of unconscious rage originally directed at his parents. Second, the attack represents an unconsciously self-punitive act because it invites reprisal by society. Third, Leites' elaboration of his analysis of Meursault's personality lays great emphasis on affectlessness as a defense. Specifically, according to Leites, "Affectlessness is here not only a defense against the various fantasied dangers of [emotional] involvement but also an instrument of aggression against (and contempt for) those persons who expect a fuller response from the hero" (254). Leites points to Meursault's detachment, to the way he generalizes his feelings (replying, "Yes, like everybody else" when asked if he loved his mother), to the way he avoids moral judgments of himself and others, and to the way Meursault's perception of emotion in others is blurred by his lack of empathy.

If one were to cast about for clinical analogues of Meursault's personality, two likely nominees would be the closely related types described as the "as-if" personality by Deutsch (1942) and as the "false-self" personality by Winnicott (1960).

Deutsch employs the label "as-if" to convey how the behavior of this type "forces on the observer the inescapable impression that the individual's whole relationship to life has something about it which is lacking in genuineness and yet outwardly runs along *as if* it were complete" and "normal" (302). Although interpersonal relations appear on the surface to be normal, the analyst discerns that such individuals are "devoid of any trace of warmth" (303). Deutsch makes a distinction between "the coldness of repressed individuals" and the falsified relations of the borderline schizophrenic, whom she sees not as guarding against forbidden impulses but as avoiding, in her terms, "a real loss of object cathexis" (304). In this type of person, according to Deutsch, aggressive tendencies are usually masked by passivity and mild amiability (305); at the same time she notes that the as-if personality is fundamentally devoid of any superego formation—to the point of being capable of serious misdeeds. To rephrase this formulation, one might say that no parental introjects of a moral kind have been internalized to constitute a control system. Thus Meursault, unable to feel remorse for his crime, wishes he had a chance to explain to the prosecutor, "in a quite friendly, almost affectionate way, that I have never been able really to regret anything in all my life." As for etiology, in the principal illustrative case Deutsch discusses, the analysand was cared for in childhood almost entirely by a series of comparative "strangers" and experienced neither tenderness nor punishment directly from her parents. "Throughout her whole childhood there was no one person who loved her and who could have served as a significant love object for her" (306). Of all the factors mentioned by Deutsch, there is one in particular that seems to be crucial to the makeup of the as-if personality, which is the tendency to be responsive to the wishes of others in a superficial way. Deutsch speaks of "a completely passive attitude to the environment with a highly plastic readiness to pick up signals from the outer world and to mold oneself and one's behavior accordingly" (304). These people are "suggestible" and exhibit "a passive readiness to be influenced" (305).

Meursault gets on well with people on the surface of everyday life. He gets on with his fellow workers, with his boss, with his neighbors. Many of his acquaintances, like Céleste, regard him as a friend. To Raymond's way of thinking, he is a "pal." Though laconic, Meursault is a pleasant, unargumentative, agreeable person. Yet it is precisely Meursault's *compliance* that betrays his fellowship with the as-if, false-self personality types. This compliance takes both trivial and extreme forms. When the keeper offers to unscrew the lid of the coffin, Meursault tells him "not to trouble" in an inappropriately accommodating way. Though technically in mourning, he goes along with Marie's desire to see a Fernandel film. Emmanuel suggests they run so as to catch a ride on the back of a truck, and Meursault obliges. Raymond asks him to concoct a letter to his Arab mistress for him (as a prelude to taking revenge), and Meursault goes along with this malicious plan. When Raymond asks "if I'd like us to be pals," Meursault replies that he has "no objection." Later, after he has written the letter, Raymond says, "So now we're pals, ain't we?" and Meursault tells us, "I didn't care one way or the other, but as he seemed so set on it, I nodded and said, 'Yes.' " Subsequently Meursault agrees to lie to the police on Raymond's behalf by saying that he knew the girl had been unfaithful to Raymond. A more extreme instance of compliance occurs when Meursault's boss asks him to take a new post in Paris: "I told him I was quite prepared to go; but really I didn't care much one way or the other," though we learn later that Meursault had lived in Paris and did not like it there. Hot, bored, and tired of being subjected to the examining magistrate's presumptions, Meursault tells us: "As I usually do when I want to get rid of someone whose conversation bores me, I pretended to agree." After the trial, when one of the lawyers says about Meursault's lawyer's performace, "Fine, wasn't it?" we are told, "I agreed, but insincerely." The instance of compliance most likely to arrest the reader's attention occurs when Marie asks Meursault if he will marry her. "I said I didn't mind; if she was keen on it, we'd get married." The peculiarity of his compliance gets underscored when Marie asks whether he would have responded in a similar way if another girl he liked had asked him to marry her. He assures her he would have.

Winnicott locates the origin of the inappropriate compliance of the False Self in the dynamics of early object relations. In essence, Winnicott characterizes the "good-enough" mother as responding (often enough) to spontaneous gestures, gestures Winnicott sees as deriving from the infant's illusion of omnipotence, in a way that gives birth to increments of a psychological True Self. In contrast, "the mother who is not good enough is not able to implement the infant's omnipotence, and so she repeatedly fails to meet the infant gesture; instead she substitutes her own gesture, which is to be given sense by the compliance of the infant. This compliance . . . is the earliest stage of the False Self" (1960, 145). Having been repeatedly "seduced" into a compliant mode of intersubjectivity, the false-self person becomes overly accepting of environmental cues and demands, and "builds up a false set of relationships" (146). It is interesting to note in regard to Winnicott's claim that "only the True Self can be creative" (148) that Meursault shows no signs of being a productive, creative person—unlike his creator, Camus.

There is no need to accept Winnicott's highly dichotomized schema of the True and False Self as a precise model of human development in order to appreciate the relevance of his idea for understanding a figure like Meursault. Neither is there any need to assume that Meursault, as an individual, corresponds exactly to the as-if or false-self personality types. No individual ever conforms exactly to type, at least not in real life, and certainly not in the case of a complex figure like Meursault. Meursault is nothing if not authentic in certain ways. For instance, he is authentic in the sense that the reader always experiences him as consistently himself— consistently functioning according to a hypothetical identity—and he is so honest a person in some respects that by the honesty of his responses to questions he contributes to his own prospective execution. In fact, Camus once referred to Meursault—years after the novel's publication— as "a man who refuses to lie" (Lottman 1979, 393).

Winnicott leads us into early object relations; this is where we must go if we are to understand the psychological correlatives of Meursault's ontological position in an absurd universe. Melanie Klein remarks that the schizoid patient "feels *estranged* and far away, and this feeling corresponds to the analyst's impression that considerable parts of the patient's personality and of his emotions are not available" (1970, 313; italics added). Such a remark helps us to see a correspondence in the real world to Meursault's estrangement in Camus's fictive one, the primary difference being that awareness of Meursault's estrangement abides with the reader, not with Meursault himself. Meursault appears to possess little, if any, consciousness of being strange, or isolated, or radically different from others. After all, he loves his mother "just like everyone else."

Regarded from the confines of attachment theory, Meursault's relationships with other people appear to fall into a permutation of what is referred to as "avoidant behavior," which in Meursault's case does not mean the avoidance of superficial relationships with acquaintances, or even sexual relationships, but rather the avoidance of emotional closeness. According to Parkes, "Two types of behavior indicative of insecure attachment in infancy are *avoidance behavior* and *clinging*" (1982, 296). The former inclines the child to become abnormally self-reliant: "Having learned that he must not make bids for attention if he is going to be tolerated at all, the young child inhibits attachment behavior." Certain consequences follow: "As with all forms of avoidance, once the child has learned to avoid the dangerous or punishing situations that result if he exhibits attachment, he has no way of finding out whether or not the danger has passed. Hence his avoidant behavior will tend to persist" (296). Parkes says concerning the predictable consequences in adult life, "The compulsively self-reliant person becomes increasingly isolated from others, who naturally interpret his lack of overt affection as a sign of *indifference*" (p. 297; italics added). What Parkes does not mention here, but what seems relevant in terms of what the reader of the novel is told about Meursault's mother, is that the child's avoidant behavior may be *modeled on the behavior of the parenting figures* as distinct from simply being a general response to a range of inappropriate parenting. In other words, Meursault's avoidant behavior serves the defensive purpose of avoiding the perceived danger of emotional closeness, and at the same time it replicates the familiar mode of intersubjectivity consituting an aberrant form of attachment behavior.

For those familiar with the details of Camus's early life, there is ample reason to infer that the circumstances of Meursault's infancy and childhood parallel those of Camus in crucial respects, although to say so is by no means to set up anything like a one-to-one correspondence between novelist and protagonist, which would be a naive reduction. The resemblance of the mothers of Meursault and Camus is close but not exact. McCarthy's version, quoted earlier, is somewhat distorted by ellipsis. In his account of the fictionalized autobiographical sketch in *L'Envers et l'Endroit,* McCarthy says that Camus "depicts her as cold" (McCarthy's paraphrase) and then he quotes these words: ". . . she never caressed her son because she wouldn't know how to" (1988, 1). The account in Lottman's biography—a more accurate and comprehensive one than McCarthy's—brings out the text's distinction between grandmother and mother: ". . . living with a grandmother without kindness and *a good and kind mother* who knew neither how to love nor to caress and so was *indifferent* . . ." (Lottman, 1979, 20; italics added). In the fictionalized sketch, the son "pities his mother, is that to love her? She had never caressed him because she would not know how. So he stares at her for long minutes. *Feeling a stranger,* he becomes conscious of her unhappiness" (Lottman, 29; italics added). As is well known, Camus's mother was half-deaf, illiterate, and generally exhausted by her work as a charwoman, labor that supported her two children and her own mother after the death of her husband in October 1914, when Albert Camus was less than one year old. Camus's mother seldom spoke, presumably because of her deafness. She also deferred to her strong-willed mother, to whom she left the rearing of her sons and control of the household. The grandmother, a proud, bitter woman, was a harsh disciplinarian who literally cracked a whip in the household, striking the children with a *nerf de boeuf* (ligament of a bull's neck; Lottman, 21).

That McCarthy's account blurs the personality of the mother by collapsing mother and grandmother into one figure is not only not surprising but almost pardonable in view of the fact that this merging is exactly what seems to happen in the novel itself, that is, Meursault's mother represents a composite of Camus' conscious memory of his mother and grandmother and his unconscious internalization of the introjects of these figures. One of the many substantial differences between novelist and protagonist is that Camus' mother did not die until after he did. And according to the account in *L'Envers et l'Endroit*, it is at the funeral of the grandmother, not the mother, that the grandson experiences difficulty mourning: "Only on the day of the funeral, because of the general explosion of tears, did he cry, *but with the fear of not being sincere.* . . ." (Lottman, 23; italics added).

Two widely recognized correspondences between Camus's life and Meursault's involve the theme of filicide and the story of the father's encounter with the spectacle of death by the guillotine. Briefly, the newspaper clipping about the story of the mother who "completely failed to recognize" her son and (with the help of his sister) murdered him out of greed becomes an obsession: "I must have read that story thousands of times." Camus himself not only clipped this story of real events out of the newspaper to use in *The Stranger;* he later based an entire play on it: *Le Malentendu*. Whatever else Melanie Klein might have found in this mixture of truth and "phantasy," she would at least have regarded the story as a projection of the rage and guilt of the greedy infant of the paranoid-schizoid position. In this hypothetical situation, the infant directs his rage at the bad-breast (withholding) mother, which precipitates a fantasied attack on her that is then projected onto the mother-figure so that it eventually takes the paranoid form of a fatal hostility directed from without at the guilty infant self. Thus Meursault's subsequent encounter with the story of a mother who fails to recognize her son presumably excites his unconscious memory of infantile death wishes directed at his mother.

The other well known correspondence lies in the fact that the story of the father Meursault says he "never set eyes on," the anecdote about seeing a murderer executed, replicates exactly the only story about his father Camus remembers having been told in his childhood. The essential correspondence is at least twofold: the obvious narrative parallel itself, and, more profoundly, the inferable unconscious infantile rage about never having a father, that is, a psychological as distinct from a biological father. In addition, the crime-and-punishment narrative as embedded in the novel may be regarded as incorporating punishment for death wishes directed at the absent father if Meursault, metonymically linked in the novel with the case of the parricide to be tried after he is, can be said to identify with the guillotined murderer. The theme of displaced patricide occurs without any buffering in "The Renegade": "One really ought to kill one's father, but after all there's no danger that *he'll* hurl himself into missionary work since he's now long dead. . . . so there's nothing left but to kill the missionary" (Camus, 1958, 36). A related difference between protagonist and novelist, in this connection, is that Meursault repeatedly comes into conflict—generally mild conflict except in the case of the priest who wants Meursault to address him as "father"—with authority figures in part 2 of the novel, such as the judge and the examining magistrate, whereas in real life Camus enjoyed a number of close friendships with supportive older men like Jean Grenier and Pascal Pia. The difference between Meursault and Camus in this regard paradoxically confirms the implied presence of the theme of the need for paternal love.

Still another correspondence, also widely recognized, between Meursault and Camus lies in the situation of being condemned to death, a theme of great significance for Camus because of the recurrent threat of death from tuberculosis. That Meursault's sentence to be guillotined constitutes a transmutation of Camus's situation can scarcely be questioned.

It has been said that Hamlet was the man Shakespeare might have been if he had not written a play called *Hamlet*. Meursault might be said to be the man Camus might have been if he had not written *The Stranger*. However meaningful that comparison may be, a kind of dynamic difference, or tension, may be found to exist between novelist and protagonist within the spectrum of their similarities. In terms of attachment theory, Camus was a man—whatever his air of reserve—capable of making all kinds of friends, of being devoted to members of his family, of being committed to causes, and in general a man profoundly engaged by social and political issues. He was a man who could distill the concept of love to its very essence, which he does in an early sketch called "Les Voix du quartier pauvre" in a passage based on his mother's affair with a married man: "Catherine's lover brought her flowers, oranges, and liqueurs which he won at carnivals. It was an adulterous relationship, but his wife was a drunkard. He was not handsome, but he was good. 'She cared about him who cared about her. Is love anything else?' " (in Lottman, 22).

Camus possessed a complexity of personality that makes Meursault appear almost one-dimensional by comparison. As McCarthy remarks, "Camus was a man of many parts: the swaggering Belcourt street-kid, the aristocratic dandy, Fouchet's cold-blooded rival [for Simone Hié, Camus's first wife], and De Freminville's miserable friend" (1982, 44), not to mention the many roles he played later in life, such as being an editor of *Combat*. "I am linked to the world by everything I do, to men with all the gratitude I feel," Camus writes in his *Notebooks* (1963, 17–18). Another passage in the *Notebooks* dramatizes Camus's sense of his own variousness: "To know yourself you must act—and this does not mean that you can then say who you are. 'The Cult of the Self'—don't make me laugh. Which self and which personality? When I look at my life and at the secret color which it has, I feel as if tears were trembling in my heart. I am just as much the lips that I have kissed as the nights spent in the 'House before the World,' just as much the child brought up in poverty as this frenzied ambition and thirst for life which sometimes carry me away. Many people who know me sometimes don't even recognize me" (1963, 63–64). In contrast to Camus's polychromatic variousness, Meursault seems monochromatic.

Meursault's weapon against the residual effect of the emotional poverty of his early life is indifference. To put back into play the passage quoted earlier, Camus lived with "a good and kind mother who knew neither how to love nor to caress and so was indifferent." By a process of identification, indifference becomes the essential ingredient of the interactional style of the son. In the novel whose working title was *L'Indifférent,* Meursault is indifferent to many things: to people, to goals (he is some sort of a clerk, with no career ambitions), to causes, and even to survival. The forms of his indifference include isolation, emotionlessness, impassivity, uninvolvement, silence, terseness, and passive compliance, the latter functioning as a mode of disengagement where engagement might be threatening to a precarious autonomy (as distinguished from the active cooperation of a mature person for whom interpersonal cooperation constitutes no psychic threat). Speaking of Camus's relationship with his mother, McCarthy says that the bond between them "was a kind of illness. . . . Camus talked of 'my profound indifference which is like a

natural infirmity.' The long hours spent with his mother [after he con-
tracted tuberculosis] were a death where Camus ceased to be a separate
person and was merged with her. Yet her mute suffering also sharpened
his desire to write. Since she could not speak he would speak for her. His
writing would be tough and concise because it would contain her silence"
(1982, 21). Meursault's profound indifference may also be regarded
as one form of the denial of a massive rage toward what Leites refers
to as "the severe deprivations which were imposed by an absent
father, an indifferent mother, and a withholding wider environment"
(1947, 248).

Whatever Leites intends to convey by the phrase "wider environment,"
it needs to be taken in this case not only as inclusive of society in general
but more particularly as embracing the natural environment, including
the climate—especially that of Algeria. On the whole, Camus himself
experienced this physical environment as benign. In one of his early
poems he represents the Mediterranean Sea as a "Blond blue cradle where
certainties balance" (in Lottman, 69). Again and again Camus relates to
the physical environment much as he relates to people, as these passages
from his notebooks show: "Seek contacts. All contacts. If I want to write
about men, should I stop talking about the countryside? If the sky or light
attract me, shall I forget the eyes or voices of those I love?" (1963, 15);
"A day of sunshine and clouds. The cold spangled with yellow. . . . The
bay trembling with light like a moist lip" (16). Such evidence tends to
confirm what everyone intuitively knows: that the natural environment
possesses object-relational significance. Harold Searles articulates this claim
at length in his pioneering work, *The Nonhuman Environment* (1960),
arguing specifically that "man is not an alien in his nonhuman environment but in kinship with it" (5), and that the nonhuman environment,
"far from being of little or no account to human personality development,
constitutes one of the most basically important ingredients of human
psychological existence" (5–6).

Although Meursault also relates to the physical environment in a positive way at times, what is much more significant in the novel is the way
he experiences it as painful, discouraging, and disorienting. On the morning of his mother's funeral the sky is "a blaze of light." As Meursault gazes
at the countryside he remarks, "Evenings in these parts must be a sort of
mournful solace. Now, in the full glare of the morning sun, with everything shimmering in the heat haze, there was something inhuman, dis-

couraging, about this landscape." On the morning of the day he kills the
Arab, Meursault feels "under the weather" and "the glare of the morning
sun hit me in the eyes like a clenched fist." In Kleinian terms, he frequently experiences the environment as a persecutory object—psychologically a function of his own projection even though the sun itself is real
enough. For Meursault, as for the protagonist of Camus's story "The
Renegade," the sun in particular exhibits the power to confuse, so that
Meursault speaks the truth in object-relational terms when he tries to
explain that he killed the Arab "because of the sun."

What needs to be considered further, because of the pivotal consequence of Meursault's physiological condition when he shoots the Arab,
is the relationship of the persecutory environment to his state of mind
and the state of his body—this in reference to his own explanation,
mentioned earlier, that his physical condition at any given moment often
influences his feelings. Stern asserts that "the sharing of affective states is
the most pervasive and clinically germaine feature of intersubjective relatedness" (1985, 138). If one assumes, hypothetically, that the form and
degree of what Stern calls "affect attunement" experienced by Meursault
in infancy and early childhood stunted not only his emotions but other
aspects of his psychological development as well, and if one takes it for
granted that the earliest stage of good-enough parenting consists largely
in regulating the homeostasis of bodily needs and functions, then one
may further suppose that Meursault's "body self," or roughly what Stern
calls "the emergent self," carries a disproportionate burden with regard to
his sense of well-being and his ability to control his own behavior. When
his limited coherence of selfhood breaks down under conditions producing bodily discomfort, Meursault's repertory of hierarchically higher defensive measures, such as indifference, prove insufficient to save him from
lapsing into the turbulence of a dangerous, regressive state of mind. "I
knew it was a fool thing to do," he says. "I wouldn't get out of the sun by
moving on a yard or so. . . ." Then a shaft of reflected light lances upward
from the Arab's knife:

> I felt as if a long, thin blade transfixed my forehead. . . . Beneath a veil of
> brine and tears my eyes were blinded; I was conscious only of the cymbals
> of the sun clashing on my skull, and, less distinctly, of the keen blade of
> light flashing up from the knife, scarring my eyelashes, and gouging into
> my eyeballs.
> Then everything began to reel before my eyes, a fiery gust came from

the sea, while the sky cracked in two, from end to end, and a great sheet of flame poured down through the rift. (1942, 75)

And then he pulls the trigger.

The diseased environment at Oran in *The Plague* exhibits persecutory elements multiplied a millionfold, but in contrast to Meursault, figures like Rieux, the physician, and Rambert, the journalist, are capable of love. What the surface of *The Plague* presents as contingent cannot in fact be accidental. What cannot be psychologically accidental is the fact that the persecutory forces of the plague arise during the absence of beloved women, though Rieux's separation from his wife is counterbalanced, in part, by the presence of his mother. Separation, as distinct from loss, becomes a major leitmotif in the novel, even though the novel's preoccupations with death would lead one to expect the reverse. One instance of this emphasis on separation can be found in the phrasing of M. Othon, the magistrate who has lost his son, when he insists that by voluntarily returning to duty within the confines of an isolation camp he will "feel less separated" from his little boy. By comparison, Meursault's physical isolation from Marie in prison breeds no yearning for her *as a person*.

In a way influenced by his own existentialist convictions, Sartre claims that "the absurdity of the human condition [in *The Stranger*] is its sole theme" (1947, 111). It was, in any case, the first to be published of a group of works, all written more or less contemporaneously, on the theme of the absurd: *Caligula*, *The Myth of Sisyphus*, and *Le Malentendu* (Lottman, 428). The word "absurd" occurs infrequently in the verbal texture of *The Stranger*, at least in Stuart Gilbert's translation, and only in what looks like a casual manner, as in the passage where Meursault thinks, ". . . the mere thought of being an onlooker who comes to see the show, and can go home and vomit afterward, flooded my mind with a wild, absurd exultation." Though scarcely the sole theme in *The Stranger*, the theme of the absurd is certainly a major one. More to the point, this theme needs to be understood in terms of Meursault's conviction of the absence of meaning in life, an absence of meaning unwittingly predicated on the absence of meaning, for him, in interpersonal relations. He believes love has no meaning: "When she laughed I wanted her again. A moment later she asked me if I loved her. I said that sort of question had no meaning, really; but I supposed I didn't." Camus, in contrast, remarks in his *Notebooks* on "the misery and greatness of the world: it offers no truths, but only objects of love." He adds, "Absurdity is king, but love saves us from it" (93).

Meursault may be said to understand but deny this truth, or, alternatively, Camus may be said to understand it while allowing Meursault to deny it. "It's common knowledge that life isn't worth living, anyhow," claims Meursault in much the same vein that Caligula remarks, "Really, this world of ours, the scheme of things as they call it, is quite intolerable" (1965, 9). Later on, in the flood of thought and emotion released in connection with his tirade at the priest in his cell, Meursault himself touches on the way the meaningfulness of life inheres in, or grows out of, personal relationships (technically, both intrapersonal and interpersonal ones): "None of his certainties [such as the existence of God] was worth one strand of a woman's hair." Even after Meursault's profoundly nihilistic claim that "Nothing, nothing had the least importance, and I knew quite well why," he reveals that he unconsciously grasps the way personal relationships constitute the ground of all meaning (Marris 1982) by the way he discusses the meaning of life in the context of such relationships: "What difference could they make to me, the deaths of others, or a mother's love, or his God; or the way a man decides to live, the fate he thinks he chooses, since one and the same fate was bound to 'choose' not only me but thousands of millions of privileged people who, like him, called themselves my brothers." If all alike are condemned to die, "what difference could it make if, after being charged with murder, he were executed because he didn't weep at his mother's funeral, since it all came to the same thing in the end?"

Two characters in the novel, Pérez, the mother's aged boyfriend ("He and your mother had become almost inseparable.") and old Salamano, Meursault's neighbor, are foils showing what difference weeping does make. Pérez's "eyes were streaming with tears. . . . But because of the wrinkles they couldn't flow down. They spread out, crisscrossed, and formed a smooth gloss on the old, worn face." And old Salamano weeps at the loss of his mangy cur, with whom he fought eight years of daily battle at the end of a leash, dragging and cursing and even beating him on their walks. When told he would have to pay a fee at the pound if the dog were found, Salamano responds, "Is it likely I'd give money for a mutt like that? No damned fear! They can kill him, for all I care." But nevertheless he weeps. When Meursault suggests he get another dog, Salamano points out that "he'd become used to this one, and it wouldn't be the same thing." Readers of the novel cannot fail to notice the ironic contrast between the depth of Salamano's attachment to his pet and the shallowness of Meursault's emotions in the face of the loss of his mother.

Meursault passes up his last opportunity for a meaningful personal attachment, even if only a symbolic one, when he rejects the overtures of the priest in his cell. After Meursault refuses the solace of faith, the priest asks if he may kiss him. Meursault refuses. When the priest asks why Meursault never addresses him as "Father," Meursault says, "I told him he wasn't my father." Shortly thereafter, provoked beyond endurance, Meursault breaks into an "ecstasy" of rage at the priest—the first state of true passion Meursault ever appears to have felt. This anger constitutes the only major exception to his sustained indifference and detachment, assuming that his impulse to kiss Céleste after his testimony ("I didn't say anything . . . but for the first time in my life I wanted to kiss a man") and his contacts with Marie constitute minor ones.

Some readers of *The Stranger* believe that Meursault experiences a fundamental change toward the end of the novel, an enlightenment. Brée writes, "Defiant and lucid, he will go to his death happy" (1959, 113), and McCarthy contends, "But the Meursault of the closing pages is innocent and he goes to the guillotine reconciled with the universe" (1982, 162). These readers miss, among other things, the irony of the closing lines. Meursault's sense of estrangement, which mirrors an experience that no human being can have escaped totally, not only endures to the end of the novel but becomes accentuated by Camus's savage, remorseless irony. Meursault feels as if his great rush of anger has washed him clean by emptying him of hope. Gazing up at the stars, he lays his heart open for the first time "to the benign indifference of the universe." He says that "to feel it so like myself, indeed, so brotherly," makes him realize that he has been "happy," and that he is happy still. Camus's austere conclusion follows: "For all to be accomplished, for me to feel less lonely, all that remained to hope was that on the day of my execution there should be a huge crowd of spectators and that they should greet me with howls of execration." Even if readers were to choose to regard this assertion, which Meursault alleges to be a new position, achieved for "the first time," as a kind of rock-bottom foundation for existential becoming on his part, Meursault's psychic position vis-à-vis the universe nevertheless remains a paranoid-schizoid one in that his conception of the essence of feeling "less lonely" in the world takes the form of being greeted with a crowd's "howls of execration."

As readers we can dissociate ourselves from our unconscious identification with Meursault at this terminal point where, as a scapegoat hero, he is driven from the community of our collective guilt by those imagined howls of execration (before his actual sacrifice at the guillotine). Yet we sense he is laden with our collective guilt. After all, it is true, as Meursault remarks, that "all normal people . . . had more or less desired the death of those they loved, at some time or another," even if only in infancy.

7.

THE SEQUESTERED
SELF OF EMILY DICKINSON

Deprived of other Banquet
I entertained Myself—
At first—a scant nutrition —
An insufficient Loaf—

But grown by slender addings
To so esteemed a size
'Tis sumptuous enough for me—
And almost to suffice

A Robin's famine able—
Red Pilgrim, He and I—
A berry from our table
Reserve—for charity—

(#773)

"Deprived of other Banquet/I entertained Myself—." Emily Dickinson often felt deprived: "God gave a Loaf to every Bird—/But just a Crumb

N.B.: Dickinson's punctuation is highly idiosyncratic; all poems are cited by number, T. H. Johnson edition (1960). Reprinted by permission of the publishers and the Trustees of Amherst College from *The Poems of Emily Dickinson,* Thomas H. Johnson, ed., Cambridge, Mass.: The Belknap Press of Harvard University Press, copyright 1951, © 1955, 1979, 1983 by President and Fellows of Harvard College and from *The Complete Poems of Emily Dickinson,* edited by Thomas H. Johnson. Copyright 1914, 1929, 1935, 1942 by Martha Dickinson Bianchi; copyright © renewed 1957, 1963 by Mary L. Hampson, Reprinted by permission of Little, Brown and Company.

—to Me—" (#791). Themes of scarcity and deprivation occur again and again in her poetry, yet in the midst of this scarcity one unfailing source of abundance is available: her imagination. Like the Spider Artist in two of her poems (#605 and #1275), she weaves the delicate tapestries of her poetry out of the abundance of her very self. In a sense, she feeds upon herself: "I entertained Myself—/At first—a scant nutrition—/An insufficient Loaf—." But with time comes accumulation: ". . . [the loaf] grown by slender addings/ To so esteemed a size/ 'Tis sumptuous enough for me —." Here, as usual, her diet is high in irony. By "sumptuous" she means "almost [able] to suffice/A Robin's famine"—with a morsel left over for charity—so that the complaint that God leaves her just a crumb remains in play.

When Dickinson elects to write the poetry constituting her letter to the world ("This is my letter to the World/That never wrote to Me—," #441), she chooses to accept the challenge of what she deems a life of consequence:

> *One Life* of so much Consequence!
> Yet I—for it—would pay—
> My Soul's *entire income*—
> In ceaseless—salary—.
>
> (#270).

One reward of such a life of consequence, when the achievement is real, must be the enhancement of self-esteem in a person who feels insufficiently loved, attended to, rewarded. What her life of consequence as a poet provides is nothing less than the attention of monarchs: "But *Monarchs*—are *perceptible*—/Far down the dustiest Road!" (#270). Images of exalted status recur in her poems, as in

> 'Tis little I—could care for Pearls—
> Who own the ample sea—
> Or Brooches—when the Emperor—
> With Rubies—pelteth me—
>
> Or Gold—who am the Prince of Mines—
> Or Diamonds—when have I
> A Diadem to fit a Dome—
> Continual upon me—.
>
> (#466)

These imagined experiences of exalted status and the plaintive objections about God's withholding of all but a crumb frequently involve the representation of self in the form of metaphorical roles: the "Prince of Mines," for example, and the Red Pilgrim (the robin)—a famished way-farer in life.

Commentators on the life and work of Emily Dickinson have followed her lead by highlighting the many roles she attributes to herself. In providing contexts for these roles they tend to stress negative factors in Dickinson's social environment and psychological makeup—even to the point of assuming the presence of psychotic disturbances. The discussion to follow emphasizes Dickinson's adaptive maneuvers in the face of adver-sity. It contends that although her art may be regarded as a showcase full of her yearnings and conflicts, her poetry may more profitably be seen as constituting a privileged, protected realm—a sequestered realm—within which she finds space to establish a superordinate conception of herself, as Bard, sufficient to embrace her multifarious voices and roles, though without necessarily effecting an integration of them. Within this enabling space she can assert the truest, most essential aspects of her being, espe-cially as they depend on her relationships to important others, including God. This same material also provides an occasion for examining certain problems in self theory, especially Winnicott's contention that even in healthy persons there lies a secret, "sacred," noncommunicating "core" at the center of the "true self"—a "secret self" within the self (1963).

Brinnin introduces us to "several strong and distinct Emily Dickinsons" (1960, 8–9; subsequent Brinnin quotations from 8–13). A role he asso-ciates more with legend than reality is Emily as The Nun in the Cloisters of Her Father's House, a person who enacts in her poems "the bittersweet resignation of thwarted love" and who accepts marriage "to nothing but the universe." This is Emily as The Perpetual Bride, forever dressed in white—as was her custom in later years. Closer to reality are Emily as Empress of Calvary ("Title divine is mine/The Wife without/The Sign./ Acute degree/Conferred on me—/Empress of Calvary"), and Emily as "The Reclusive Bride of Silence," a radiant but isolated girl "who tarries in the world like an ethereal visitor and associates on speaking terms with birds, bees, butterflies, lilacs, and gentians as her only equals." Then there are Emily as Dutiful Daughter, as Affectionate Sister, and as Compassion-ate Neighbor. Already alluded to is what Brinnin typifies as The Senti-mentalist Writer of Flowered Verses, who is closely related, in Brinnin's view, to The Saucy Rebel in God's Back Yard "who teases words into the shapes of rococo valentines." She is a far cry from the Emily who tells

T. W. Higginson that her business is circumference, this being a Dickinson whose mind, for Brinnin, "plays like lightning between the immediate and the ultimate" in her poems about God and eternity. Even though they may often be grossly oversimplified, these rolelike constellations of selfhood do convey, as a group, some sense of the protean variety of Dickinson's personae.

Feminist critics have been especially concerned in recent years with the multifariousness of Dickinson's roles. Gilbert and Gubar (1979) look at her writing more as *mimesis* (enactment) than as *poesis* (making) because they regard her masks and poses, in life as in the poetry, as part of a concerted, liberating strategy for "a *woman* poet" in a repressive patriarchy. When they remark that "Emily Dickinson herself became a madwoman," they see her as both cunning and victimized: she becomes "both ironically a madwoman (a deliberate impersonation of a madwoman) and truly a madwoman (a helpless agoraphobic, trapped in a room in her father's house)" (pp. 583–86). In addition to The Madwoman in the Attic, Gilbert and Gubar speak of a number of "impersonations" involving whiteness: The Little Maid in White, The Fierce Virgin in White, The Nun in White, The Bride in White, The Madwoman in White, The Dead Woman in White, and The Ghost in White, adding, "Dickinson seems to have split herself into a series of incubae haunting not just her father's house but her own mind, for, as she wrote in one of her most openly confessional poems, 'One need not be a Chamber—to be Haunted' " (621–622). Other roles specified by authors represented in a collection of essays entitled *Feminist Critics Read Emily Dickinson* (Juhasz 1983) are The Priestess of Daily Domesticity (Gilbert), The Wayward Nun (Gilbert), Alice of Amherst: The Perpetual Child (Mossberg, alluding to Lewis Carroll's Alice), and The Only Kangaroo among the Beauty (Keller, picking up on the playful note of self-deprecation sounded in one of Dickinson's letters).

The editor of this collection insists on the marriage of gender and art: "The central assumption of feminist criticism is that gender informs the nature of art, the nature of biography, and the relation between them. Dickinson is a woman poet, and this fact is integral to her identity" (1). Something disjunctive may lurk in these remarks. Dickinson's gender cannot be divorced from her social and psychological identities, to be sure. But the phrase "woman poet," as employed by Juhasz, Gilbert, and Gubar operates in an ideologically exclusionary way. Many readers may prefer to see Dickinson as *a poet who happens to be a woman* rather than simply as a *woman poet*. Later Juhasz stands on firmer ground when she observes that "woman" and "poet" are not to be viewed as mutually exclusive terms, which is very different from designating Dickinson as a "woman poet." "From the feminist perspective," Juhasz adds, "Dickinson's life was neither a flight, nor a cop-out, nor a sacrifice, nor a substitution, but a strategy, a creation, for enabling her to become the person she was" (10). She quotes Adrienne Rich as saying that Dickinson's poetry represents the work of a "mind engaged in a lifetime's musing on essential problems of language, identity, separation, relationship, the integrity of the self; a mind capable of describing psychological states more accurately than any poet except Shakespeare" (Juhasz, 10). The phrasing of this statement is notably free of gender markers. Obviously a great proportion of Dickinson's poetry may legitimately be characterized as gender oriented insofar as it exhibits female roles and consciousness in various ways. Yet to say so should not obscure the fact that much of her work transcends gender in that it was evidently written for the world—that is, by a person, for people, as distinct from by a woman, for women.

Dickinson informed Higginson in one of her letters, "When I state myself, as the Representative of the Verse—it does not mean—me—but a supposed person" (*Letters* 2: 412). Wolff writes about Dickinson's supposed persons in terms of Voice rather than Role, remarking that the presence of many voices has sometimes puzzled readers: "One poem may be delivered in a child's Voice; another in the Voice of a young woman scrutinizing nature and the society in which she makes her place. Sometimes the Voice is that of a woman self-confidently addressing her lover in the language of passion and sexual desire. At still other times, the Voice of the verse seems so precariously balanced at the edge of hysteria that even its calmest observations grate like the shriek of dementia" (1986, 177). When the speaker is a child, sometimes the child is a boy, not a girl, as in #986, where the voice says, "Yet when a Boy, and Barefoot—/I more than once at Noon/Have passed, I thought, a Whip lash/Unbraiding in the Sun." And in #1201 we have a disobedient boy who "Went to Heaven perhaps at Death/And perhaps he didn't." Quite often the voice we hear is an indeterminate one: "Many of Dickinson's poems, especially the late poems, seem to issue from a speaker whose gender and station in life are indifferent" (239). This voice, which Wolff associates with Ecclesiastes, can be regarded as the voice of the Prophet, or omniscient Poet—a genderless voice issuing from afar, sometimes even from beyond the grave.

* * *

Commentaries alleging the presence of pathological elements in Dickinson's personality, such as the psychoanalytic biography by Cody (1971), call for a sharper scrutiny than the foregoing discussions of voices, roles, masks, poses, and personae. Broadly speaking, Cody regards Dickinson as falling within the stereotype of the sick genius. What he specifically claims is that "threatening personality disintegration compelled a frantic Emily Dickinson to create poetry—for her a psychosis-deflecting activity" (391). He further claims, but does not satisfactorily demonstrate, that "the letters, poems, and biographical data all indicate that during her psychotic breakdown [this "breakdown" being more in the nature of an inference than a fact] Emily Dickinson's unconscious life forged into awareness accompanied by the fear that aggressive and libidinal drives would get out of control" (404). Two flaws in Cody's argument need to be mentioned at this point. The first flaw is an inconsistency. He infers that Dickinson probably (he says, *must* have) experienced "what she interpreted as a cruel rejection by her mother" (2), but then he adds, lamely, "However, there exists no record of any concrete instance in which Mrs. Dickinson took such an attitude toward her daughter." Cody assumes that this "rejection" was experienced early, during the first two years, and he talks about it, along Freudian lines, almost entirely in terms of *oral* deprivation, citing, as supporting evidence, the presence of oral imagery in the poetry (naturally without entering into any speculations about how poets could possibly manage *without* using such imagery). A second and more serious flaw occurs when he writes, "And when Emily Dickinson says in a poem (#280, referring to herself): 'And then a Plank in Reason broke' (that is, rational faculties gave way to psychosis), why should we not believe her?" (29). Cody finds it convenient for his purposes to treat a figurative assertion as a literal one. He takes Dickinson's "supposed person" here as her real, whole self rather than as a representation of what was presumably only an image for an *aspect* of an emotion recollected in tranquility.

As for the already mentioned portrait of Dickinson as the madwoman in the attic, Gilbert and Gubar (1979) rely, in part, on Cody's book, first for the connection he tries to establish between psychosis and agoraphobia and second for the breakdown hypothesis (606, 625). In their view, "As a girl, Dickinson had begged to be kept from 'what they call households,' but ironically, as she grew older, she discovered that the price of her salvation was her agoraphobic imprisonment in her father's household, along with a concomitant exclusion from the passionate drama of adult sexuality" (595). What they choose to ignore, here, is that both of these behavioral patterns were essentially voluntary and were based on a more complex set of personal circumstances than their melodramatic metaphor ("agoraphobic imprisonment") implies. Gilbert and Gubar write plausibly of a Soul/Goblin split in the poems (622–23), but they go on from there to assert that the speaker/addressee dichotomy in a poem alluding to the theme of suicide involves a "murderous madwoman" goblin, assuming, in the process, that anyone who even thinks of suicide, let alone writes a poem about such an impulse, must necessarily be categorically psychotic. The issue at hand can be summed up by suggesting that while no one on earth may be totally free of traces of psychotic experience, the ill-substantiated assertion that Emily Dickinson was virtually committable does not markedly enhance our understanding of the complexities of her personality.

Observations about neurotic features of Dickinson's behavior have sometimes—but by no means always—been more meaningful. They generally focus on assumptions about repressed sexuality. Cody unsympathetically describes Dickinson in the 1860's as "loveless [certaintly untrue except in a narrow, sexual sense], excluded [it was she who limited her contact with others], almost burned out as a poet [demonstrably untrue], and reduced to the status of a queer, hypochondriacal, and depressed old maid" (1971, 438). He argues that she "avoided heterosexuality out of fear" (261), by which he means —mainly—that she identified with males rather than females (a contestable oversimplification), though he stops short of claiming she was homosexual (103). The primary manifestation of what Cody refers to as her "voracious love-hunger" (101) appears in what he takes to be her "predominantly 'oral' personality" (101), orality being, of course, essentially sexual (a "component-instinct") in traditional psychoanalytic thinking.

Keller takes a much different route. In an audacious, inventive, but sometimes silly essay entitled "Notes on Sleeping with Emily Dickinson," he openly celebrates the passion he finds in her work, saying, "The poems on sleeping with someone are instructions, I believe, on how to 'take' her. When she writes about wild nights, she is not only describing her ecstasy but also instructing us how to react to her, what to expect, what to get. She thus couples with the critic" (1983, 67). Keller suggests that "there may have been men in her mind but, except for God, there are hardly any men to speak of in her poetry. Much of her poetry is poetry in which she wishes there were, or she fantasizes about there being, or she documents the absence of . . . Yet a man can put himself there as a reader quite easily." Keller adds, "She created the space for someone to understand her, enclose her, love her. . . . She lets one in lovingly" (70). Keller arrives at a conclusion of sorts when he remarks, "Hard for a man to see, I think, what is erotic about Emily Dickinson's poetry [all of which he lumps together at this point]. Having slept with her once, I found it more masturbatory than anything else. Her art, I think, became a kind of orgasm withheld, though lusting still after the concealed and tantalizing, after the incomprehensible, after fantasy. She plays, but she does not climax with you" (72). By this point, Keller's readers may wonder whose fantasies he is examining, Dickinson's or his own.

The reader of Keller's earlier commentary on Dickinson (1979) gets a better sense of what he means by describing her art as "masturbatory" when he discusses, together, the two poems quoted side by side on page 144.

Keller argues, "Both phallic creatures are extremely attractive to her, even though she finds her genitals alarmed, feeling what she calls 'tighter breathing/And Zero at the Bone' in one case and 'creeping blood' in the other" (269). He sees her as both shocked and fascinated by the male erections, "aroused," and even "penetrated" ("He fathomed me"). And yet, Keller goes on, "as much as she might desire it, she does not connect well, dismissing the encounter with the snake as merely a boy's brief summertime adventure and the encounter with the worm-snake as merely a housewife's daydream. There is no significance in the sex; it is fun and games" (269). What he means by "fun and games" emerges more clearly when he remarks, "The sex in her poems forms no program but is made up of individual bold moments, flashes of desire, mainly masturbatory" (270). After quoting "Wild Nights!—Wild Nights!/ Were I with thee/ Wild Nights should be/Our luxury!" he adds, "She could play with it on wild nights in her poems without any consequences. It is, I believe, another of her areas of freedom" (271). Another instance of what he means he provides by quoting from #213: "Did the Harebell loose her girdle/To the lover Bee/Would the Bee the Harebell *hallow*/Much as formerly?" If I understand him, Keller cherishes the erotic playfulness he finds in some of Dickinson's poems even as he limits his approbation because he feels the eroticism is "without any consequences," only "fun and games." His ambivalent epithet, "masturbatory," expresses in nontechnical terms his reservations about his perception of inhibition in Dickinson's eroticism.

A narrow Fellow in the Grass
Occasionally rides—
You may have met him—did you not
His notice sudden is—

The Grass divides as with a Comb—
A spotted shaft is seen—
And then it closes at your feet
And opens further on—

He likes a Boggy Acre
A Floor too cool for Corn—
Yet when a Boy, and Barefoot—
I more than once at Noon
Have passed, I thought, a Whip lash
Unbraiding in the Sun
When stooping to secure it
It wrinkled, and was gone—

Several of Nature's People
I know, and they know me—
I feel for them a transport
Of cordiality—

But never met this Fellow
Attended, or alone
Without a tighter breathing
And Zero at the Bone—
                                    (#986)

In Winter in my Room
I came upon a Worm
Pink lank and warm
But as he was a worm
And worms presume
Not quite with him at home
Secured him by a string
To something neighboring
And went along.

A Trifle afterward
A thing occurred
I'd not believe it if I heard
But state with creeping blood
A snake with mottles rare
Surveyed my chamaber floor
In feature as the worm before
But ringed with power
The very string with which
I tied him—too
When he was mean and new
That string was there—

I shrank—"How fair you are"!
Propitiation's claw—
"Afraid he hissed
Of me"?
"No cordiality"—
He fathomed me—
Then to a Rhythm *Slim*
Secreted in his Form
As Patterns swim
Projected him.

That time I flew
Both eyes his way
Lest he pursue
Nor ever ceased to run
Till in a distant Town
Towns on from mine
I set me down
This was dream—   (#1670)

Willbern (1989) deals with the same "snake poems" except that he does so mainly within the context of psychoanalytic theory and with considerably more finesse. Although his readings of the imagery coincide with

Keller's for the most part, Willbern is careful not to insist that the meanings of the poem are exclusively sexual in nature. He construes "A narrow Fellow in the Grass" as relating to the experience of "the momentous (re)discovery of genital difference": "A reading after Freud, then, reconstructs Emily Dickinson's famous poem about a snake as a poem about the female discovery of genital difference, perceived as an anxious absence. The traditional psychoanalytic terms here are *castration anxiety* and *penis envy*" (167). Willbern remarks that Dickinson "is not a barefoot boy, with an easily secured appendage of mastery; in fact she possesses (or feels she possesses) an absence, a lack [in the Lacanian sense]: 'Zero [no/thing] at the [pubic] Bone.' " He further suggests, following Wolff's interpretation, that the poem registers anxiety concerning "male sexuality or even phallic brutality" in addition to concern about the attributes of her own body. Willbern employs these psychobiographical interpretations as illustrations of his assumption that Freud's depiction of a dynamically repressed unconscious whose "deepest roots" emerge from "sexual life" still constitutes the "bedrock" of psychoanalytic theory (160). That is an assumption I have repeatedly called into question in this book. The issue immediately at hand is not the presence of sexual imagery in the poems mentioned but rather the potential distortion of the larger psychobiographical picture that results when only two poems, in Willbern's paper, or just a few, in Keller's discussion, are treated as substantially representative of the mind of the author. Of the nearly two thousand poems she composed, only a small percentage can be considered "love poems" by any ordinary measure, and of this limited group only a very small fraction can legitimately be characterized as *erotic* to any significant degree. The poetry of Emily Dickinson simply does not transact much of what Freud called "the sexual business." What it does transact, pervasively, is that commerce of the mind known in psychoanalysis as object relations.

Bollas observes that what we call self "is the history of many internal relations" and that each individual experiences innumerable "parts" of the self "articulated through the interplay of internal and external reality" (1987, 9). We know enough about Dickinson's childhood to begin to understand how the multifarious aspects of her self exhibited in her poetry constitute permutations of early interpersonal relationships. We know enough to begin to appreciate what she was driving at when she told Higginson, "Could you tell me what home is"? "I never had a mother. I suppose a mother is one to whom you hurry when you are troubled" (*Letters* 2: 475).

Cody, who intuitively appreciates the gravity of these remarks, tries to force their implications into his traditional explanatory framework by arguing that the most powerful undercurrent in Dickinson's personality was "a ravenous search for affection," that she "craved love," and that "her insatiable love needs and their frustration saturate the poetry and the letters" (1971, 39)—which is partly correct, of course, except for the negatively toned phrasing and Cody's tendency to set up equivalencies between love and nourishment, and love and sexuality. As was mentioned earlier, he hypothecates that Dickinson probably experienced "what she interpreted as a cruel rejection by her mother," yet he asserts that "there exists no record of any concrete instance in which Mrs. Dickinson took such an attitude" (2). Although there may be no record of any negative attitude of the mother toward her daughter, there was in fact a situation that Emily almost certainly did construe as implying a cruel rejection by her mother.

Emily Dickinson suffered a separation from her mother for a period of three or four months beginning at the age of two years and two months, that is, precisely during that phase of development when, according to Bowlby, the pain of separation is most likely to be acute and the effects most lasting. The occasion for this separation was the difficult birth of Emily's baby sister, Lavinia, and its aftermath. Because Emily's aunt, Lavinia Norcross, could not come to Amherst to aid her sister during the postpartum period, Emily was sent to stay with her Aunt Lavinia, who would probably have seemed a virtual stranger to Emily at the beginning of her stay. What complicates the emotional picture presented by this situation is that Emily behaved well under the circumstances, as one would *not* have expected from a securely attached child. Emily did not appear to miss her mother but only her brother, Austin. That Emily soon became attached to her aunt seems apparent from what Aunt Lavinia writes to her sister: "She thought everything of me—when any thing went wrong she would come to me" (in Cody 1971, 51). In contrast to the devoted attentiveness of Aunt Lavinia, here is a portrait of Emily's mother: "A talented housewife whose custards and baked goods would be remembered with pleasure, Mrs. Dickinson was nontheless isolated by her tearful withdrawals and obscure maladies. Although she was undoubtedly loving and well intentioned, she did not have an intimate relationship with any of her three children. Despite her constant presence, there was an abiding sense of emotional separation" (Wolff 1986, 64).

Matching all of these circumstances with Emily Dickinson's adult behavior suggests certain inferences about her emotional history. Emily probably *did* experience pain on being separated from her mother, hating her for the rupture without showing it. It seems likely that she had already put some emotional distance between herself and a mother who, though devoted, was not likely, judging from what we know about her phlegmatic personality, to have been a sufficiently sensitive, responsive one in terms of what Stern calls "affect attunement" (especially in view of the mother's tendency to be depressed and the extraordinary sensitivity of her daughter's constitutional endowment). If Emily did form a strong attachment to her Aunt Lavinia, she must have re-experienced the pangs of separation once again on being parted from her affectionate aunt. Emily undoubtedly relied heavily for support throughout her life on her siblings: "The children had learned early to band together fiercely because Mother and Father were generally so unavailable to them. . . . Emily Dickinson could feel she was securely *herself* only when Austin and Vinnie were there to listen and respond to her meditations or to share the complex sense of humor that never [for them] required explanation" (Wolff 1986, 109–10). The fervor of Emily's quest for attention and affection from various people in her youth, so evident in her early correspondence, probably represents an attempt, well within the bounds of normal social behavior, to seek compensation for her sense of being "deprived" of sufficient emotional contact in her childhood. That Emily repeatedly wove the threads of her attachments, to males and females, real and imaginary, into the warp of her poetry appears to be beyond question.

It is not true that Emily never had a mother to hurry home to when she was troubled. Her father was her mother in this regard, as she reveals in another letter to Higginson, for whom—transferentially—she reserves so many intimate disclosures: "I always ran Home to Awe when a child, if anything befell me. He was an awful Mother, but I liked him better than none" (*Letters* 2: 517–18). The outrageous pun in "awful" bears witness to her ambivalence: her worship and her pain. She idealizes her father, yet resents his emotional distance. She also rebels against his authority in unobtrusive ways, just as she does against the God of her religious upbringing. One hint of her rebelliousness emerges in a letter to

Austin: "We do not have many jokes tho' *now* [that you are away]; it is
pretty much all sobriety, and we do not have much poetry, father having
made up his mind that it's pretty much all *real life* [that matters]. Father's
real life and *mine* sometimes come into collision, but as yet [we] escape
unhurt!" (*Letters* 1: 161). To Higginson she wrote, "My father was not
severe I should think but remote" (*Letters* 2: 404). He was emotionally
remote even when he was around, apparently, but mostly he was away: at
the office, or in Boston, or in the legislature. "My Mother does not care
for thought—and Father [is] too busy with his Briefs—to notice what
we do" (*Letters* 2: 404). The only member of the family Edward Dickinson noticed much was his son, Austin. He doted on him. As Emily writes
to her brother, "Father says your letters are altogether before Shakespeare,
and he will have them published to put in our library (*Letters* 1: 122).
But there is no evidence that Edward Dickinson ever gave any heed to
his daughter's literary efforts. The day after he died she wrote, "His
Heart was pure and terrible and I think no other like it exists" (*Letters*
2: 528).

The act of writing, especially letters and poetry, constitutes a special
feature of Emily's relationship to her beloved brother. When Austin sends
her a poem he composed, she responds (at the age of twenty-one) with
rivalry masked by affectionate playfulness: "And Austin is a Poet. . . . Out
of the way, Pegasus, Olympus enough 'to him,' and just say to those 'nine
muses' that we have done with them!" She continues: "Now Brother
Pegasus, I'll tell you what it is—I've been in the habit *myself* of writing
some few things, and it rather appears to me that you're getting away
[with] my patent, so you'd better be somewhat careful, or I'll call the
police!" (*Letters* 1: 235).

Wolff helps us to understand the depth of the emotional issues underlying Emily's badinage. She was an ambitious young woman disenfran-
chised by a patriarchal family and culture. "How, then, could Emily
Dickinson assert an empowered, autonomous 'self' while continuing to
live in Father's house?" Wolff answers, "Having forfeited society's cooperation in defining self when she rejected the roles usually available to
women, she discovered that *this* 'I,' the 'poet,' was in some ways better
than the roles offered by Amherst to anyone (man or woman), a secret,
privileged inner self that could observe life to analyze and criticize with
complete safety" (1986, 128). Emily also understood that, although Austin was the indisputable heir to the public offices and material prizes

constituting the patriarchal House of Dickinson, "her writing was a profound act of rebellion against Father and an unbeatable form of competition with Austin: in the matter of authorship, *she* intended to win unquestioned ascendancy" (130).

When Wolff employs the term "self" in discussing Dickinson's life, she uses the term in a general-purpose, non-technical sense. A couple of noteworthy exceptions occur in the passage quoted above when Wolff writes about Dickinson's discovery of "a secret, privileged inner self that could observe life to analyze and criticize with complete safety," and when, more particularly, she mentions a *sequestered* self shortly thereafter: "Dickinson's poetry apotheosizes this central human paradox: the poignant, inevitable isolation of each human being—the loneliness and the yearning to be seen, acknowledged, and known—on the one hand; on the other, the gleeful satisfaction in keeping one part of the self sequestered, sacred, uniquely powerful, and utterly inviolate—the incomparable safety in retaining a secret part of the 'self' that is available to no one save self" (130). At this point in her book Wolff draws directly on the psychoanalytic model of selfhood presented by Winnicott in a paper about communication. The most essential passage reads,

> I suggest that in health there is a core to the personality that corresponds to the true self of the split personality; I suggest that this core never communicates with the world of perceived objects, and that the individual person knows that it must never be communicated with or be influenced by external reality. . . . Although healthy persons communicate and enjoy communicating, the other fact is equally true, that [at the core of] *each individual is an isolate* [entity], *permanently non-communicating, permanently unknown,* in fact unfound. . . . At the centre of each person is an incommunicado element, and this is sacred and most worthy of preservation. . . . Traumatic experiences that lead to the organization of primitive defences belong to the threat to the isolated core, the threat of its being found, altered, communicated with. The defence consists in a further hiding of the secret self. . . . Rape and being eaten by cannibals, these are mere bagatelles as compared with the violation of the self's core, the alteration of the self's central elements by communication seeping through the defences. (1963, 187)

Readers familiar with Winnicott's other work (as Wolff gives no sign of being; she cites only this one paper, only at this point in her book) will realize at once that the ideas mentioned derive in part from the rather special conception of selfhood, presented three years earlier by Winnicott

(1960), in the form of the dichotomous model he calls the True and False Self. These readers may also notice that the-self-with-a-hidden-core is predicated on what is understood to be an unintegrated, pathological personality structure (the hidden core, as he says, corresponding to the true self "of the split personality"). There are certain difficulties and inconsistencies here. To begin with, Winnicott generalizes a model derived from a primitive defense (splitting) in a way that makes its key feature representative for all individuals, that is, these noncommunicating cores lurk at the center of even healthy persons. Is this a universal paradox, as he implies, or simply a contradiction in his conceptualization? A related contradiction crops up on the next page of his paper when Winnicott reminds his readers that normal ego development, including a sense of reality, depends on "communicating with subjective phenomena," meaning subjective objects, including interpersonal communication (1960, 188); this position implies that the absence of communication and interaction is unhealthy, so why should a healthy self possess a secretive, noncommunicating core?

The term "core" presents two obstacles to creating an acceptable model of selfhood: mythical centeredness and misplaced concreteness. When Winnicott speaks of the danger of "the violation of the self's core," for example, this reifying statement differs radically from speaking, more abstractly, of an experience that violates an individual's senses of security, self-esteem, and identity (assuming "identity" to be an operational term implying systemic integrity). The most serious deficiency of Winnicott's assumptions about a precious, sacred, secret "core" of selfhood that "must never be communicated with or be influenced by external reality" can be understood in the light of the more dyadic model of self-development exemplified by Stern's discussion (1985, 101–11) of what he calls "we-experiences," which are essentially shared, joyful, and authentic experiences. The problem is that when Wolff buys into Winnicott's assumptions about a secret-self core, she purchases more than she bargains for.

The valuable elements of Wolff's application of Winnicott's model are not represented by her references to a *secret, inner* self, or to what she calls the "central human paradox" of the *"inevitable isolation* of each human being—the *loneliness"* of a self that is *"utterly inviolate. . . available to no one"* save the self itself. The valuable elements of Wolff's application of the model lie in her emphasis on a *privileged* self that can *observe* self and society "with complete *safety."* This is a *sequestered* self but not a totally disengaged, isolated one. It is a self "yearning to be seen, acknowledged, and known"—and succeeding! When I say "succeeding" I mean succeeding artistically in communicating with the world of her imagined audience. Dickinson's self is not a secret one "available to no one save herself." On the contrary, she enjoys access to all aspects of her personality and she manages, magnificently, to share these aspects of herself with her audience. We need to understand that *sequestration* is a means to the end of enabling her to compose poetry (essentially an individual task as distinguished from an emotionally isolated one). It provides her with a tranquil "potential space" where she can make contacts with those aspects of her self and her relationships with important others by no means readily negotiated, at least by her, in ordinary social space. The prototype for this kind of playful, creative activity, as Winnicott, Mahler, and others tell us, is the sequestered playspace children find when they feel secure by virtue of the presence or nearness of their mothers—a secure space mature artists may be said to have internalized. As Winnicott well knew, emotional isolation does not engender creativity. The way that children learn to tolerate being alone—alone enough to play creatively—is in the presence of their mothers: "Thus the basis of the capacity to be alone is a paradox; it is the experience of being alone while someone else is present" (1958, 30).

This is not to say that Dickinson never feels degrees of loneliness and emotional deprivation as a result, in part, of her chosen path, but only that "Deprived of other Banquet," she entertains herself. As poem #777 reveals, she fears loneliness, as we all do:

The Loneliness One dare not sound—
And would as soon surmise
As in its Grave go plumbing
To ascertain the size—.

She fears

The Horror not to be surveyed—
But skirted in the Dark—
With Consciousness suspended—
And Being under Lock—.

But she recognizes that this loneliness has different potentials, one being ultimate isolation, perhaps that of madness, and the other that of *illumination,* or soul-making:

I fear me this—is Loneliness—
The Maker of the soul
Its Caverns and its Corridors
Illuminate—or seal—.

(#777)

By staying at home—in deliberate, measured isolation from others but
not from family—she creates a privileged abode characterized by imagination, beauty, and voluntary access to the outer world; at the same time,
this world is sheltered and secure:

I dwell in Possibility—
A Fairer House than Prose—
More numerous of Windows—
Superior—for Doors—

Of Chambers as the Cedars—
Impregnable of Eye—
And for an Everlasting Roof
The Gambrels of the Sky—.

(#657)

As for Dickinson's so-called agoraphobia, it should be remembered
that in her youth she was nothing if not sociable and outgoing; that she
was never, at any time in her life, intellectually isolated from the world of
culture; that the onset of her reclusiveness was gradual, as Lavinia stresses;
that her eye trouble may have been a contributing factor in causing her to
avoid people; that she did not isolate herself from members of her immediate family; that even in her forties she was attractive enough as a woman
to receive a proposal of marriage from the eminent Judge Otis Lord; and
that even in her late years she maintained significant emotional contact,
mainly through correspondence, with people who continued to be important to her.

The contact was important but so was the distance. In the same letter
in which she wrote to Higginson, in her humble yet queenly way, "Could
it please your convenience to come so far as Amherst I should be very
glad, but I do not cross my Father's ground to any House in town," she
also wrote, "A letter always feels to me like immortality because it is the
mind alone without corporeal friend" (*Letters* 2: 460). Distanced relationships maintained through written communication allow her the security
of her chamber and at the same time enable her to be more at liberty,
more spontaneous, more herself than she could manage face to face. An
early hint of this preference appears in a chatty letter to her brother

written when she is twenty: "We miss you more and more, we do not become accustomed to separation from you. . . . and then again I think that it is pleasant to miss you if you must go away, and I would not have it otherwise, not even if I could" (*Letters* 1: 160–61). What appears to be a simple contradiction or a masochistic desire, superficially considered, may in fact reveal a form of object-relational behavior evolving from the early emotional distancing from her mother, the connection-at-a-distance with Aunt Lavinia, the distanced intimacy of her experience of living with an emotionally remote father, and the experience of many other situations, known and unknown, such as the frequent experience of losing friends and relatives by death (with astonishing frequency), the "loss" of people she felt close to in her youth who moved away from Amherst, sometimes because of matrimony, and the sense of losing suitors, whether because of their apathy or her ambivalence. Separation and loss become major themes in her poetry, as in "My life closed twice before its close—" (#1732), which ends grimly:

> Parting is all we know of heaven,
> And all we need of hell.

Yet closeness could be suffocating, as this note to Susan Gilbert Dickinson implies: "I must wait a few Days before seeing you—You are too momentous. But remember it is idolatry, not indifference" (*Letters* 2: 631).

Wolff helps us to understand some of the biographical coordinates of the theme of distance in Dickinson's life and art. Instead of matrimony "she embraced the vocation of poet and took up battle with the Lord. . . . She chose *words* rather than people as her ultimate source of comfort, and she valued the creation of a permanent, unchanging Voice over the shifting, unpredictable relationships that make up a varied ordinary life. Instead of descendants, she would have readers" (1986, 386). Wolff points out that Dickinson's love poetry builds on separation: "The same poetry that postulates marriage as the ideal also accepts as a given that this 'marriage' can never take place. It is not that the lovers are joined only to discover that they are unhappy together; rather, two lovers, perfectly matched and deeply in love, are not permitted to remain together" (387). Absence, or distance, appears to be an "enabling virtue" in her relationships (390). "Deep affection for anyone outside the immediate family and passionate love both"—even for Judge Lord—"necessarily entail separation" (404).

* * *

Dickinson remarks that as a child she was "always attached to Mud, because of what it typifies—also, perhaps, a Child's tie to primeval Pies" (*Letters* 2: 576). When she graduated from making mud pies to creating poems, she continued to make an investment of self in her creations. To be sound, the investments had to possess psychological integrity:

> The Soul unto itself
> Is an imperial friend—
> Or the most agonizing Spy—
> An Enemy—could send—
>
> Secure against its own—
> No treason it can fear—
> Itself—its Sovereign—of itself
> The Soul should stand in Awe—.

(#683)

One mark of the consistency of the psychological integrity of self exhibited in these poems is that she holds nothing back—not in any of the poems that matter. There is nothing essentially hidden or secret in her poetic representations of self and other.

Of the handful of poems especially illuminating with regard to Dickinson's use of her self as an object that remain to be discussed, the two "Dollie poems" possess psychological interest as illustrations of transitional phenomena. Emily, at the age of twenty, alludes to a doll in the context of separation when she writes to Austin about how much she misses him. After concocting a playful fantasy about waiting for him at the gate, she writes, "If I hadn't been afraid that you would 'poke fun' at my feelings, I had written a *sincere* letter, but since the 'world is hollow, and Dollie is stuffed with sawdust,' I really do not think we had better expose our feelings" (*Letters* 1: 112). The first Dollie poem raises the question of the fidelity of the subjective object's attachment to the articulating self:

> You love me—you are sure—
> I shall not fear mistake—
> I shall not *cheated* wake—
> Some grinning morn—
> To find the Sunrise left—
> An Orchards—unbereft—
> And Dollie—gone!

I need not start—you're sure—
That night will never be—
When frightened—home to Thee I run—
To find the windows dark—
And no more Dollie—mark—
Quite none?

(#156)

The final stanza admonishes Dollie to "Be sure you're sure" and, if not, to tell her now. The other Dollie poem, written from the perspective of a child dying in a state of great anxiety, stresses the sense of security Dollie's presence will insure:

Dying? Dying in the night!
Won't somebody bring the light
So I can see which way to go
Into the everlasting snow?

And "Jesus"? Where is *Jesus* gone?
They said that Jesus—always came—
Perhaps he doesn't know the House—
This way, Jesus, Let him pass!

Somebody run to the great gate
And see if Dollie's coming! Wait!
I hear her feet upon the stair!
Death won't hurt—now Dollie's here!

(#158)

The psychological interest of the next poem lies in Dickinson's imaginative identification with the caretaking role of Mother Nature:

Nature—the Gentlest Mother is,
Impatient of no Child—
The feeblest—or the waywardest—
Her Admonition mild—.

(#790)

This idealized portrait of a maternalized nature concludes, after two intervening stanzas:

Her Voice among the Aisles
Incite the timid prayer
Of the minutest Cricket—
To most unworthy Flower—

When all the Children sleep—
She turns as long away
As will suffice to light Her lamps—
Then bending from the Sky—

With infinite Affection—
And infiniter Care—
Her Golden finger on Her lip—
Wills Silence—Everywhere—.

If the psychological relationship of self to environment does possess the object-relational valency attributed to it in the previous chapter, then Dickinson's attachment to, and identification with, a natural environment perceived as responsive and protecting, as in the poem above, contradicts the absoluteness of her claim to Higginson, "I never had a mother" (*Letters* 2: 475). While her easy, tonic identifications with emblematic creatures, such as robins and hummingbirds, exhibit a range of emotional states, they are generally positive and sometimes even ecstatic in their representation of the creatures' experience of their natural environment, as in,

I taste a liquor never brewed—
From Tankards scooped in Pearl—
Not all the Vats upon the Rhine
Yield such an Alcohol!

Inebriate of Air—am I—
And Debauchee of Dew—
Reeling—thro endless summer days—
From inns of Molten blue—.

(#214)

The more austere vision of selfhood exhibited in the following poem shows another, probably more representative, side of Dickinson:

I think the Hemlock likes to stand
Upon a Marge of Snow—
It suits his own Austerity—
And satisfies an awe

That men, must slake in Wilderness—
And in the Desert—cloy—
An instinct for the Hoar, the Bald—
Lapland's—necessity—

The Hemlock's nature thrives—on cold—
The Gnash of Northern winds
Is sweetest nutriment—to—him—
His best Norwegian Wines—.

(#525)

This and the previously quoted poems feature identifications by the poet with plants and creatures of the natural environment. The poetic renderings of these identifications can be understood, object-relationally, as *handlings* of aspects of self that reflect earlier relational experiences in the sense articulated by Bollas: "Our handling of our self as an object partly inherits and expresses the history of our experience as the parental object [as the parent's object], so that in each adult it is appropriate to say that certain forms of self perception, self facilitation, self handling, and self refusal express the internalized parental process still engaged in the activity of handling the self as an object" (1987, 51).

In Dickinson's poetry these "handlings" are various in tone: sometimes peaceful, sometimes ecstatic, sometimes triumphant, often austere. And often agonized, as in "I like a look of Agony,/Because I know it's true—" (#241). And often numb, as in "Pain—has an Element of Blank" (#650). These poems may also be regarded as exemplifying manifestations of what Bollas calls "the aesthetic moment," which he thinks of as involving "an evocative resurrection of an early ego condition often brought on by a sudden and uncanny rapport with an object, a moment when the subject is captured in an intense illusion of being selected by the environment for some deeply reverential experience. . . . It is a pre-verbal, essentially pre-representational registration of the mother's presence" (1987, 39). The term "aesthetic moment" presumably applies both to the poet's exercise of the creative process and the reader's experience of literary work.

Richard Chase remarks that what interests Dickinson most is "the achievement of status through crucial experiences" (1951, 121), the achievement, by undergoing pain, of the exalted status of Queen of Calvary, for instance. Perhaps the most remarkable group of her poems exhibiting the theme of exalted status revolves around the achievement of some form of immortality by the process of dying, as in "I felt a Funeral, in my Brain" (#280), "I died for Beauty" (#449), "I heard a Fly buzz—when I died—" (#465), and "Because I could not stop for Death" (#712). References to eternity and immortality often remain ambiguous in such poems in that they presumably refer to artistic as well as spiritual immortality. In any case, the transformation from the precarious state of life into the more stable state involving a permanent relation to God may be understood to represent, in terms of psychobiography, Emily's achievement of recognition by her father, certainly, and perhaps by her mother as well—the achievement of immortality as a poet being a permutation of this need to be recognized by important others.

Dickinson discovered that the path to her complex experience of recognition ran through the woods of sequestration. Freud would have thought that path a highly overdetermined one. In terms of a contemporary paradigm, it was not so much overdetermined as highly *probable* that an individual in Dickinson's circumstances would learn to make a virtue of emotional distance and psychological autonomy. Deprived of other banquet, she entertained herself. She did so by writing poems. She persisted until her initially "insufficient Loaf" had "grown by slender addings" to "so esteemed a size" that it became "sumptuous" enough for her —and a feast for posterity.

8.

SELF AND OTHER IN SHAKESPEAREAN TRAGEDY

Sometimes many are one in dreams and other works of the imagination. Angus Fletcher suggests that "the allegorical hero is not so much a person as he is a generator of other personalities [that] are partial aspects of himself. . . . By analyzing the projections we determine what is going on in the mind of the highly imaginative projector" (1964, 35). If readers want to understand Redcrosse in *The Faerie Queene,* for example, they can list the tests and adventures—essentially the other figures encountered—"so as to see, literally, what aspects of the hero have been displayed" (35–36). The related phenomenon of "doubles" in literature, that is, when two or more characters represent a psychological whole, has often been discussed along psychoanalytic lines (Rogers 1970). Thinking about fragmentations of self and other along semiotic lines, which assumes that the most important signifying unit in art is the text itself, the whole work being a supersign composed of a hierarchy of lesser sign elements (Lotman 1977; Riffaterre 1978), also leads naturally to the theoretical possibility that important characters in literary works often represent aspects of a single self, a self that may be designated holistically in the title of the work.

It will be convenient to assume three working hypotheses, one literary and two psychological, during the following exploration of configurations of self and other in *Hamlet, Othello, Macbeth,* and *Lear.* First, in each of these plays the essential intactness, or wholeness, or psychological integrity of the titular hero at the beginning of each narrative can be thought of as breaking up into constellations of self and other that enact through the medium of interpersonal relationships the predispositions to conflict present in a single personality. Thus Hamlet, for example, as a character *in* the play, represents both the composite (titular) Hamlet and a component thereof (the unconsciously rebellious oedipal son guilty of wishing his father dead), while Laertes can be regarded as another aspect of the composite (the loyal, uncritical son quick to take revenge for his father's death). Second, these tragedies can be regarded as revolving around the deep-seated depression or anxiety each protagonist experiences as a result of some form of separation or loss. Third, "when the loved figure is believed to be temporarily absent the response is one of anxiety, [and] when he or she appears to be permanently absent it is one of pain and mourning" (Bowlby, 1980, 27). Hamlet's loss is evident, his depression manifest. Othello, to the extent that he loves "not wisely but too well," may be said to love anxiously in a story where anxiety about possible loss ironically brings about actual loss. The intensity of the anxiety Macbeth displays can be regarded as deriving not so much from fear and guilt concerning Duncan's murder as from "loss" taking the form of counterfeit nurture and maternal aggression. And the story of King Lear dramatizes, with greater profundity than any in literature perhaps, the disastrous psychological effects of loss taking the form of abandonment.

As I present fresh interpretations of these representative Shakespearean tragedies, I shall have occasion to revise some of my own earlier readings in order to emphasize the greater degree of illumination that can be derived from a person-oriented theory of object relations.

How well does Freud's drive-oriented theory of the oedipus complex illuminate the dynamics of *Hamlet?* One reason why Hamlet seems so oedipal is that Freud explicitly mentions *Hamlet* when he formulates his theory of the oedipus complex, first in a letter to Fliess (1954, 227) and later in *The Interpretation of Dreams* (1900: 261–66), so that in a sense the theory can be said to be based on *both* the Oedipus myth and Shakespeare's play. For Freud there is not much difference between the Oedipus Complex and the Hamlet Complex except that Oedipus literally consummates incest with his mother, however unintentionally, whereas Hamlet represses his incestuous desire. And Oedipus literally kills Laius whereas Hamlet only symbolically murders his father when he kills Polonius and Claudius. In any case, Freud's oedipal reading of *Hamlet,* including the elaborations of it by Jones (1949) and many others, has been so influential that it constitutes a necessary point of departure for alternative readings.

When I discussed the topic of Hamlet's losses in an earlier paper (Rogers, 1982), much of my commentary addressed sexual factors germane to the standard oedipal interpretation. I even went so far as to argue that if words heard from the stage signify every bit as much as actions performed on the stage, and if the images of ears and daggers in the text of the play acquire vaginal and penile connotations *in this text,* then Hamlet can be said symbolically to commit incest with his mother when he speaks daggers to her in her bedroom: "I will speak daggers to her, but use none." Part of this speech involves his elaborate, almost masochistic rehearsal of the sexual crimes he charges her with:

> Nay, but to live
> In the rank sweat of an enseamèd bed,
> Stewed in corruption, honeying and making love
> Over the nasty sty—.
>
> (3.4.92–95).

Gertrude's plea for mercy ("O, speak to me no more./These words like daggers enter in mine ears") constitutes both an admission of her guilt and a sign, to the audience, that Hamlet has penetrated the portals of her body with his erotically charged language.

Instead of accentuating the sexual overtones of this scene, my present inclination is to emphasize the rage expressed by Hamlet's daggered speech while treating the erotic elements as adultomorphic permutations of an earlier and fundamentally nonerotic, nonincestuous set of feelings and needs. Considered in this perspective, a line like "Frailty, thy name is woman," while it obviously refers to sexual fidelity in adult relationships, can be seen to exhibit attachment concerns underlying the oedipal phase. In this view Hamlet's angry feelings toward his mother, Claudius, Polonius, and Ophelia stem not from reexcited yet frustrated *libidinal* impulses but from his profound sense of loss because of the death of his father; from the loss—just when he needs her most—of the internalized good mother, a loss resulting from Gertrude's transformation in Hamlet's mind into someone no better than a whore; and from the psychologically comparable loss of Ophelia because of Polonius's edict. There is also the temporary loss of his birthright, the crown, to Claudius (loss of the role of ruler being the loss of an aspect of the internalized good father). What makes it all so wrenching is that Hamlet's very selfhood partly disintegrates as a consequence of his object losses, as Ophelia tells us when she laments: "O, what a noble mind is here o'erthrown!"

Besides serving in part as a model for the oedipus complex, Hamlet also functions as a model for melancholia. Freud mentions only one individual in "Mourning and Melancholia" (1917), other than the analysts he cites, and that is Hamlet. Hamlet furnishes Freud the model for an individual who redirects toward himself the reproaches he unconsciously directs toward the lost object who is perceived as an abandoning object. The result, says Freud, is that loss of the object becomes transformed into an "ego loss" as the conflict between the ego and the loved person becomes transformed into "a cleavage between the critical activity of the ego and the ego as altered by identification [with the lost object]" (249)—transformations Freud accounts for in terms of libidinal dynamics. "If the love for the object—a love which cannot be given up though the object itself is given up—takes refuge in narcissistic identification, then the hate comes into operation on this substitutive object, abusing it, debasing it, making it suffer and deriving sadistic satisfaction from its suffering" (251). According to Freud, "the melancholic's erotic cathexis in regard to his object has thus undergone a double vicissitude: part of it has regressed to identification, but the other part . . . has been carried back to the stage of sadism. . . . It is this sadism alone that solves the riddle of the tendency to suicide which makes melancholia so interesting —and so dangerous" (251–52). Although Freud does not mention in "Mourning and Melancholia" the probable connection between Shakespeare's loss of his father shortly before writing *Hamlet* and the theme of the loss of fathers in the play, Freud does make much of this conjunction in his discussion of the play in *The Interpretation of Dreams*.

Sharpe (1929) picks up on this connection in her discussion of splitting in *Hamlet*. She assumes that the conflicts in the play reconstitute elements of conflict in the author's mind so that "in externalizing the introjected objects in dramatic form," Shakespeare experiences something like a catharsis of these introjects:

> The poet is not Hamlet. Hamlet is what he might have been if he had not written the play of *Hamlet*. The characters are all introjections thrown out again from his mind. He is the murdered majesty of Denmark, he is the murdered Claudius, he is the Queen, Gertrude, and Ophelia. He is Hamlet. . . .He has ejected all of them symbolically and remains a sane man, through sublimation that satisfies the demands of the super-ego and the impulses of the id. (205)

Sharpe makes no distinction here between the splitting of self and the splitting of other, which is understandable enough, given her emphasis. That Freud makes no such distinction in his discussion of splitting in melancholia seems rather more surprising. Freud concentrates on subjective splitting, a splitting of the ego, as he refers to it, an idea that will lead him in due course to his formulation of the superego. It does not occur to him—in spite of the fact that he has Hamlet in mind—that a splitting of the *object* might also be one of the consequences in mourning. In short, it does not occur to him that the work of mourning needs to be talked about in terms of the splitting of *both* self and other. For that one must turn to Melanie Klein.

Even Klein does not make a direct connection between splitting of the object and the work of mourning, but the connection is indirectly implied in various ways in her work. Whenever grief arises, writes Klein, "it undermines the feeling of secure possession of the loved internal objects, for it revives the early anxieties about injured and destroyed objects" (1952a, 217). Thus mourning involves "a repetition of the emotional situation the infant experiences during the depressive position" (218) when the infant struggles to reconcile good with bad internalized objects. This is when ambivalence sets in. "Ambivalence, carried out in a splitting of the imagos, enables the small child to gain more trust and belief in its real objects and thus in its internalized ones" (Klein 1940, 132). How does ambivalence *enable* the child to do what is in part the work of mourning? Ambivalence does so by facilitating a process that is incremental rather than sudden:

> It seems that at this stage of development the unification of external and internal, loved and hated, real and imaginary objects is carried out in such a way that each step in the unification leads again to a renewed splitting of the imagos. But as the adaption to the external world increases, this splitting is carried out on planes which gradually become increasingly nearer and nearer to reality. This goes on until love for the real and the internalized objects and trust in them are well established. (132)

What can be said about adult experience of loss in view of Klein's ideas is that real loss inevitably reactivates the processes of what Klein calls the depressive position, including object splitting, idealization, and "omnipotent phantasies, both the destructive and the reparative ones" (131).

Applied to Shakespeare, virtually all of the text of *Hamlet* exhibits a complex set of splittings (idealizations and denigrations): a set of omnipotent fantasies eventuating in the destruction of self and other—except, of course, that young Fortinbras, who succeeds Hamlet, can be read as an aspect of Hamlet himself. Shakespeare responds to the loss of his father in part by generating a radically split pair of paternal imagos, the gist of his fantasy being: "I must destroy my bad father in order to revenge [make reparation to] my good father [for the hatred I feel toward him for leaving me]." But because the genre is tragedy, this and other splittings rush toward disaster instead of leading toward reconciliation and integration. Paralleling in *Hamlet* the splitting of the psychological father into an idealized figure and his evil counterpart ("so excellent a king, that was to this/Hyperion to a satyr"), and into a beloved and comic Yorick versus a scorned and ridiculous Polonius, is the splitting of maternal figures: the mother who "would hang on him [Hamlet senior]/As if increase of appetite had grown/By what it fed on" as compared to the faithless, shameless, lecherous matron Hamlet attacks in the bedroom scene. To mention but one of the many subjective splits discernible in the play, one notes the disjunction between the "noble mind" of the courtier-soldier-scholar passionately dedicated to his father's call for revenge and the mental turmoil of the "rogue and peasant slave," an "ass," who "must like a whore unpack [his] heart with words/And fall a-cursing like a very drab" instead of taking action. It is the rogue and peasant slave who compares his own mourning so unfavorably to that of the actor who merely imitates grief:

> Tears in his eyes, distraction in his aspect,
> A broken voice, and his whole function suiting
> With forms to his conceit? And all for nothing,
> For Hecuba!
> What's Hecuba to him, or he to Hecuba,
> That he should weep for her?
>
> (2.2.539–44)

If loss is so crucial to understanding the psychology of *Hamlet,* how far does that assumption go toward explaining Hamlet's delay in executing revenge on Claudius, a problem the Freudian interpretation solves with great economy by attributing it to Hamlet's unconscious identification with Claudius as an oedipal criminal? It is worth noting in this regard that the first thing Hamlet accuses his mother of—well before he has heard from the ghost—is her failure to mourn long enough:

> O God, a beast that wants discourse of reason
> Would have mourned longer.
>
> (1.2.150–51)

There is a sense in which Gertrude stands for Hamlet here. So short a period has passed since the death of his father that Hamlet himself has had insufficient time to perform the labor of mourning, the difficulty of which, in his case, is commensurate with the depth of his unconscious ambivalence toward the psychological father that is dramatized throughout the play. The mere "trappings and the suits of woe" do not help much in performing this arduous labor:

> 'Tis not alone my inky cloak, good mother,
> Nor customary suits of solemn black,
> Nor windy suspiration of forced breath,
> No, nor the fruitful river in the eye,
> Nor the dejected havior of the visage,
> Together with all forms, moods, shapes of grief,
> That can denote me truly. These indeed seem,
> For they are actions that a man might play,
> But I have that within which passeth show—
> These but the trappings and the suits of woe.
>
>   (1.2.77–86).

What Hamlet needs above all is time to deal with that within which passeth show, time for working through his grief, which is exactly what he does not have when the cascading events represented in the play begin. In his discussion of mourning Bowlby repeatedly emphasizes that one of the most important factors in handling loss is the prolonged duration of the mourning process, even in normal as distinguished from abnormal mourning (1980, 8, 10, 100–103, 130). And as Freud so well understood, what is so painful about mourning is that it is always conflictful. Loss begets hatred toward *the abandoning other* before the work of mourning can eventuate in a benign internalization of *the departed other*. It may therefore be that Hamlet's delay in taking revenge, a delay he himself experiences as intolerable, corresponds in part to the time-consuming restructuring of representations of self and other that the mourning process requires of us.

Loss begets anger at the lost object. This anger takes the irrational form of wishing for the death of the lost object, a wish that gives rise, in turn, to fear of losing the precious object, a fear at odds with the impulse to destroy that object, thereby creating an unconscious conflict that produces the kinds of inaction and deflected action—such as play-acting— that constitute the very stuff and matrix of the play, not just with regard to Hamlet and his father-surrogates but also with respect to his relationship with his "lost" mother and the "lost" Ophelia. In other words, this reading attributes Hamlet's indecision both to the *conflict* involved in mourning his losses—the oedipal conflict between warring impulses being a spinoff of that process—and to the *time* required to deal with that conflict. Hamlet devotes much of the time required for working through his conflicts to verbalizing them. For Hamlet, words are both an expression of the problem and a solution to the problem. With words he creates the idealized good object ("See what a grace was seated on his brow:/ Hyperion's curls, the front of Jove himself,/An eye like Mars, to threaten and command") and the denigrated bad object (Claudius is "a mildewed ear"). Hamlet's omnipotence of thought becomes omnipotence of speech: "A man may fish with the worm that hath eat of a king, and eat of the fish that hath fed of that worm." The Prince of Wordplayers plays with words transferentially, as transitional objects, showing us, in this instance, "how a king may go a progress through the guts of a beggar," that is, showing us the bad object (Claudius) reduced to feces from a beggar's bowels.

A reading of *Hamlet* stressing loss differs markedly though not completely from the traditional, incest-oriented, mainly oedipal interpretation of Freud. What it offers is another kind of Freudian reading, the object-relational one partly implicit in but not elaborated on in "Mourning and Melancholy."

Like *Hamlet, Othello* can profitably be viewed as a macrosign within which Othello and other characters in the play represent components of a complex set of conflicting inclinations symbolized by the titular hero. A number of commentators notice that Othello and Iago appear to be differing aspects of the same person, an hypothesis that explains how a deeply jealous person who believes his wife has been unfaithful (Iago) can so readily convince "one not easily jealous" (as Othello describes himself) that Desdemona has been cheating on him. Among the commentators, James Joyce has Stephen Dedalus say of Shakespeare, "in *Othello* he is bawd and cuckold. . . . His unremitting intellect is the hornmad Iago ceaselessly willing that the moor in him shall suffer" (1934, 219). And F. R. Leavis contends that the source of Iago's power over Othello comes from representing something in Othello: "The essential traitor is within the gates" (1937, 264).

During the course of developing this line of interpretation further (Rogers 1969), I have suggested, among other things, that Cassio also functions as a component of the Othello Complex. Much of that argument hinges on a demonstration that male figures in the play subscribe to the sexual double standard by either idealizing or denigrating women. As for Cassio, I point out that Shakespeare allows him an overelaborate verbiage in speaking of Desdemona that Cassio does not ordinarily use elsewhere in the play—one distinctly artificial as compared to Othello's sublime yet controlled praise of Desdemona—such as the hyperbolical speech with which Cassio announces Desdemona's arrival in Cyprus:

> Tempests themselves, high seas, and howling winds,
> The guttered rocks and congregated sands,
> Traitors ensteeped to clog the guiltless keel,
> As having sense of beauty, do omit
> Their mortal natures, letting go safely by
> The divine Desdemona.
>
> (2.1.68–73).

Cassio gives further evidence of his idealization of women during Iago's futile attempts to arouse in Cassio an erotic interest in Desdemona. When Iago speculates about how voluptuous Desdemona must be in bed, Cassio, the perfect gentleman, responds primly with polite compliments about the "exquisite lady." Yet Cassio has his whore. He laughs about Bianca's passion for him when Iago mentions the possibility of marriage: "I marry her? What, a customer? Prithee bear some charity to my wit; do not think it so unwholesome."

I argue that this division of female objects present in so exaggerated a way in Cassio can be discerned in Othello as well, in both subtle and extreme forms. In this connection I note that Kirshbaum calls Othello a romantic idealist who overvalues Desdemona: "He loves not Desdemona but his image of her" (1944, 292). In contrast to Othello's inclination to see Desdemona as either a saint or a whore, Shakespeare presents her to the audience as lovely and devoted but at the same time as a real and hence fallible human being, one who prevaricates about losing the handkerchief when straightforwardness might have saved her, and who somewhat basely begs for her life as Othello is about to kill her ("Kill me tomorrow; let me live tonight"). I then go on to claim that the play as a whole enacts the endopsychic drama of a composite Othello whose principal components can be understood as a Psychotic Othello, personified by Iago, who can experience neither affection nor lust except in perverted form; a Romantic Othello, a refined, sensitive, idealistic person whose impulses in these respects are exaggerated in Cassio; and a Normal Othello, a man more gifted than the average, but normal and healthy psychologically in that he possesses control ("Keep up your bright swords, for the dew will rust them"), awareness of reality, and self-respect. This is the "noble Moor whom our full senate/Call all in all sufficient," the man "whom passion could not shake." He is good and trusting, "of a free and open nature/That thinks men honest that but seem to be so." He is a manly, masculine man, a more or less integrated, sensual man who under ordinary circumstances can combine the currents of affection and lust.

One of the revisions I would like to impose on my earlier reading of the play has to do with the motivation of Iago. My earlier assessment of him was based upon the interpretations of Wangh (1950) and Smith (1959). They regard Iago as a paranoid personality suffering from repressed homosexuality who unknowingly perceives Desdemona as a rival for the love of Othello, an interpretation depending heavily on the views about paranoia, especially in regard to delusional jealousy, that Freud expounds in the Schreber case. Diagnosing Iago as a psychotic of the paranoid type (his suspicions about Emilia are quite literally delusional) still makes sense to me, but Freud's claim about the etiology of paranoia in repressed homosexual impulses no longer holds up. Besides that, Wangh's idea that Iago's interpersonal relationship with Othello represents an *object* relation, however unconsciously, does not jibe with the view that theirs is a *subject* relation (as components of a divided self). What defines the relationship of Othello and Iago, as I thought all along but did not understand clearly enough before, has to do with the differing ways they relate to women.

Another revision I would like to impose on my earlier reading is to shift the emphasis of the relation of men to women in the play from a focus on adult interpersonal relations, especially sexual relations, to a concentration on the early needs and structures those adult permutations reflect. As part of that shift I would pay more attention to the pre-oedipal features of Desdemona's function as a maternal surrogate in contrast to my earlier discussion of the idealization of sexual purity in women as it relates to the oedipal son's false attribution of sexual purity to his mother. I wrote earlier, "One trifle light as air, the handkerchief, tends to confirm because of its history and multiple symbolism that Desdemona enjoys the natural position of being a surrogate of Othello's mother" (Rogers, 1969, 213). In addition, I would now call attention to the obviously maternal cast of Desdemona's lines as she defends the insistence of her suit to Othello to restore Cassio to his former position:

> Why, this is not a boon;
> 'Tis as I should entreat you wear your gloves,
> Or feed on nourishing dishes, or keep you warm,

Or sue to you to do a peculiar profit
To your person.

(3.3.76–80)

I would point especially to the psychological overtones of the part-object and whole-object imagery of a speech in which Othello appears to equate the integrity of his faith in Desdemona with the place of his earliest origin, the person/breast/womb/vagina he refers to as the "fountain" from which his current runs and from which he cannot stand to be displaced:

> But there where I have garnered up my heart,
> Where either I must live or bear no life,
> The fountain from which my current runs
> Or else dries up—to be discarded thence,
> Or keep it as a cistern for foul toads
> To knot and gender in—.

(4.2.57–62)

These possibilities he cannot bear.

Considered in the context of separation anxiety, Othello's fear of being abandoned appears to be expressed in an especially significant way elsewhere in the play. "She's gone," he says when he begins to believe his fears:

> Haply, for I am black
> And have not those soft parts of conversation
> That chamberers have, or for I am declined
> Into the vale of years—yet that's not much—
> She's gone. I am abused, and my relief
> Must be to loathe her.

(3.3.263–68).

The passage "She's gone. I am abused" treats Desdemona's imagined sexual departure metaphorically as a departure in space. It is precisely the correct metaphor for expressing the literal departure in space that can generate so much anxiety in young children, especially in children already made into anxiously clinging ones because of prior experiences of their mothers' departures—the point being not to insinuate that Othello is childlike but rather to illuminate the origin of the emotional value he attaches to Desdemona's sustaining presence as represented in the play by her faithfulness.

According to this line of thinking, one can scarcely overestimate the psychological importance of the otherwise minor scene of Othello's reunion with Desdemona after their separation during the sea voyage—a

scene that falls so naturally into the story's sequence of events as to excite
comparatively little notice. Shakespeare does not tell us that this separation made Othello anxious, at least not directly. What he does tell us
about is Othello's joy at being reunited with Desdemona:

> It gives me wonder great as my content
> To see you here before me. O my soul's joy!
> If after every tempest come such calms,
> May the winds blow till they have wakened death!
> And let the laboring bark climb hills of seas
> Olympus-high, and duck again as low
> As hell's from heaven! If it were now to die,
> 'Twere now to be most happy; for I fear
> My soul hath her content so absolute
> That not another comfort like to this
> Succeeds in unknown fate.

> (2.1.181–88)

This representation of separation from and reunion with a maternal figure
in the narrative present of the play reinforces the idea that Othello's "loss"
of Desdemona later in the play re-enacts at the deepest levels of his being
some prior, painful separation from his mother as a child, an experience
of separation that led him to become an anxiously clinging, jealous man
in the field of love even though he is an otherwise stable, confident man,
one well able to tolerate deprivations and travails of all kinds on the
"flinty and steel couch of war." If Klein is to any degree correct about
idealization being a defense against persecution anxiety (1957, 193), then
Othello's proneness to idealize his wife as the "cunning'st pattern of
excelling nature" and as a heavenly creature ("If she be false, O, then
heaven mocks itself!") serves to defend him against the persecutions
imagined by Iago. The Iago part of him defends in an alternative way by
externalizing the danger, that is, by projecting the jealousy onto someone
else. It never works, of course, because, as Leavis says, the essential traitor
remains within the gates.

Whereas Hamlet reacts to actual loss by mourning rather than with
anxiety, and Othello responds to the threat of loss by becoming anxious,
Macbeth, who at the outset of the story seemingly faces gains rather than
losses, may in fact be seen to experience a special kind of object-relational
threat, one that generates in him a maddening anxiety. Macbeth experiences a paradoxical form of loss: loss of the other in the presence of the
other. I describe his loss at the beginning of this chapter as deriving

primarily from counterfeit nurture and maternal aggression. He also suffers the loss of a dimension of his selfhood—his autonomy—because the intensity of the anxiety provoked by the manipulations of the witches and his wife obliges him to comply with the dictates of a ruthless, suffocating maternal introject.

Various discussions of psychological splitting portrayed in *Macbeth* provide a useful avenue of approach to comprehending the problem. Freud calls attention to the way Shakespeare's apparent inconsistency in characterizing Macbeth and his wife exhibits an extraordinary complementarity such that "the hesitating, ambitious man" becomes an "unbridled tyrant" while his "steely-hearted instigator" turns into "a sick woman gnawed by remorse":

> The germs of fear which break out in Macbeth on the night of the murder do not develop further in *him* but in *her*. It is he who has the hallucination of the dagger before the crime; but it is she who afterwards falls ill of a mental disorder. It is he who after the murder hears the cry in the house: "Sleep no more! Macbeth does murder sleep . . ." and so "Macbeth shall sleep no more"; but we never hear that *he* slept no more, while the Queen, as we see, rises from her bed and, talking in her sleep, betrays her guilt. It is he who stands helpless with bloody hands, lamenting that "all great Neptune's ocean" will not wash them clean, while she comforts him: "A little water clears us of this deed"; but later it is she who washes her hands for a quarter of an hour and cannot get rid of the bloodstains: "All the perfumes of Arabia will not sweeten this little hand." . . . Together they exhaust the possibilities of reaction to the crime, like two disunited parts of a single psychical individuality. (1916, 322–24)

Jekels (1952) subsequently writes that in an oedipal context Macbeth, Banquo, and Macduff are all son figures, with Macbeth switching to the role of the psychological father when he becomes king, a lead I follow when I argue that Macbeth and Macduff thus form a composite hero such that the latter part of the drama depicts symbolic restitution for the crime committed in the first part (Rogers 1970, 49).

Barron's interpretation adds an entirely new dimension to the psychoanalytic reading of *Macbeth*. Although he explicitly opposes his interpretation to Freud's by claiming that Macbeth and Lady Macbeth cannot be regarded as a composite personality because they represent "a mother and son who have failed to achieve separate identities" (1960, 151), Holland notes that the two interpretations are not so much conflicting as complementary because Barron "is showing beneath the oedipus conflict . . . an earlier, oral understructure that shapes the form of the phallic or oedipal conflict in development" (1966, 227). Barron links the influence of the witches as evil mother figures with that of Lady Macbeth on her husband-son, shows that the witch-mother is not only treacherous but treacherous in the feeding situation, sees the bearded weird sisters and the "unsexed" Lady Macbeth as domineering, masculine women who instill their own "vaulting ambition" into the husband-son, and argues that Macbeth has qualms about his masculinity because he submits to the maternal author-ity of the witches and Lady Macbeth rather than to the paternal authority of Duncan.

As I read it now, the fundamental strength of Barron's interpretation stems from its person-oriented object-relational features, such as when he observes that Macbeth progressively tries to cut himself off from his wife's influence (first murdering Duncan at her instigation, then murdering Banquo after giving her no more than a hint, and finally killing Macduff's wife and children without prior communication), so that by the end of the play her death elicits no more than a remark that "she should have died hereafter." The main weakness of Barron's interpretation derives from its Freudian posture with respect to sexuality, especially orality. The title of his paper, "The Babe that Milks" (alluding to Lady Macbeth's "I have given suck, and know/How tender 'tis to love the babe that milks me") reflects this emphasis. In contrast, I would now contend that the many oral images in the text of the play should be read broadly, as analogical metaphors encoding *relationships,* rather than narrowly, as signs that characterize the nature of these relationships in a literal way. I would say the same thing about the innumerable phallic images of the play that once seemed so sexually significant; they now appear more meaningful for the way in which they define Macbeth's intrapersonal failure to iden-tify with the oedipal father except in a manner that incorporates the pre-oedipal mother's subversive, ruthless dictates. And whereas I formerly construed Macbeth's anxiety in the Freudian, mainly oedipal context of castration anxiety, as Barron does in part, I would now emphasize early interactional sources of anxiety, as Barron also does, though he tends to see the problem to a considerable extent in terms of *oral* deprivation.

The extent to which Macbeth exhibits anxiety can scarcely be over-stated. Though fearless in battle *prior* to seeing the witches, Macbeth becomes anxious almost immediately afterward when he thinks about killing the king:

> Why do I yield to that suggestion
> Whose horrid image doth unfix my hair

And make my seated heart knock at my ribs
Against the use of nature? Present fears
Are less than horrible imaginings.

(1.2. 135–39)

Lady Macbeth, who berates him for being a coward for hesitating to kill Duncan, deals with his fear of failure by saying, "But screw your courage to the sticking place/And we'll not fail." After murdering Duncan, Macbeth refuses to take the bloody daggers back to the scene of the crime: "I am afraid to think what I have done;/Look on't again I dare not." After Lady Macbeth mocks him for his fears, she exits and then he hears Macduff's knocking at the gates: "How is't with me when every noise appals me?" When Lady Macbeth returns, she exclaims, "My hands are of your color, but I shame/To wear a heart so white." After the murderers fail to kill Fleance along with Banquo, Macbeth declares,

But let the frame of things disjoint, both the worlds suffer,
Ere we will eat our meal in fear and sleep
In the affliction of these terrible dreams
That shake us nightly.

(3.2. 16–19)

By act 5 Macbeth has become so anxious he cannot resist mocking a servant for being a "cream-faced loon" and "lily-livered boy" whose "linen cheeks" are "counselors to fear." He shouts, "What soldiers, whey-face?" Shortly thereafter he orders, "Hang those that talk of fear," and announces, "I will not be afraid of death and bane/Till Birnam Forest come to Dunsinane."

The concept of castration anxiety can by no means account for the whole of Macbeth's anxiety, including that represented by his wife. In terms of attachment theory, Lady Macbeth's command that her bedroom be continuously lighted at night betokens not so much provision for seeing her way as she sleepwalks as it does her fear of the dark—a form of separation anxiety. There is one feature of attachment theory that goes a long way toward explaining the ultimate sources of Macbeth's anxiety, an anxiety so intense as to breed his psychotic delusion of the hallucinated dagger and his vision of Banquo's ghost at the banquet, not to mention the apparitions of act 4. The feature in question is the paradox that "threats of separation from the mother, acts of physical rejection by her, and alarming conditions in the environment are presumed to activate the system [of attachment behavior] at particularly high intensities" (Main and Weston, 1982, 33). In other words, when an attached infant is subjected to threats from an attachment figure who simultaneously rejects physical contact, he is placed in a theoretically irresolvable and indeed self-perpetuating conflict situation. This is because threats of any kind, stemming from any source, arouse tendencies to withdraw from the source of the threat and to approach the mother. If (as is the case with mothers of avoidant infants) the mother is not only threatening but also forbids approach and contact, the conflict is not resolvable. The mere fact that approach is forbidden when it is most necessary should activate still further the attachment behavior system; it should also activate angry behavior; but approach is still not possible; and this should activate still further the system. Thus, on a theoretical level, a kind of [destablizing] positive feedback loop develops. (ibid., 53)

Assuming the underlying maternal cast of Lady Macbeth's relationship to her husband, exactly this general situation obtains between them, especially in the famous scene where she attacks him for hesitating to carry out the plan to kill Duncan:

> I have given suck, and know
> How tender 'tis to love the babe that milks me.
> I would, while it was smiling in my face,
> Have plucked my nipple from his boneless gums
> And dashed the brains out, had I so sworn
> As you have done to this.
>
> (1.7.54–59)

The only significant difference between the scene hypothecated by Main and Weston and the one dramatized by Shakespeare is that the threat is one of total annihilation. As Macbeth *is* this babe in arms, he has no choice but to comply with her demands. What he never does do, anywhere in the play, is to exhibit any anger toward his "dearest partner of greatness," no matter how often she belittles him by saying things like "Are you a man?", "What, quite unmanned in folly?", and "O, these flaws and starts/ (Imposters to true fear) would well become/A woman's story at a winter's fire."

What I have been explaining from the rather outside-oriented perspective of attachment theory Willbern comments on from the more inside-oriented view of classical object relations theory, particularly Winnicott's concepts of mirroring and potential space. Willbern observes that Lady Macbeth's phrase, "while it was smiling in *my* face," replicates in language "the perfect mirroring of other and infant that founds familial harmony: it locates the infant's smile 'in' the mother's face" (1986, 527). Willbern reads this "perfect mirroring" as symbiotically destructive: "This paradox-

ical pathology suggests a potential hazard of the necessary reciprocity
between mother and infant in human development. . . . Perfect reciprocity institutes no difference. Individuation is therefore a process of
breaking out of this exact mirroring without breaking the mirror (the
reflecting relationship)" (530–31), a process that Winnicott says requires
gradual "dis-illusionment." Lady Macbeth provides a suffocating symbiotic fusion instead of the "potential space" of developing difference,
Willbern is saying, her only alternative offer being that of the catastrophic
disruption of plucking her nipple from the boneless gums of her nursing
infant in order to dash his brains out: "Here the space of difference is
neither initiated by the infant nor mutually sustained by the mother, but
suddenly and catastrophically created by her: from mother's breast un-
timely ripped" (531). Willbern concludes that "in the play of *Macbeth*
Shakespeare provides his audience with a framed potential space where-
in he presents a character, Macbeth, for whom such space is closed
off" (535).

Stern's discussion of "affect attunement" in the development of intersubjectivity distinguishes, along lines similar to Willbern's discussion,
between the perfect "imitation" of mirroring and the "cross-modal" differ-
ential matching that instantiates difference in affect attunement. Stern
specifically defines affect attunement as "the performance of behaviors
that express the quality of feeling of a shared affect state without imitating
the exact behavioral expression of the inner state" (1985, 142). If one
looks at Macbeth's problem in terms of Winnicott and Stern, and also in
the context of Lichtenstein's concept of mothers who "imprint" identity
themes on their infants (discussed in chapter 4 above), one is tempted to
regard Macbeth as a psychological clone of his mother. After Lady Macbeth asks "murth'ring ministers" to "Come to my woman's breasts,/And
take my milk for gall," which is virtually what Macbeth does, she adds,

> Come thick Night,
> And pall thee in the dunnest smoke of Hell,
> That my keen knife see not the wound it makes,
> Nor Heaven peep through the blanket of the dark.
>
> (1.6.48–51)

Her keen knife cannot see to see. As Brooks (1947) notices, Macbeth is
her knife, her tool. Brooks means this only in the sense that she succeeds
in manipulating him. But the connection lies deeper than that. Macbeth
is his wife's knife—a lethal extension of her destructive personality. Her
own fell phallicism has been "imprinted" on him in a way that obliges

him to screw his courage to the sticking place, thereby complying with an imposed identity theme, or psychological mission, in much the same way that Winnicott's false-self personalities conform to the will of others.

Lear's agony leads him into madness. That is something he has more or less in common with Hamlet, Othello, and Macbeth. Sooner or later, in one form or another, they all exhibit some signs of psychotic behavior, though the other three do so less obviously than Lear. One sign of Hamlet's madness, other than what he feigns, is that whereas Horatio and the guards also see the "real" ghost at the beginning of the play, Hamlet hallucinates the ghost in the bedroom that Gertrude cannot see. Othello's madness appears not so much in the "fits" that take hold of him as in the way the demonic Iago takes possession of his mind, Iago himself being clinically paranoid in his delusional jealousy. In a way that parallels the example given from *Hamlet,* both Macbeth and Banquo perceive the "real" witches in act 1, but no one except Macbeth sees Banquo's ghost at the banquet.

Where does madness come from? The answer provided by Winnicott, mentioned in chapter 5 in relation to Pip's being temporarily lost at sea, is that traumatic separation in childhood can induce madness: "If the mother is away more than x minutes, then the image fades. . . . The baby is distressed but this distress is soon *mended* because the mother returns in x plus y minutes. . . . But in x plus y plus z minutes the baby has been *traumatized*" (1971, 97). "Madness here simply means a *break-up* of whatever may exist at the time of *a personal continuity of existence,*" madness being a set of primitive defenses organized to defend against any repetition of such an "unthinkable anxiety" (97). Whereas *Hamlet, Othello,* and *Macbeth* glance at the origins of madness rather indirectly in terms of varying responses to widely differing situations of loss, *King Lear* dramatizes in a relatively direct way that madness ensues as a consequence of "departures" of attachment figures. What the play veils is that the purest and most radical form of all departures is the *abandonment* of a helpless infant by its mother. It veils this theme by presenting us with the helpless infant masked as an aged man in his second childhood, and with mothers masked as daughters.

Some interpretations of the play pay heed to the theme of childhood, but none that I am aware of sufficiently recognizes the importance of separation as the vortex of recirculating pain, a vortex out of which emerge lines as various as Gloucester's despairing "As flies to wanton boys

are we to the gods;/They kill us for their sport" and Lear's cosmic cry of
"Howl, howl, howl!" The psychoanalytic interpretations considered by
Holland fall into three categories: statements about the play's mythic
implications, notably Freud's paper on the theme of the three caskets;
claims that Lear is a childish, narcissistic person; and contentions that
Lear suffers from unconscious sexual impulses towards his daughters
(Holland 1966, 218). One recent instance of the many analyses falling
into the third category may serve as representative: "I see in the play the
outbreak of a lifelong, unconscious, incestuous passion. When that passion emerges late in life, it is by no means weakened by age. On the
contrary, passion in the elderly can irrupt more strongly than in the
young" (Blechner 1988, 323). As for the other two viewpoints, I will
pass over the mythic one for now in order to concentrate on the one that
looks upon Lear as a child. What should be born in mind about these
commentaries is that the child they perceive is very much a Freudian
Child, that is, a narcissistic, oral-incestuous, pre-oedipal Oedipus as distinguished from the potentially anxious Interactive Infant of Sullivan,
Bowlby, and Stern.

The most significant of the commentaries on childhood in the play is
that of Ella Freeman Sharpe (1946). She suggests that *King Lear* represents "a conflict not of age but of childhood and infancy re-activated in
the poet's maturity" (218), that psychically Lear regresses "to the loves
and hates of early childhood" (219), that "Child Lear's phantasies are
dramatized in the play" (223), and that Lear's daughters represent different aspects of Child Lear's mother (223). So far, so good. What does not
become clear until later in the chapter is that what Sharpe refers to as
"Child Lear" is really a condensation of Lear's hypothetical childhood and
Shakespeare's actual childhood. Whatever the theoretical perils of such an
assumption, they might not pose an insuperable problem were it not that
paralleling the hypothetical separations and frustrations young William
Shakespeare may have experienced at the advent of siblings born when he
was two-and-a-half and five years old are what Sharpe assumes to be
similar events occurring at a similar time in the life of Child Lear. Sharpe
declares, "Categorically I have to assert that mother-Goneril's pregnancy
is the cause of child Lear's 'storm' in the play," that is, her pregnancy
constitutes "the reason for his anger" (225). No shred of textual evidence
supports Sharpe's notion that Goneril is pregnant, and even if she were,
Sharpe provides no effective argument to support her claim that *that* is
the primary basis for Lear's rage. Her claim rests entirely on the supposi-

tion that Child Lear stands in for Child Shakespeare, who *must* have been angry about his mother's pregnancies (as well he may have been).

Besides presenting Goneril's supposed pregnancy as the main basis for Child Lear's anger, Sharpe offers a number of other reasons for it. These include certain traumata, "observed menstruation" of the mother being one, and another being Child Lear's tantrum about an unseen primal scene—his grievance being that the parental bedroom doors are bolted against him. Sharpe also mentions the hate-generating "frustrations" of "loss of the breast" and loss of attention to "His Majesty the Baby," grievances constituting "a subtle defence used *unconsciously* to fool his *father* and to hide from him and himself his knowledge of the father's sexual love for the mother" (231). Besides taking it for granted that Child Lear desires his mother as a "sexual object," Sharpe insists that "rejection and hate of the mother is a confession of incestuous desire" (231). That Sharpe's Child Lear is essentially a child of Freudian theory becomes clear in the context of her discussion of the banishment motif: "Everyman resents 'banishment' from the Garden of Eden of infancy and phantasy to a world of reality" (224), that is, banishment as Sharpe imagines it is from an indulgent, oral-incestuous paradise as distinct from banishment in the sense of separation.

I believe Sharpe might have read the play rather differently had she had a more scientific object-relational paradigm available to her. While continuing to insist that the drama depicts "a conflict not of age but of childhood," I think she might have dispensed with the incest theme and the various supposed sexual traumata. Without insisting on the presence of a pregnant female in the cast, Sharpe might have realized that Goneril does not have to be pregnant to be experienced as a cruelly rejecting maternal figure by a man who, as the Fool says, has made mothers of his daughters. Goneril—and Regan, too—are not so much absent mothers as depriving ones, though they do effectively become abandoning ones, abandonment being symbolized in the play mainly by Lear's "unbonneted," exposed, shelterless condition on the moor during the storm, and by his extreme isolation in madness. Sharpe might have become more aware that what accounts for Lear's special vulnerability to abandonment is not a latent set of revivable oedipal impulses so much as the inevitable dependency of an aged man in his second childhood who must, as he himself says, "unburdened crawl toward death." Sharpe, who has surprisingly little to say about Cordelia other than designating her as a good mother figure, might have paid more attention to the attachment implications of Lear's remark about Cordelia: "I loved her most, and thought to set my rest/On her kind nursery." Sharpe might eventually have come to realize that Lear feels abandoned by Cordelia not so much because she seems to withhold affection in saying "Nothing" in response to his greedy call for expressions of love in the opening scene but because he creates the separation himself when he banishes her by saying, "Hence and avoid my sight!"—the same words he uses as he banishes Kent a few moments later. Besides realizing, in Goneril's words, that "old fools are babes again," what I think that Sharpe might have noticed above all is that *King Lear* is a story about a parent who, having abandoned his "children" (including Kent), is represented with devastating dramatic irony as being punished for this crime by having to experience, as a child, the maddening emotional consequences of being abandoned by the children who now serve him as parents.

While it might be said that Lear as a component figure in the play is, as he sees himself, more sinned against than sinning, the titular Lear, a great tragic figure, must suffer for the primal parental crime of abandoning his children. What misleads so many readers is the theme of "filial ingratitude." But this play is no more about "How sharper than a serpent's tooth it is/To have a thankless child" than *Macbeth* is simply a play about "vaulting ambition." *King Lear* is a play about the emotional turbulence of the aftermath of abandonment. Individuals (of varying chronological age) representing children in some sense abandoned by their primary attachment figures include—besides Lear—Cordelia, Kent, Edgar, the Fool, and Gloucester. Cordelia is literally a daughter abandoned by her father. Kent, who assumes a care-taking role after his banishment, is the symbolic son of his king. Edmund "arranges" for Edgar's abandonment by his insufficiently trusting father, and Edgar, as Poor Tom, suffers in a way that parallels Lear's madness. Because of Cordelia's absence, we are told, the Fool "hath much pined away." And Gloucester experiences abandonment in the form of almost total helplessness after being blinded, a dependency comparable to what Lear experiences in his madness. Lear also "abandons" Goneril and Regan by totally rejecting them; that the rejection is deserved does not alter the tyrannical tempestuousness of Lear's manner of dealing with his dog-hearted daughters.

At one point in his three-caskets essay Freud brings up the problem of accounting for the "overpowering effect" of *King Lear*. His own explanation of the power of the play involves his perception of its mythic dimensions. At the end, Lear is an old man, a dying man, and when Lear carries the dead body of Cordelia onto the stage she is Death herself: "If we reverse the situation it becomes intelligible and familiar to us. She is the Death-goddess who, like the Valkyrie in German mythology, carries away the dead hero from the battlefield. Eternal wisdom, clothed in primaeval myth, bids the old man renounce love, choose death and make friends with the necessity of dying" (1913, 301). A complementary way of understanding the overpowering effect of the play is to regard death as another abandonment, an irreversible separation, an irrevocable loss, a final parting from all loved persons.

The theme of abandonment becomes a sounding board that magnifies the power of all painful scenes and wrenching lines in the play. "O thou side-piercing sight!" exclaims Edgar when he encounters Lear on the moor, mad and bedecked with flowers. When he feels utterly abandoned, Lear can no longer love. He says to blinded Gloucester, "I remember thine eyes well enough. Dost thou squiny at me? No, do thy worst, blind Cupid; I'll not love." The scenes of reunion, of Edgar and Gloucester and of Lear and Cordelia, achieve an indescribable poignancy against the backgrounding resonance of the separation motif. Edgar and Gloucester are not simply reunited. They bond again, with roles reversed, the blinded Gloucester stoically dependent on a madman's guidance, as he thinks, and the filial Edgar stoutly leading his father's faltering footsteps to the edge of the imaginary precipice, Gloucester despairing at his failed suicide ("Is wretchedness deprived that benefit/To end itself by death?"), and Edgar sustaining and encouraging him after the imaginary fall:

> Men must endure
> Their going hence, even as their coming hither;
> Ripeness is all.

> (5.2.9–11)

At the reunion of Cordelia and Lear, in contrast to Lear's severing command at the beginning of the play—"hence and avoid my sight!"—Cordelia says simply to the kneeling, bowing Lear:

> O look upon me, sir,
> And hold your hand in benediction o'er me.
> You must not kneel.

> (4.7.57–59)

As for the unutterable pathos of Lear's final loss of Cordelia, no words but Shakespeare's can register the pain of such a severance following so close upon reunion:

Howl, howl, howl! O, you are men of stones.
Had I your tongues and eyes, I'd use them so
That heaven's vault should crack. She's gone for ever.
I know when one is dead, and when one lives.
She's dead as earth. Lend me a looking glass.
If that her breath will mist or stain the stone,
Why then she lives.

(5.3.258—264)

REFERENCES

Aristotle, 1958. *On poetry and style*. trans. G. M. A. Grube. New York: Bobbs-Merrill.

Arvin, N. 1950. *Herman Melville*. New York: Viking.

Atwood, G. and Stolorow, R. 1984. *Structures of subjectivity*. Hillsdale, N. J.: Analytic Press.

Barratt, B. 1984. *Psychic reality and psychoanalytic knowing*. Hillsdale, N.J.: Analytic Press.

Barron, D. B. 1960. The babe that milks: an organic study of *Macbeth*. *American Imago* 17: 133–61.

Basch, M. F. 1988. *Understanding psychotherapy*. New York: Basic Books.

Beebe, B. 1986. Mother-infant mutual influence and precursors of self- and object representation. In *Empirical Studies of Psychoanalytic Theories*, vol. 2. Ed. J. Masling. Hillsdale, N.J.: Analytic Press.

Bernheimer, C., and Kahane, C. 1985. *In Dora's case: Freud—hysteria—feminism*. New York: Columbia University Press.

Bertalanffy, L. von. 1968. *General system theory*. New York: George Braziller.

Bettelheim, B. 1967. *The empty fortress: infantile autism and the birth of the self*. New York: The Free Press.

Blechner, M. J. 1988. King Lear, King Leir, and incest wishes. *American Imago* 45: 309–25.

Bollas, C. 1987. *The shadow of the object*. New York: Columbia University Press.

Bowlby, J. 1969. *Attachment*. New York: Basic.

———.1973. *Separation*. New York: Basic.

———.1979. *The making and breaking of affectional bonds*. London: Tavistock/Routledge.

———.1980. *Loss*. New York: Basic.

———.1982. *Attachment*, 2d ed. New York, Basic.

———.1988. *A secure base*. New York: Basic.

Brée, G. 1959. *Camus*. New Brunswick, N. J.: Rutgers University Press.

Breger, L. 1981. *Freud's unfinished journey*. London: Routledge and Kegan Paul.

Brinnin, J. M. 1960. *Emily Dickinson*. New York: Dell.

Brooks, C. 1947. The naked babe and the cloak of manliness. In *The well wrought urn*. New York: Harcourt, Brace & World.

Brown, N. O. 1966. *Love's body*. New York: Basic.

Campbell, J. 1949. *The hero with a thousand faces*. Cleveland: World, 1956.

Camus, A. 1942. *The stranger*. Trans. Stuart Gilbert. New York: Random House, 1946.

————.1958. The renegade. In *Exile and the kingdom*. Trans. Justin O'Brien. New York: Knopf.

————.1963. *Notebooks: 1935–1942*. Trans. Philip Thody. New York: Modern Library, 1965.

————.1965. *The collected plays of Albert Camus*. Trans. Stuart Gilbert. London: Hamish Hamilton.

Chase, R. 1949. *Herman Melville*. New York: Macmillan.

————.1951. *Emily Dickinson*. New York: William Sloane.

Cody, J. 1971. *After great pain: the inner life of Emily Dickinson*. Cambridge, Mass.: Harvard University Press.

Deutsch, H. 1942. Some forms of emotional disturbance and their relationship to schizophrenia. *Psychoanalytic Quarterly* 11: 301–21.

Dickinson, E. 1958. *The letters of Emily Dickinson*. 3 vols. Ed. Thomas H. Johnson. Cambridge Mass.: Harvard University Press.

————. 1960. *The complete poems of Emily Dickinson*. Ed. Thomas H. Johnson. Boston: Little, Brown.

Eagle, M. N. 1981. Interests as object relations. In *Empirical studies in psychoanalytic theories,* vol. 1. Ed. J. Masling. Hillsdale, N. J.: Lawrence Erlbaum, 1982.

————.1984. *Recent developments in psychoanalysis*. Cambridge, Mass.: Harvard University Press, 1987.

Edelson, M. 1988. *Psychoanalysis: a theory in crisis*. Chicago: University of Chicago Press.

Erikson, E. H. 1950. *Childhood and society*. 2d ed. New York: W. W. Norton, 1963.

Faber, M. D. 1989. *The withdrawal of human projection: a study of culture and internalized objects*. New York: Library of Art and Social Science.

Fairbairn, W. R. D. 1952. *Psychoanalytic studies of the personality*. London: Routledge and Kegan Paul, 1966.

————.1963. Synopsis of an object-relations theory of the personality. *International Journal of Psycho-Analysis* 44: 224–25.

Fiedler, L. 1962. *Love and death in the American novel*. Cleveland: World.

Fletcher, A. 1964. *Allegory: the theory of a symbolic mode*. Ithaca, N.Y.: Cornell University Press.

Freud, S. Unless otherwise noted, all references are to *The standard edition of the complete psychological works of Sigmund Freud,* vols. 1–24. London: Hogarth Press, 1953–1974, abbreviated SE.

————.1893–1895. *Studies on hysteria*. SE 2.

————.1900. *The interpretation of dreams*. SE 4 and 5.

————.1905a. Fragment of an analysis of a case of hysteria. SE 7: 3–122.

————.1905b. *Three essays on the theory of sexuality*. SE 7: 125–245.

————.1906. My views on the part played by sexuality in the aetiology of the neuroses. SE 7: 271–79.

————.1909a. Analysis of a phobia in a five-year-old boy. SE 10: 3–149.

————.1909b. Notes upon a case of obsessional neurosis. SE 10: 153–318.

————.1910. Five lectures on psycho-analysis. SE 11: 3–55.

————.1911. Psycho-analytic notes on an autobiographical account of a case of paranoia (dementia paranoides). SE 12: 3–82.

————.1913. The theme of the three caskets. SE 13: 289–301.

————.1916. Some character-types met with in psycho–analytic work. SE 14: 309–33.

————.1917. Mourning and melancholia. SE 14: 237–58.

————.1918. From the history of an infantile neurosis. SE 17: 3–122.

————.1921. *Group psychology and the analysis of the ego*. SE 18: 67–143.

————.1923. The libido theory. SE 18: 255–59.

————.1940. *An outline of psycho-analysis*. SE 23: 141–207.

————.1954. *The origins of psychoanalysis*. Trans. Eric Mosbacher and James Strachey. Garden City, N. Y.: Doubleday, 1957.

Gardiner, M. 1971. *The wolf-man by the wolf-man*. New York: Basic.

Gedo, J. 1979. Theories of object relations: a metapsychological assessment. *Journal of the American Psychoanalytic Association* 27: 361–74.

Gilbert, S. M. and Gubar, S. 1979. *The madwoman in the attic*. New Haven: Yale University Press.

Greenberg, J. R. and Mitchell, S. A. 1983. *Object relations in psychoanalytic theory*. Cambridge, Mass.: Harvard University Press.

Grosskurth, P. 1986. *Melanie Klein*. New York: Knopf.

Grotstein, J. S. 1982. Newer perspectives in object relations theory. *Contemporary Psychoanalysis* 18: 43–91.

Guntrip, H. 1951. First training analysis, with W. R. D. Fairbairn. Topeka, Kans.: Menninger Foundation, n.d. In Hughes, J. M., *Reshaping the psychoanalytic domain*. Berkeley: University of California Press, 1989.

————.1969. *Schizoid phenomena, object-relations, and the self*. New York: International Universities Press.

————.1971. *Psychoanalytic theory, therapy, and the self*. New York: Basic.

————.1975. My experience of analysis with Fairbairn and Winnicott. *The International Review of Psycho-Analysis* 2: 145–56.

Hadley, J. L. 1985. Attention, affect, and attachment. *Psychoanalysis and Contemporary Thought* 8: 529–50.

————.1989. The neurobiology of motivational systems, and a theory of cure. In Joseph D. Lichtenberg, *Psychoanalysis and motivation*. Hillsdale, N.J.: Analytic Press.

Hamilton, V. 1982. *Narcissus and Oedipus*. London: Routledge & Kegan Paul.

Hartmann, H. 1964. *Essays on ego psychology*. New York: International Universities Press.

Holland, N. N. 1966. *Psychoanalysis and Shakespeare*. New York: McGraw Hill.

————.1968. *The dynamics of literary response*. New York: Oxford University Press.

Holt, R. 1965. A review of some of Freud's biological assumptions and their influence on his theories. In *Psychoanalysis and current biological thought*, ed. Norman S. Greenfield and William C. Lewis. Madison: University of Wisconsin Press.

————.1976. Drive or wish? A reconsideration of the psychoanalytic theory of motivation. In *Psychology versus metapsychology* (*Psychological Issues*, monograph 36). New York: International Universities Press.

————.1989. *Freud reappraised*. New York: Guilford.

Hughes, J. 1989. *Reshaping the psychoanalytic domain*. Berkeley: University of California Press.

Hughes, T. 1971. *Crow*. New York: Harper & Row.

Jacobson, E. 1964. *The self and the object world*. New York: International Universities Press.

Jekels, L. 1952. The riddle of Shakespeare's *Macbeth*. In *Psychoanalysis and literature*, ed. Hendrick M. Ruitenbeek. New York: Dutton, 1964.

Jones, E. 1949. *Hamlet and Oedipus*. Garden City, N. Y.: Doubleday.

Joyce, J. 1934. *Ulysses*. New York: Random House.

Juhasz, S. ed. 1983. *Feminist critics read Emily Dickinson*. Bloomington: Indiana University Press.

Kazin, A. 1956. Preface to *Moby Dick*, by H. Melville. Boston: Houghton Mifflin, 1956.

Keller, K. 1979. *The only kangaroo among the beauty*. Baltimore: Johns Hopkins University Press.

————.1983. Notes on sleeping with Emily Dickinson. In *Feminist critics read Emily Dickinson*, ed. S. Juhasz. Bloomington: Indiana University Press, 1983.

Kernberg, O. 1976. *Object relations theory and clinical psychoanalysis*. New York: Jason Aronson.

Kimball, S. 1987. Uncanny narration in *Moby-Dick*. *American Literature*. 59: 528–47.

Kirschbaum, L. 1944. The modern Othello. *English Literary History* 2: 283–96.

Klein, G. S. 1976. *Psychoanalytic theory*. New York: International Universities Press.

Klein, M. 1932. *The psycho-analysis of children*. London: Hogarth Press, 1959.

————.1940. Mourning and its relation to manic-depressive states. *International Journal of Psycho-Analysis* 21: 125–53.

————.1952a. Some theoretical conclusions regarding the emotional life of the infant. In *Developments in psycho-analysis*, ed. Joan Riviere. London: Hogarth, 1970.

————.1952b. The origins of transference. In *Envy and gratitude and other works, 1946–1963*. New York: Delacorte Press/Seymour Lawrence, 1975.

————.1957. Envy and gratitude. In *Envy and gratitude and other works, 1946–1963*. New York: Delacorte Press/Seymour Lawrence, 1975.

Kohut, H. 1971. *The analysis of the self.* New York: International Universities Press.

———.1977. *The restoration of the self.* New York: International Universities Press.

Lacan, J. 1949. The mirror stage as formative of the function of the I as revealed in psychoanalytic experience. In *Ecrits.* Trans. Alan Sheridan. New York: Norton, 1977.

———.1977. *The four fundamental concepts of psychoanalysis.* Trans. Alan Sheridan. New York: Norton, 1981.

Laplanche, J. and Pontalis, J.-B. 1973. *The language of psychoanalysis,* Trans. D. Nicholson-Smith. New York: Norton.

Leavis, F. R. 1937. Diabolic intellect and the noble hero. *Scrutiny* 6.

Leites, N. 1947. The stranger. In *Art and psychoanalysis,* ed. William Phillips. Cleveland: World, 1963.

Lichtenberg, J. D. 1989. *Psychoanalysis and motivation.* Hillsdale, N.J.: Analytic Press.

Lichtenstein, H. 1961. Identity and sexuality. *Journal of the American Psychoanalytic Association* 9: 179–260.

———.1977. *The dilemma of human identity.* New York: Jason Aronson.

Little, M. 1985. Winnicott working in areas where psychotic anxieties predominate: a personal record. *Free Associations: Psychoanalysis, Groups, Politics, Culture* 3: 9–42.

Lotman, J. 1977. *The structure of the artistic text.* Trans. Gail Lenhoff and Ronald Vroon. Ann Arbor, Mich.: Michigan Slavic Contributions.

Lottman, H. R. 1979. *Albert Camus.* Garden City, N. Y.: Doubleday.

McCarthy, P. 1982. *Camus.* London: Hamish Hamilton.

———.1988. *Albert Camus: the stranger.* Cambridge: Cambridge University Press.

Mahler, M., Pine, F., and Bergman, A. 1975. *The psychological birth of the human infant.* New York: Basic.

Mahony, P. 1986. *Freud and the rat man.* New Haven: Yale University Press.

Main, M., and Weston, D. R. 1982. Avoidance of the attachment figure in infancy: descriptions and interpretations. In *The place of attachment in human behavior.* ed. C. M. Parkes, and J. Stevenson-Hinde. New York: Basic, 1982.

Marris, P. 1982. Attachment and society. In *The place of attachment in human behavior,* ed. C. M. Parkes and J. Stevenson-Hinde. New York: Basic, 1982.

Meissner, W. W. 1978. *The paranoid process.* New York: Jason Aronson.

———. 1981. *Internalization in psychoanalysis.* New York: International Universities Press.

Melville, H. 1851. *Moby Dick.* Boston: Houghton Mifflin, 1956.

Milner, M. 1969. *The hands of the living god.* New York: International Universities Press.

Mitchell, S. A. 1988. *Relational concepts in psychoanalysis.* Cambridge, Mass.: Harvard University Press.

Niederland, W. G. 1984. *The Schreber case: psychoanalytic profile of a paranoid personality.* Hillsdale, N.J.: Analytic Press.

Olson, C. 1947. *Call me Ishmael*. San Francisco: City Lights.

Ovesey, L. 1969. *Homosexuality and pseudohomosexuality*. New York: Science House.

Parkes, C. M. 1982. Attachment and the prevention of mental disorders. In *The place of attachment in human behavior*, ed. Collin Murray Parkes and Joan Stevenson-Hinde. New York: Basic, 1982.

Parkes, C. M. and Stevenson-Hinde, J. (eds.), 1982. *The place of attachment in human behavior*. New York: Basic.

Peterfreund, E. 1971. *Information, systems, and psychoanalysis*. New York: International Universities Press.

———.1983. *The process of psychoanalytic therapy*. Hillsdale, N. J.: Analytic Press.

Pine, F. 1988. The four psychologies of psychoanlaysis and their place in clinical work. *Journal of the American Psychoanalytic Association* 36: 571–96.

Prescott, J. W. 1979. Deprivation of physical affection as a primary process in the development of physical violence. In *Child abuse and violence*, ed. David G. Gil. New York: A.M.S. Press.

Rheingold, J. C. 1967. *The mother, anxiety, and death*. Boston: Little, Brown.

Riffaterre, M. 1978. *Semiotics of poetry*. Bloomington: Indiana University Press.

Riviere, J. 1955. The unconscious phantasy of an inner world reflected in examples from literature. In *New directions in psychoanalysis*, ed. M. Klein, et al. London: Tavistock Publications, 1971.

Rogers, R. 1969. Endopsychic drama in *Othello*. *Shakespeare Quarterly*, 20: 205–215.

———.1970. *The double in literature*. Detroit: Wayne State University Press.

———.1982. Hamlet's tongue. *Psychoanalytic Review*, 69: 534–55.

Rosenblatt, A. D. & Thickstun, J. T. 1970. A study of the concept of psychic energy. *International Journal of Psycho-Analysis*, 51: 265–78.

———.1977. *Modern psychoanalytic concepts in a general psychology*. New York: International Universities Press.

Rubinstein, B. B. 1967. Explanation and mere description: a metascientific examination of certain aspects of the psychoanalytic theory of motivation. In *Motives and thought*, ed. Robert R. Holt. New York: International Universities Press.

Sartre, Jean-Paul. 1947. An explication of the stranger. In *Camus: A collection of critical essays*, ed. Germaine Brée. Englewood Cliffs, N. J.: Prentice-Hall, 1962.

Schafer, R. 1968. *Aspects of internalization*. New York: International Universities Press.

———.1973. Concepts of self and identity and the experience of separation-individuation in adolescence. *Psychoanalytic Quarterly*, 42: 42–59.

———.1976. *A new language for psychoanalysis*. New Haven: Yale University Press.

———.1978. *Language and insight*. New Haven: Yale University Press.

———.1983. *The analytic attitude*. New York: Basic.

Schatzman, M. 1973. Paranoia or persecution: the case of Schreber. *History of Childhood Quarterly*, 1: 62–88.

Searles, H. 1958. Positive feelings in the relationship between the schizophrenic and his mother. In *Collected papers on schizophrenia and related subjects*. New York: International Universities Press, 1965.

————.1960. *The nonhuman environment in normal development and in schizophrenia.* New York: International Universities Press.

————.1966. Concerning the development of an identity. *Psychoanalytic Review* 53: 507–30.

Sechehaye, M., (ed.). 1951a. *Autobiography of a schizophrenic girl.* New York: Signet, 1970.

————.1951b. *Symbolic realization: a new method of psychotherapy applied to a case of schizophrenia.* New York: International Universities Press.

Sharpe, E. F. 1929. The impatience of Hamlet. In *Collected papers on psychoanalysis.* London: Hogarth Press, 1950.

————.1946. From *King Lear* to *The Tempest.* In *Collected papers on psycho-analysis.* London: Hogarth Press, 1950.

Sherwood, M. 1969. *The logic of explanation in psychoanalysis.* New York: Academic Press.

Smith, G.R. 1959. Iago the paranoiac. *American Imago* 16: 155–67.

Stern, D. N. 1985. *The interpersonal world of the infant.* New York: Basics.

Stoller, R. J. 1985. *Presentations of gender.* New Haven: Yale University Press.

Sullivan, H. S. 1953. *The interpersonal theory of psychiatry.* New York: Norton.

Thompson, L. 1952. *Melville's quarrel with God.* Princeton: Princeton University Press.

Wangh, M. 1950. *Othello:* the tragedy of Iago. *Psychoanalytic Quarterly* 19: 202–12.

Willbern, D. 1986. Phantasmagoric *Macbeth. English Literary Renaissance* 16: 520–49.

————.1989. Reading after Freud. In *Contemporary literary theory,* ed. G. D. Atkins and L. Morrow. Amherst: University of Massachusetts Press.

Winnicott, D. W. 1952. Anxiety associated with insecurity. In *Through paediatrics to psycho–analysis.* London: Tavistock, 1975.

————.1958. The capacity to be alone. In *The maturational processes and the facilitating environment.* New York: International Universities Press, 1965.

————.1960. Ego distortion in terms of true and false self. In *The maturational processes and the facilitating environment.* New York: International Universities Press, 1965.

————.1962. A personal view of the Kleinian contribution. In *The maturational processes and the facilitating environment.* New York: International Universities Press, 1965.

————.1963. Communicating and not communicating leading to a study of certain opposites. In *The maturational processes and the facilitating environment.* New York: International Universities Press, 1965.

————.1971. *Playing and reality.* New York: Basic.

————.1977. *The piggle.* Madison, Conn.: International Universities Press.

Wolff, C. G. 1986. *Emily Dickinson.* New York: Knopf.

INDEX

Printed in the United States
By Bookmasters